TILBURY LANDING STAGE
THROUGH TIME

Geoff Lunn

AMBERLEY

First published 2019

Amberley Publishing
The Hill, Stroud
Gloucestershire, GL5 4EP

www.amberley-books.com

ISBN 978 1 4456 8923 4 (print)
ISBN 978 1 4456 8924 1 (ebook)

British Library Cataloguing in Publication Data.
A catalogue record for this book is available from the British Library.

Typeset in 9.5pt on 12pt Celeste.
Typesetting by Aura Technology and Software Services, India. Printed in the UK.

Introduction

Situated approximately 41 kilometres (26 miles) downriver from the heart of London, Tilbury Landing Stage is the Port of London's principal passenger terminal. It handles the largest cruise ships visiting the Thames and, furthermore, is a fine vantage point for viewing other shipping passing to and from upriver berths.

Records show there has been a ferry link between Tilbury and the north Kent town of Gravesend for many centuries. In 1854, when a station was built at Tilbury as part of the development of the London, Tilbury & Southend Railway, a landing stage facility was provided to enable rail passengers to join the ferry either to Gravesend or to passenger liners moored in the river. A year later paddle steamers replaced the traditional sail and row boats and since then, up until this day, a regular ferry service has been maintained.

In 1886 a new set of docks was completed at Tilbury, part of a huge nineteenth-century dock complex constructed along the Thames to serve London. At the docks' entrance a new 110-bed hotel named the Tilbury Hotel was built. It was primarily used for overnight stays by passengers arriving and departing on liners operating out of the docks. After the First World War the number of passengers coming through these docks was notably increasing and it was decided that a dedicated passenger terminal should be built. The Port of London Authority and the Midland Railway promoted a Bill in Parliament for a new passenger landing stage at Tilbury. The Bill was passed in 1922, with construction work due to start two years later, but by this time the Midland Railway had been absorbed into the London, Midland & Scottish Railway and work was delayed until 1926.

Construction and Opening

Construction work was carried out by the Cleveland Bridge & Engineering Company. Designed by Sir Edwin Cooper, it featured a floating platform secured to the riverbank by four hinged steel booms, allowing a rise and fall of 21 feet with the tide. Its total length was 1,142 feet (348 m), with 842 feet (256.5 m) reserved for passenger liners and 300 feet (91.5 m) for ferries. Five bridges connected the landing stage to a new enlarged station, while access roads and a bridge over the railway tracks were built by Sir William Arrol & Co. A cupola-topped baggage hall, almost 100 metres long, was constructed and the new station featured a turret with a weather vane and clock. The station would be named Tilbury Riverside four years later.

Tilbury Landing Stage was officially opened by Prime Minister J. Ramsay MacDonald on 16 May 1930. The Prime Minister and invited guests travelled down from London on the paddle steamer *Crested Eagle* and the ceremony ended with the arrival of the P&O liner *Mongolia*, which took on passengers bound for Australia.

Thereafter, liners of P&O and the Orient Line regularly used the landing stage, their passengers including actors and film stars and members of the touring England cricket team. So busy was the new terminal that on 4 July 1932 some 2,470 passengers disembarked from six ships.

The Second World War

Just before the Second World War the region around Tilbury was designated a danger area and local schoolchildren were evacuated to Suffolk by sea from Tilbury Landing Stage. The docks survived unscathed, but a V2 rocket struck railway sidings near Tilbury Riverside, destroying freight wagons and numerous passenger coaches, while the station itself was hit, damaging the goods yard and two ferries. However the worst loss was that of the Tilbury Hotel, which was destroyed by German incendiary bombs on 4 February 1944.

Post-War Years

After the war Tilbury Landing Stage was once more busy with liner traffic, reaching 300 calls a year. With the introduction of the Assisted Passage Scheme in 1947, under which migrants could travel to Australia for a £10 fare, the Landing Stage became the point of farewell for thousands of 'Ten Pound Poms'. But, by the 1960s, when long-haul air travel was taking off, passenger liner calls dropped dramatically, with just the occasional visit by Soviet-flagged ships sailing in from the USSR.

However, as ocean liner travel changed to cruising, ship calls began to recover, thanks in no small part to UK company CTC Lines, which based its ships at Tilbury, becoming – in many ways – the landing stage's saviour. In 1981, though, British Rail ended the running of through trains to London and Southend from Tilbury Riverside and from then on passengers were shuttled to nearby Tilbury Town station to join trains there. Tilbury Riverside formally closed in November 1992 and the railway lines to the station have since been truncated.

Cruise ship calls continued to increase in the 1990s and Tilbury Landing Stage was upgraded and formally reopened in 1995 as the London Cruise Terminal. The former Riverside station building is now an indoor car park for the use of cruise ship passengers. Nowadays, cruise ships of various nationalities make seasonal calls each summer, while the flagship of UK-based Cruise & Maritime Voyages is based there year-round.

Ships Passing By

In addition to the London Cruise Terminal, the Port of London has two other cruise ship moorings. Greenwich Ship Pier, the world's first floating cruise terminal, can accommodate vessels of up to 228 metres in length, while smaller ships up to 158 metres long moor alongside HMS *Belfast* near Tower Bridge. Ships using these moorings make a fine sight as they pass Tilbury through Gravesend Reach.

Meanwhile, some of the world's largest vehicle carriers berth at a car import facility that has evolved immediately upstream from the landing stage. Just downriver, bulk carriers used to bring coal to Tilbury power station, which has now closed down.

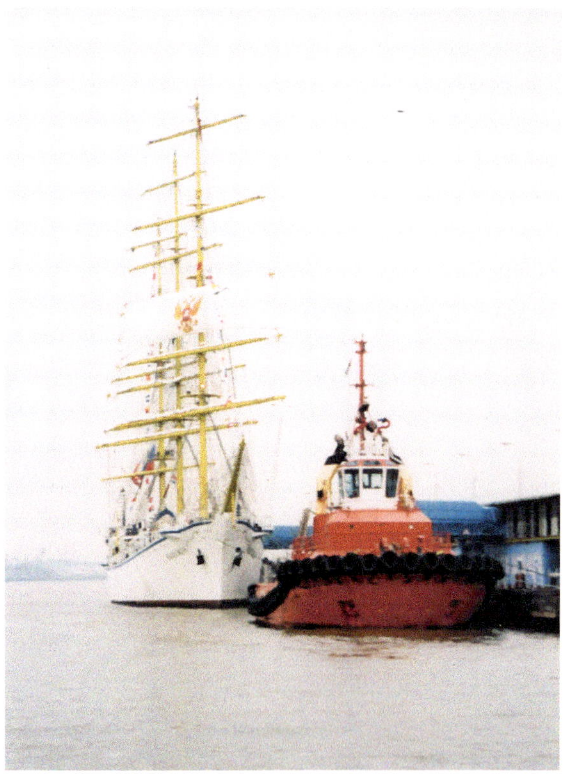

Modern and traditional: a powerful tug, designed for handling the large cruise liners and container ships of today, moored ahead of a Russian tall ship at Tilbury Landing Stage.

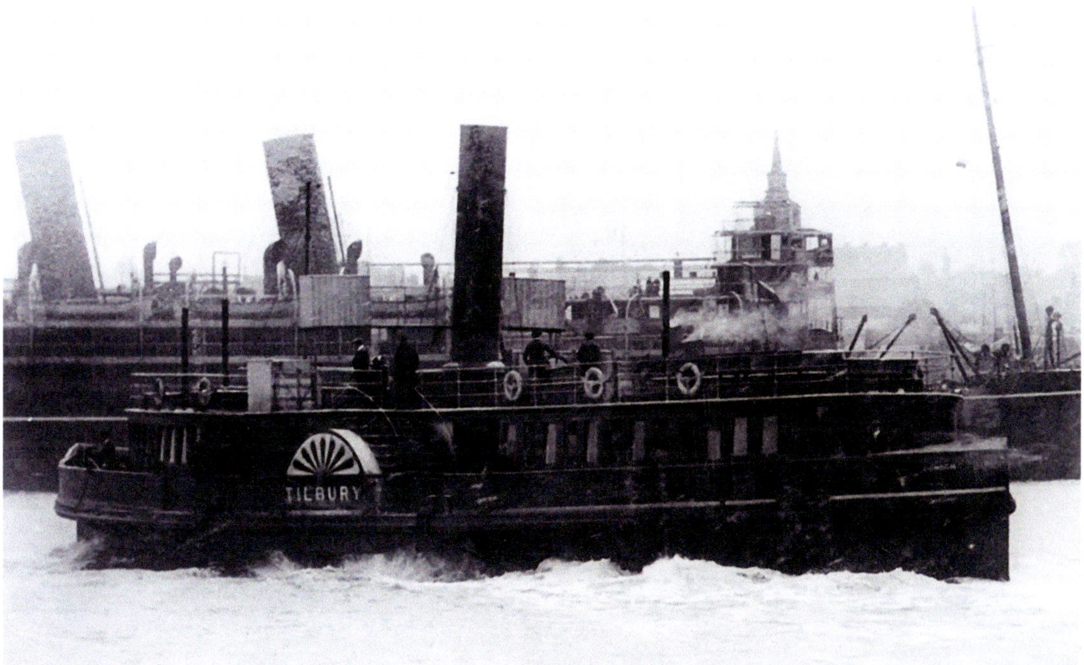

The aptly named paddle steamer *Tilbury* joined the Tilbury–Gravesend ferry service in 1883, serving the route until 1922. Note the two-funnelled P&O liner behind her.

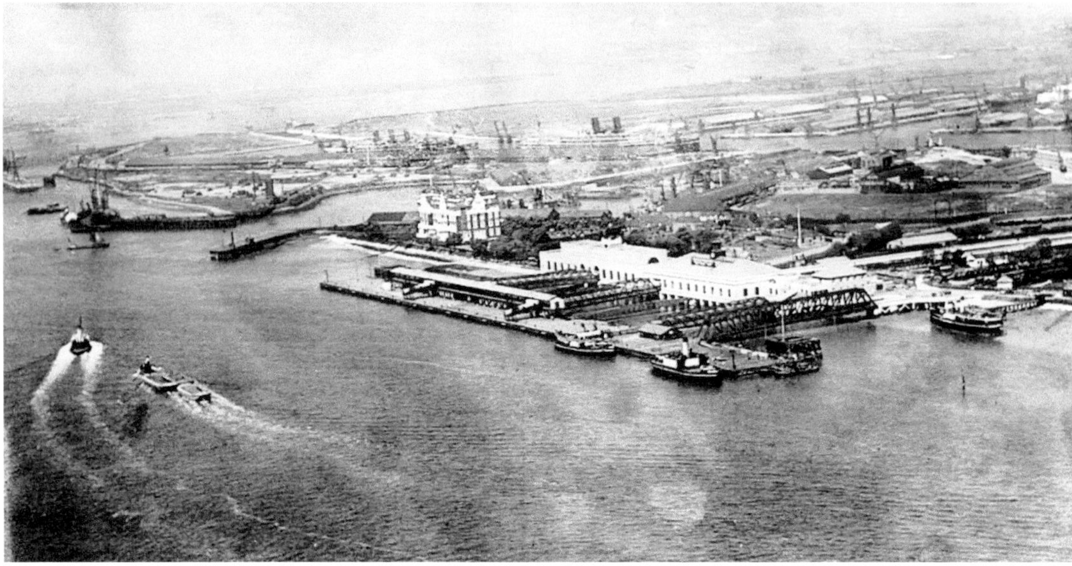

Looking upriver across Tilbury in the early years of the landing stage. Three ferries take on passengers and cars while the Tilbury Hotel, destroyed in 1944, stands just beyond Tilbury Riverside station and the baggage hall. In the background, passenger liners are berthed in Tilbury Docks. The entrance lock basin has since been filled in and the dock entrance moved upstream.

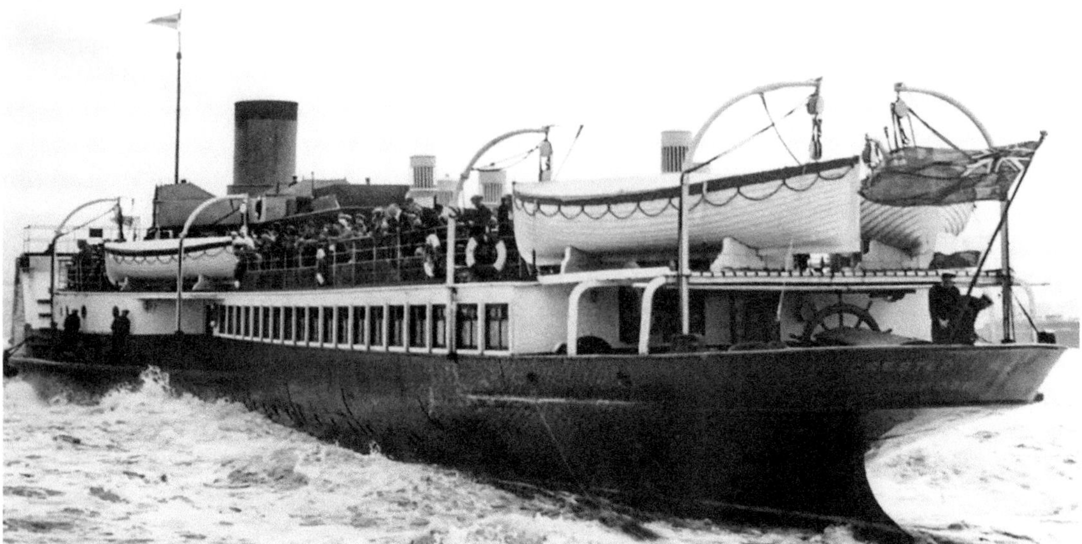

The paddle steamer *Crested Eagle,* which brought Prime Minister J. Ramsay MacDonald and guests down the Thames to Tilbury for the official opening of the landing stage. Built in 1925 for the General Steam Packet Company, the 1,110 gross registered ton (grt) *Crested Eagle* operated summer excursions from London to the Kent coast. Sadly, while participating in the Dunkirk evacuation in 1940, she was bombed with the loss of 300 soldiers and crew. Her wreck can be seen at low tide off the French shoreline even to this day.

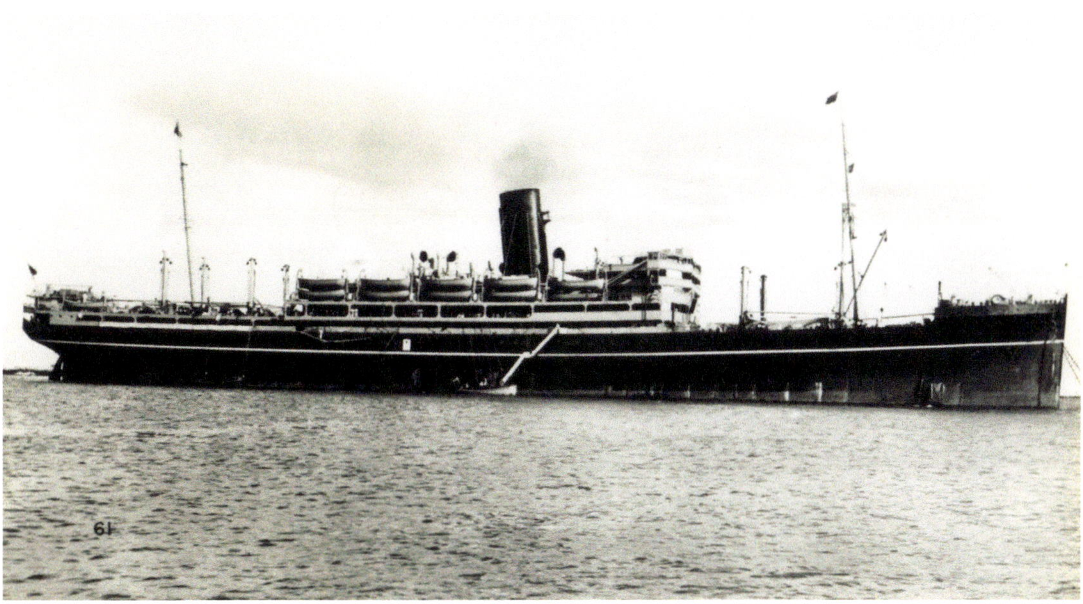

The 16,504 grt P&O ship *Mongolia* was awarded the accolade of being the first liner to board passengers at Tilbury Landing Stage following its opening. Built in 1923, she was chartered out in 1938 as SS *Rimutaka* and after the war led a varied career, becoming an immigrant carrier in 1950 under the name *Europa*. A year later, as a cruise ship, she was renamed *Nassau* and in 1961 she became the *Acapulco* before being scrapped in 1965.

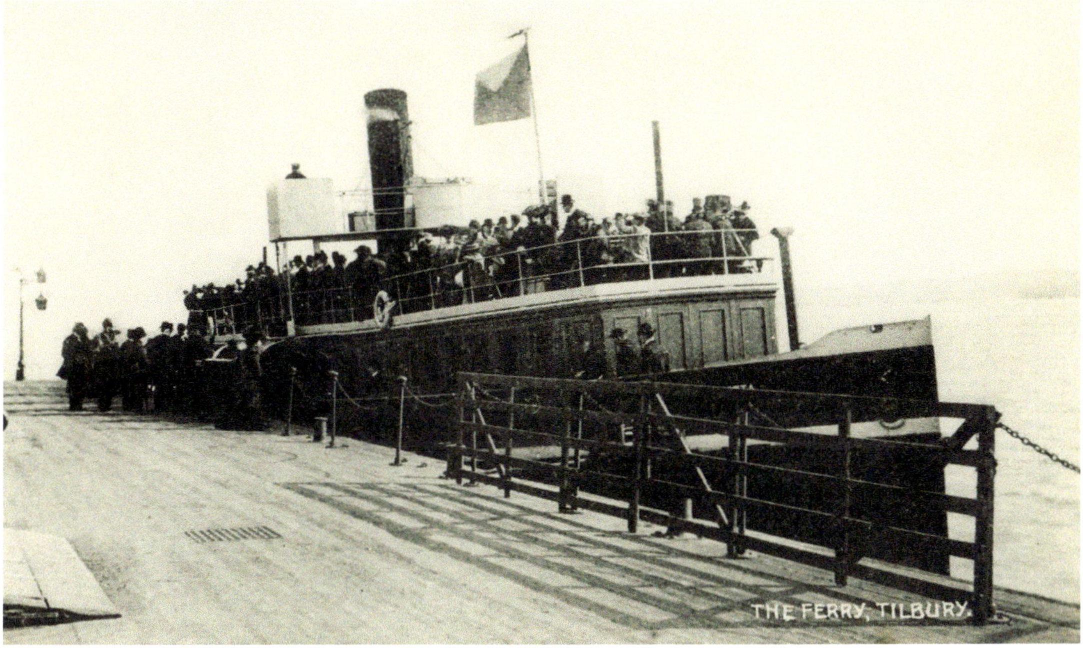

Pictured around 1904, several years before the construction of Tilbury Landing Stage, the Tilbury–Gravesend ferry *Carlotta* takes on passengers for Gravesend. Built in 1893 with an iron hull, the vessel measured 261 grt and remained in service until 1930.

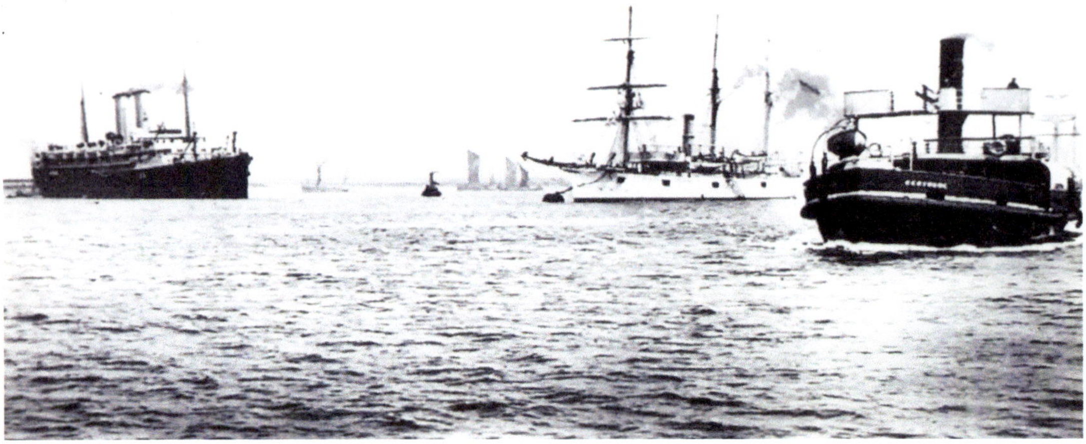

A scene from the 1920s: the Tilbury–Gravesend ferry *Gertrude* steams through Gravesend Reach, very likely acting as a tender for the Orient Line ship on the left, while a classic three-masted steamship is moored midstream.

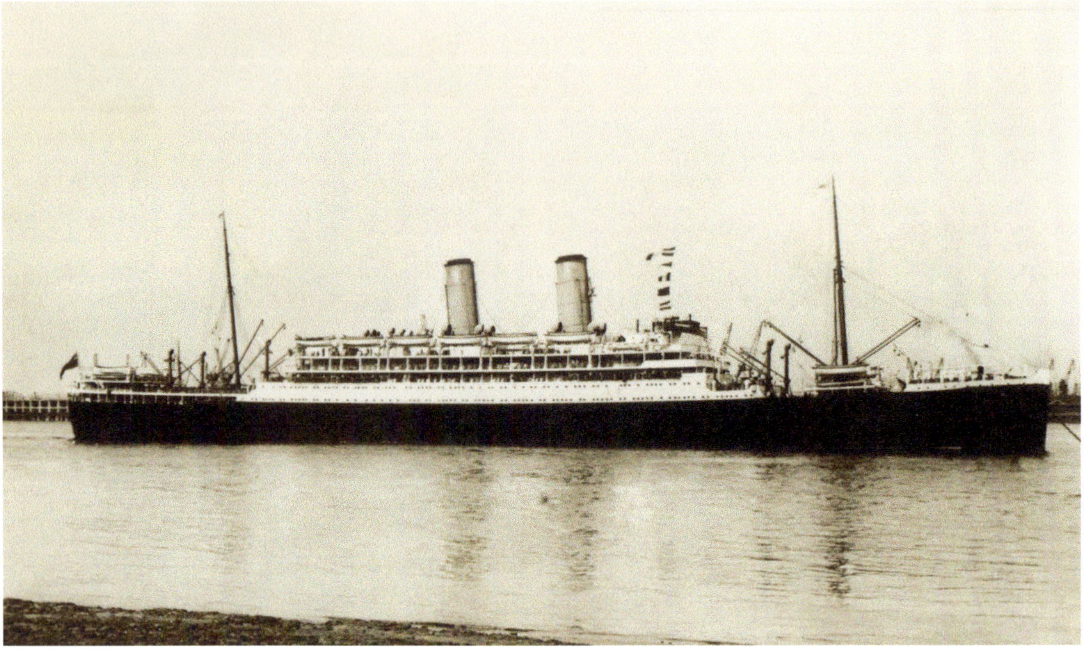

Passenger liners of P&O and the Orient Line sailed between Tilbury and Australian ports for many years and before Tilbury Landing Stage came into operation they were often seen moored in the river. One of these, the 20,043 grt *Oronsay*, was delivered to Orient Line in 1925 and could carry 1,836 passengers. In 1942, while undertaking wartime trooping duties, she was sunk off North Africa and was succeeded by a new *Oronsay* in 1951.

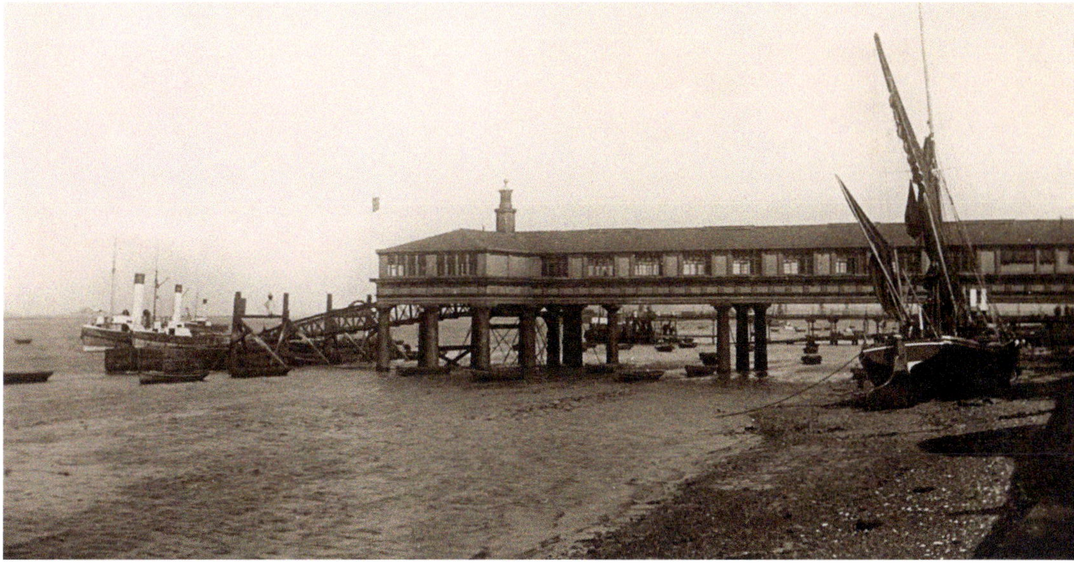

An early twentieth-century view of the Royal Terrace Pier at Gravesend, situated almost opposite Tilbury Landing Stage. Two steam tugs await instructions. The pier has been the base for river pilots since the late nineteenth century and nowadays is part of the Port of London Authority's main operations centre.

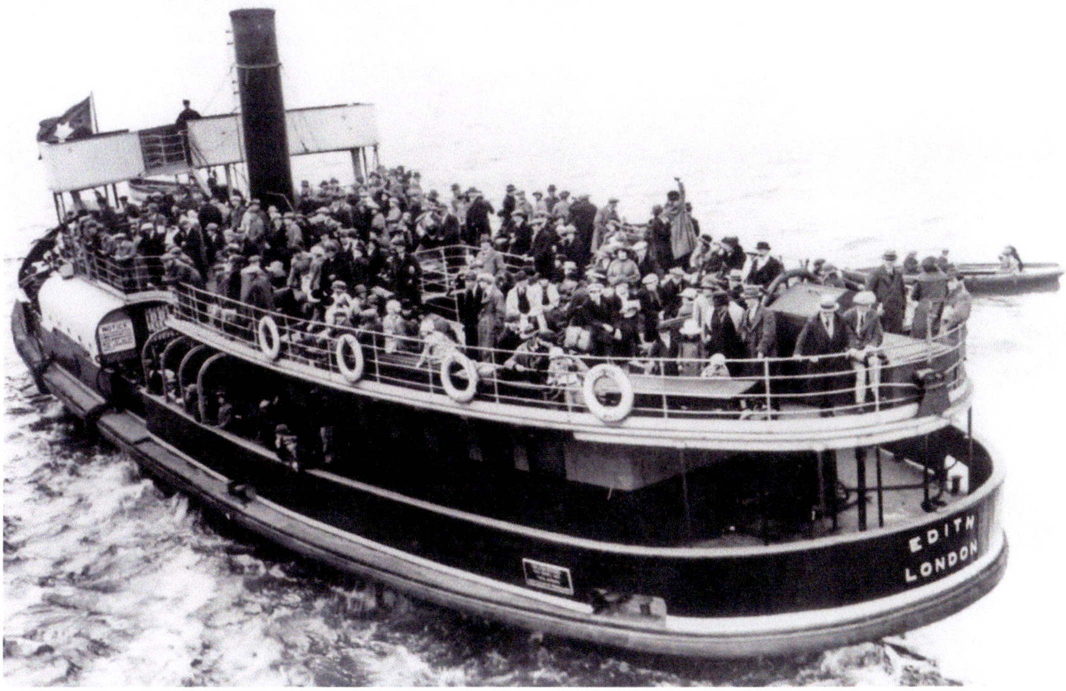

End of long day: the ferry *Edith*, her upper decks packed with workers, makes an evening crossing from Tilbury to Gravesend. Built in 1911, she was the largest of the passenger ferries and remained in service until 1961, when she was replaced by a diesel version of the same name.

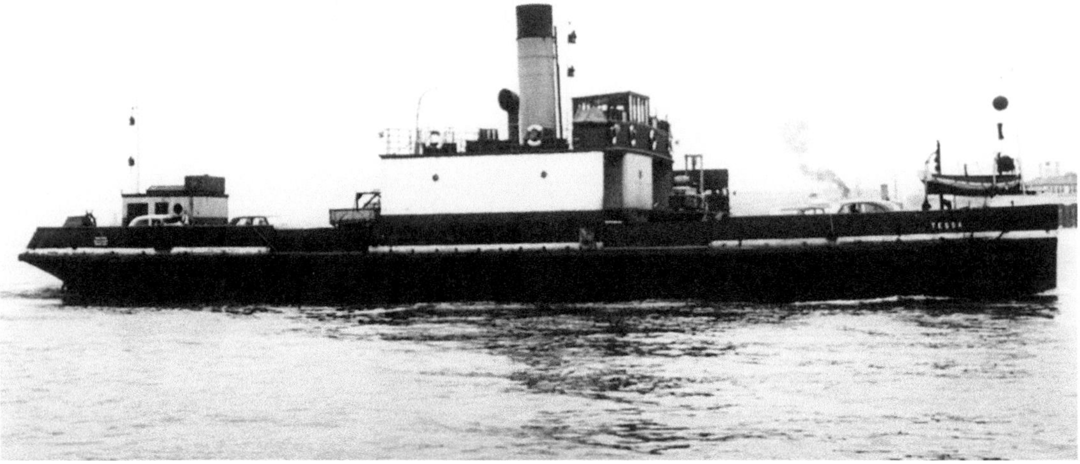

Two car ferries, the *Mimie,* built in 1929, and *Tessa,* 1924 (above), ran regularly between Tilbury Landing Stage and Gravesend until the opening of the Dartford Tunnel in 1968 led to a shortage of vehicular business. The pair were subsequently withdrawn from service.

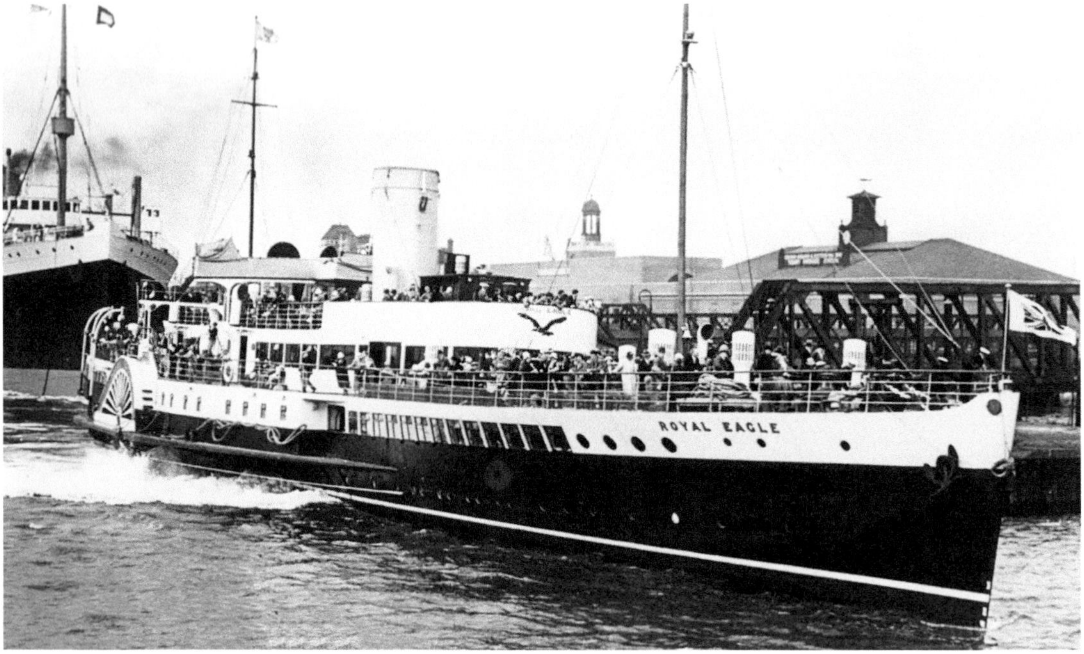

The popular paddle steamer *Royal Eagle* at Tilbury Landing Stage in August 1933. Built just a year earlier, she measured 1,539 grt and could carry up to 2,000 passengers. Unlike her unfortunate near-sister *Crested Eagle,* the *Royal Eagle* survived the war, making three successful trips to Dunkirk. From 1946 she ran excursions from London to Margate before being broken up in 1953.

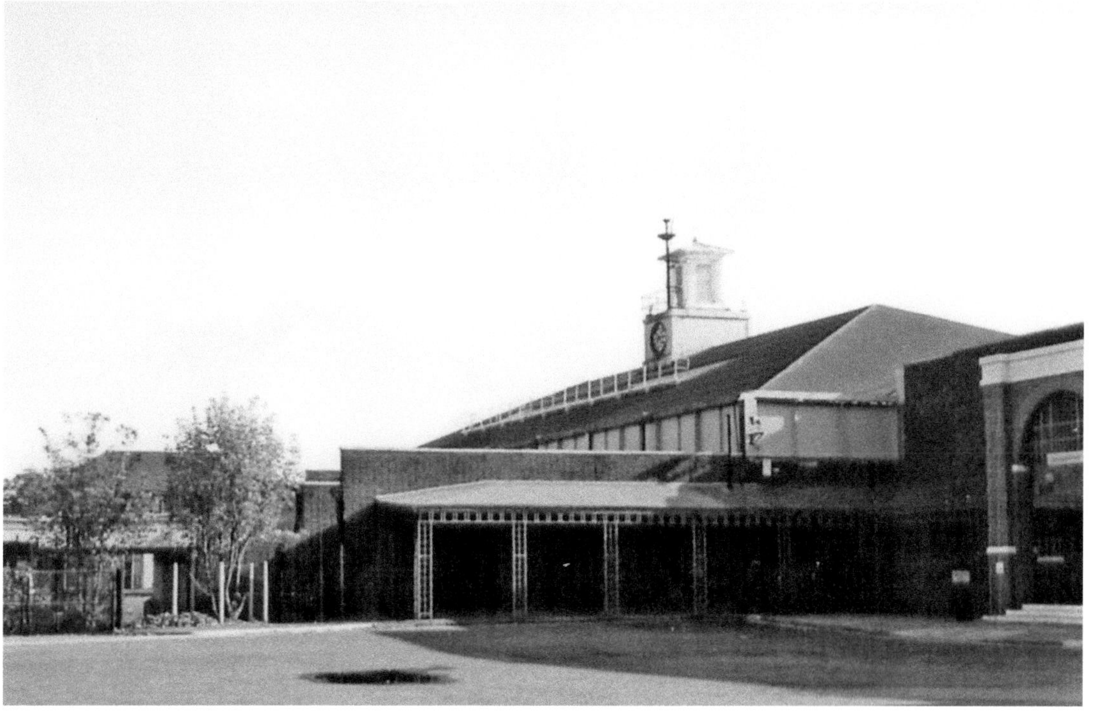

A view of Tilbury Riverside station and part of the baggage hall. The turret with its weather vane and clock can clearly be seen on the roof of the station building.

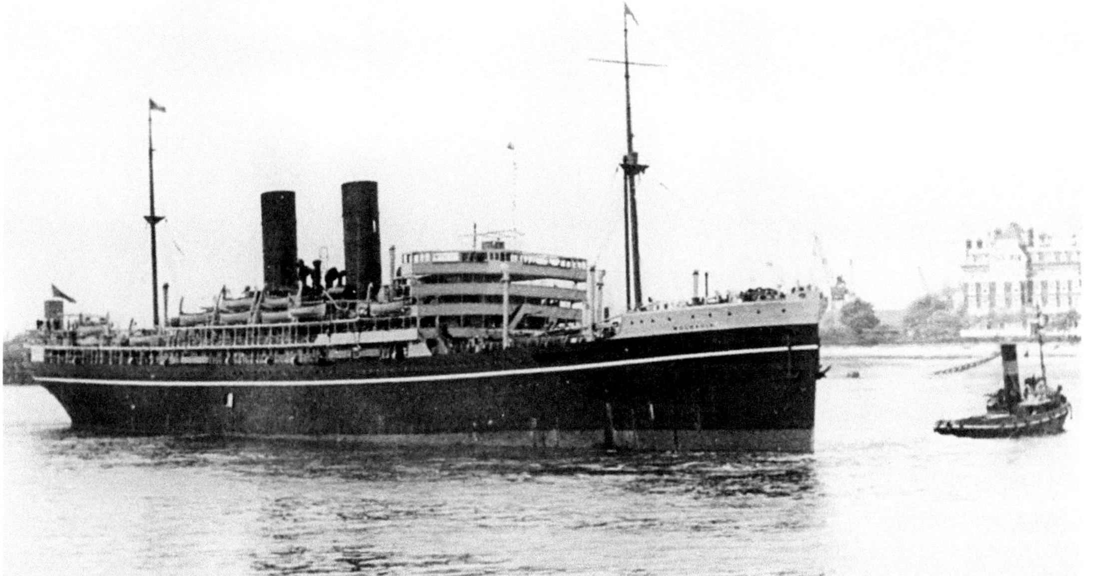

Sailing past Tilbury, the 16,500 grt P&O liner *Moldavia* sets off for Australia in August 1934. In the background, behind the tug, is the Tilbury Hotel.

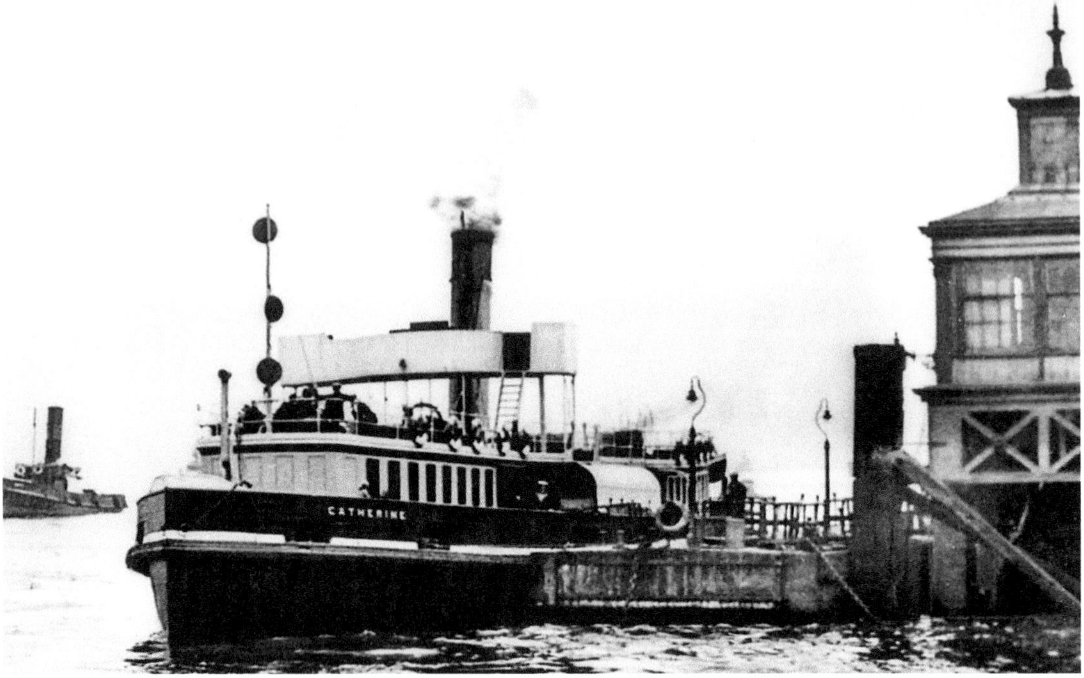

On the other side: the Tilbury–Gravesend ferry *Catherine*, built in 1903, at Gravesend's Town Pier in her early years. She was retired in 1960, when she was renamed *Catherine II* and towed to Belgium for breaking up.

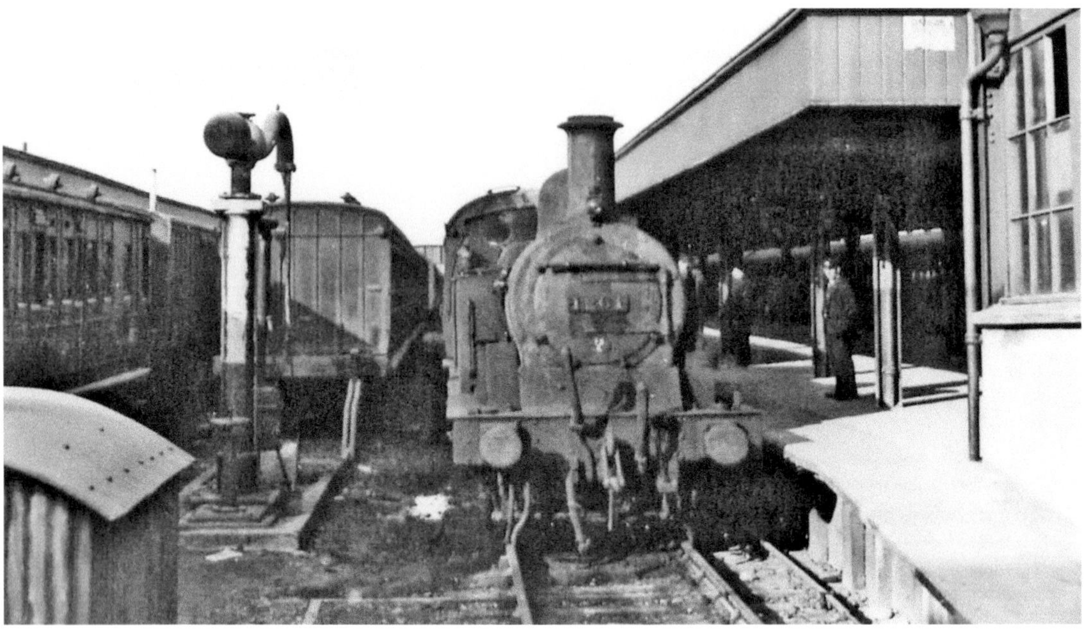

In the good old days of steam: a locomotive creates interest for station staff at Tilbury Riverside as it waits alongside passenger rolling stock sitting in the sidings. Electrification of the line to Tilbury came into effect in 1961.

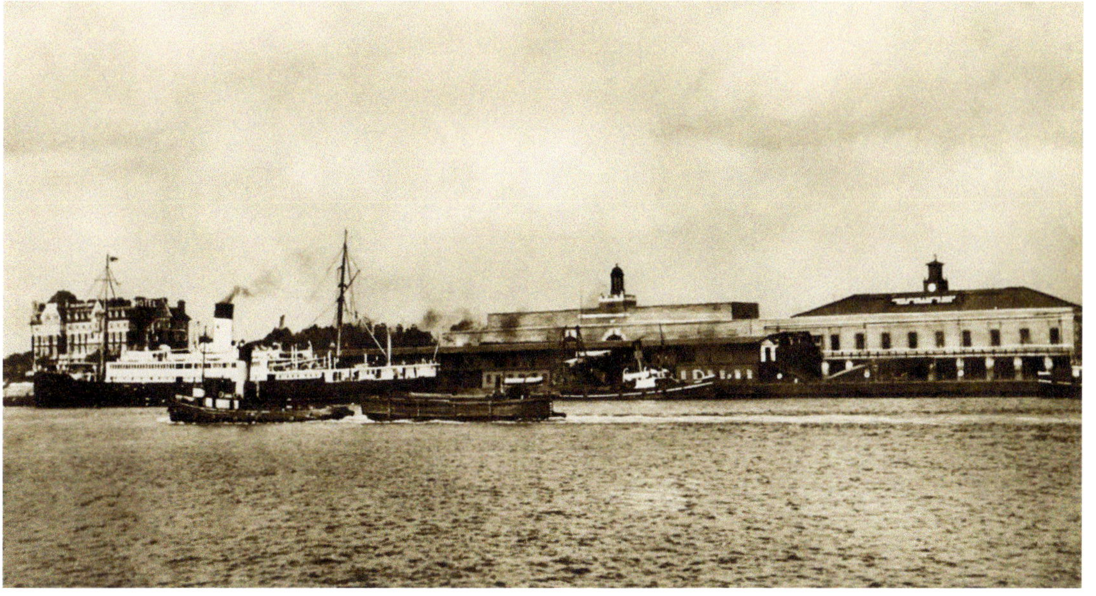

Tilbury Landing Stage pictured shortly before the outset of the Second World War. A Swedish Lloyd passenger vessel, the *Suecia* or *Britannia*, is at the stage, while to the left, immediately upriver, is the Tilbury Hotel.

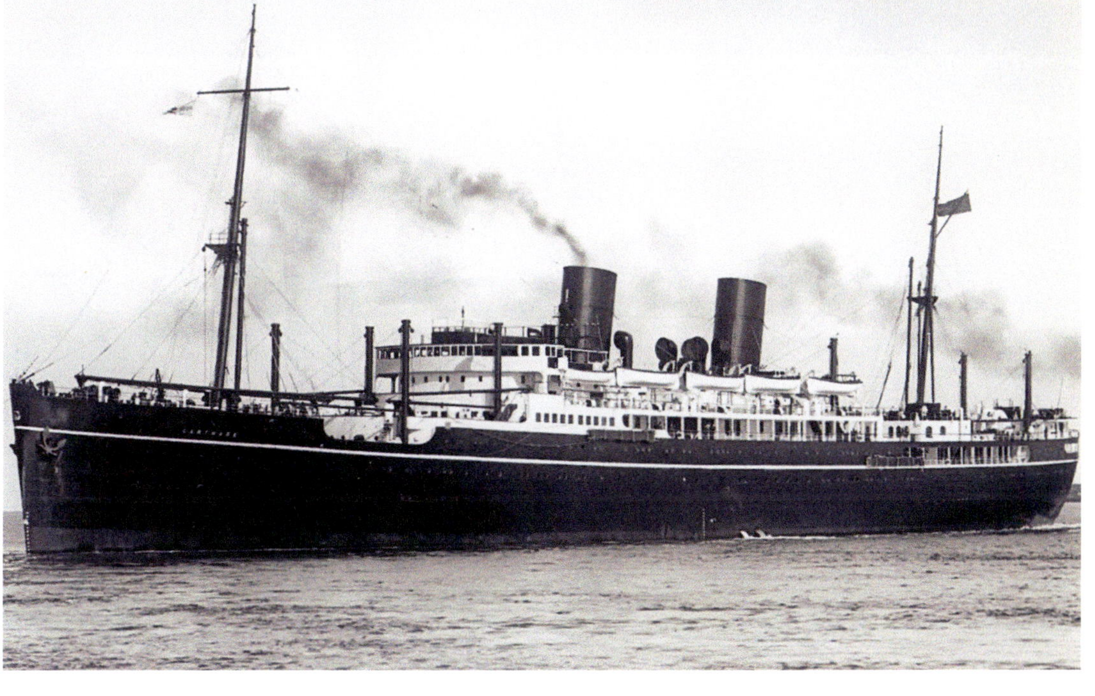

Happy day: launched in 1931 to serve P&O's India and Far East route, the 14,304 grt *Carthage* proudly displays her two black funnels and black hull as she sails up the Thames towards Tilbury. She could accommodate almost 400 passengers, whom she would offload at Tilbury Landing Stage before continuing upriver to the Royal Docks.

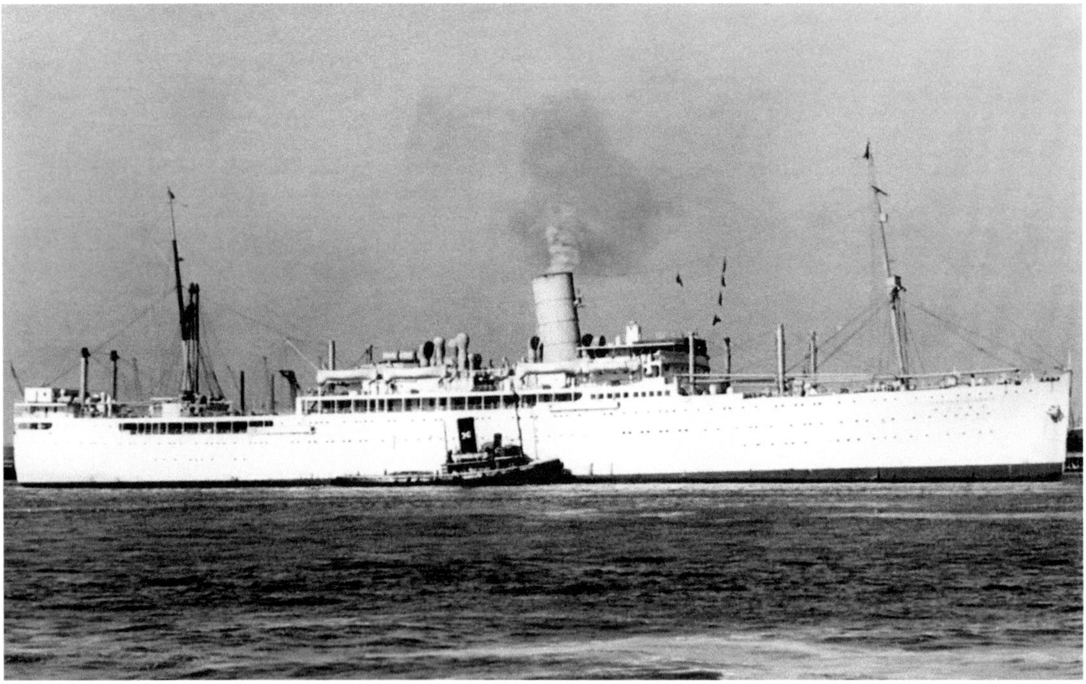

Sad day: like her identical sister *Corfu,* the *Carthage* had her second funnel removed after the war and was repainted with a buff funnel and white hull. In 1961, under the name *Carthage Maru,* she quietly slipped past Tilbury for the last time, en route for Japanese breakers.

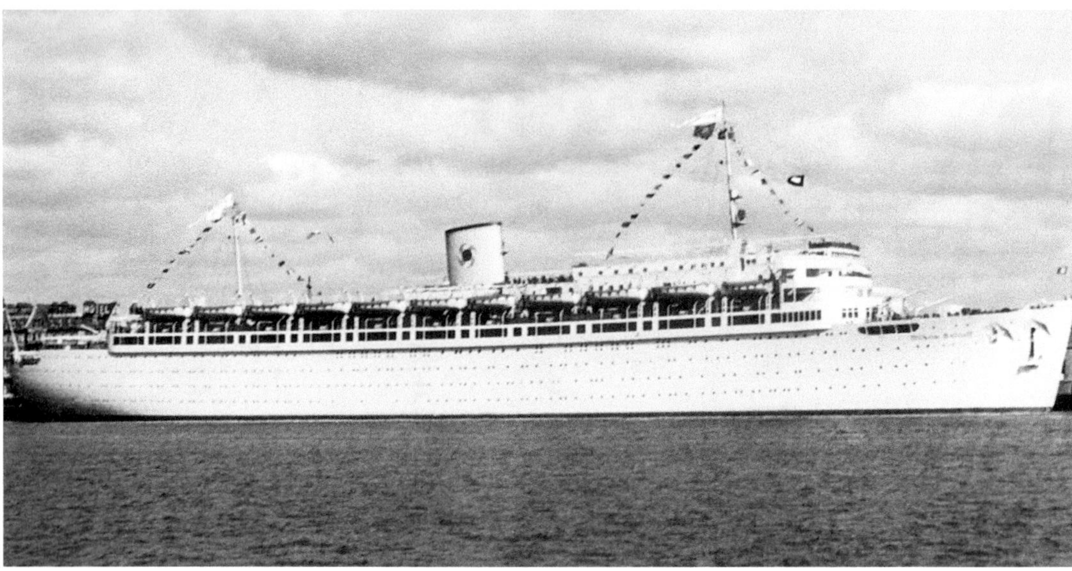

The 25,484 grt German liner *Wilhelm Gustloff* was just a month old when she made her one and only call at Tilbury Landing Stage on 10 April 1938. She was being used as a floating polling station for the 2,000 Germans residing in England to vote on the inclusion of Austria as part of Germany. On 30 January 1945 she was sunk by Soviet submarine *S-13* with the loss of more than 9,000 German civilian refugees, the worst maritime disaster in history.

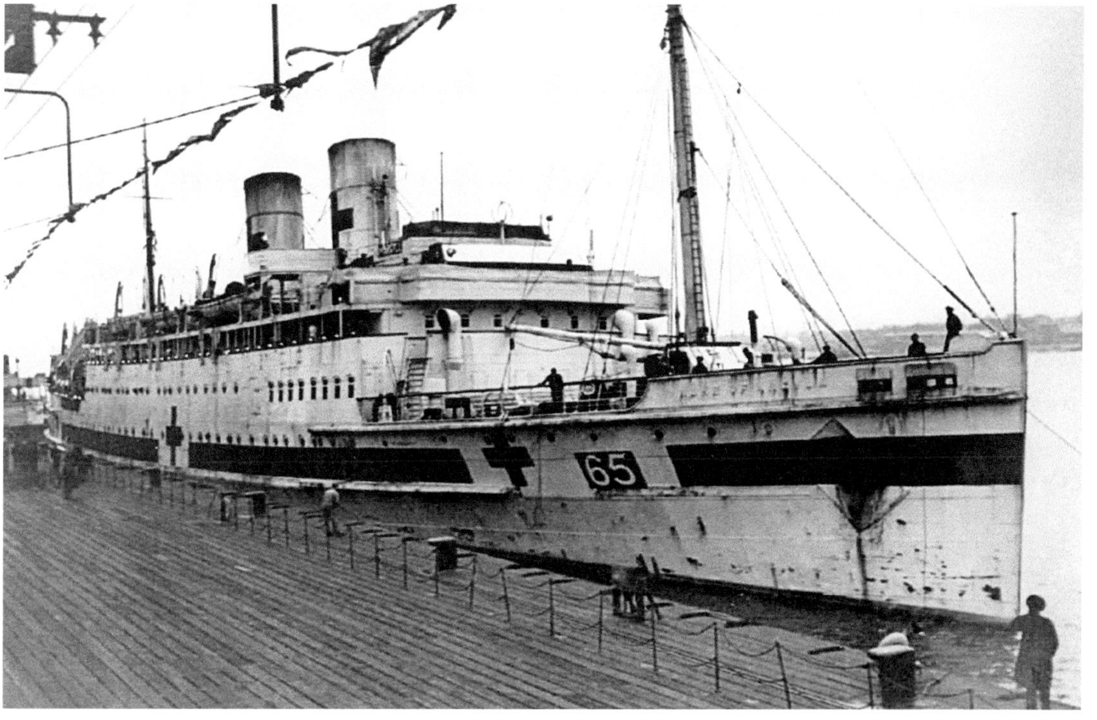

Wartime at Tilbury: *Hospital Ship 65* lies at Tilbury Landing Stage. In peacetime she was the ferry *Duke of Argyll,* which sailed the Irish Sea from 1928 to 1956.

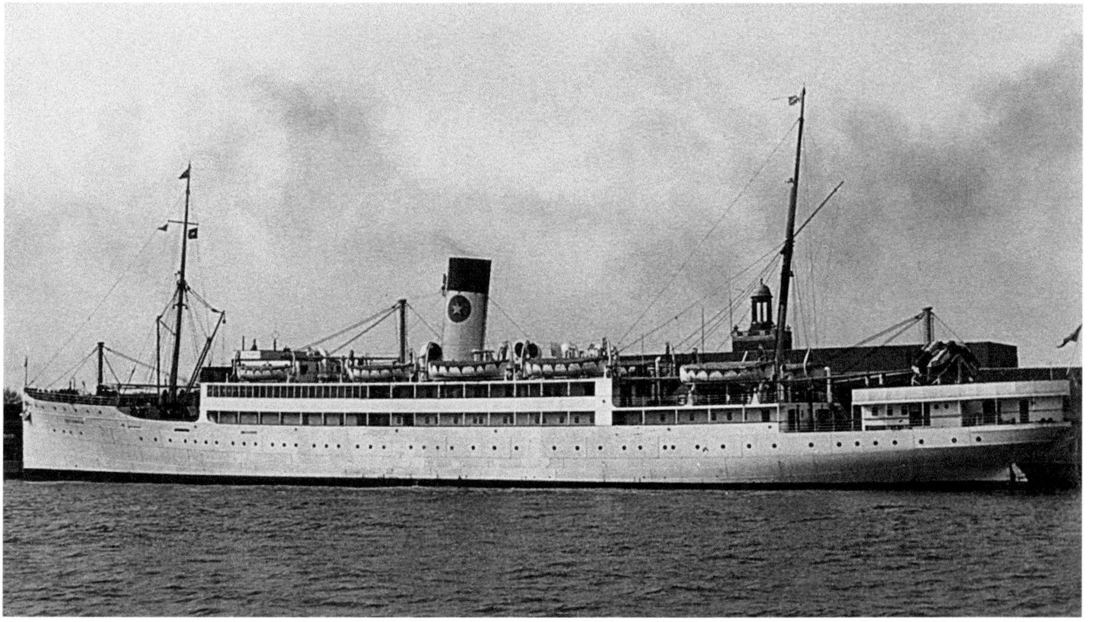

The little short-sea passenger ship *Britannia* plied between Gothenburg and Tilbury Landing Stage with her sister *Suecia* until 1966. Built for Swedish Lloyd in 1929, she could accommodate 265 passengers. She was painted all-white on reinstating the service after the Second World War.

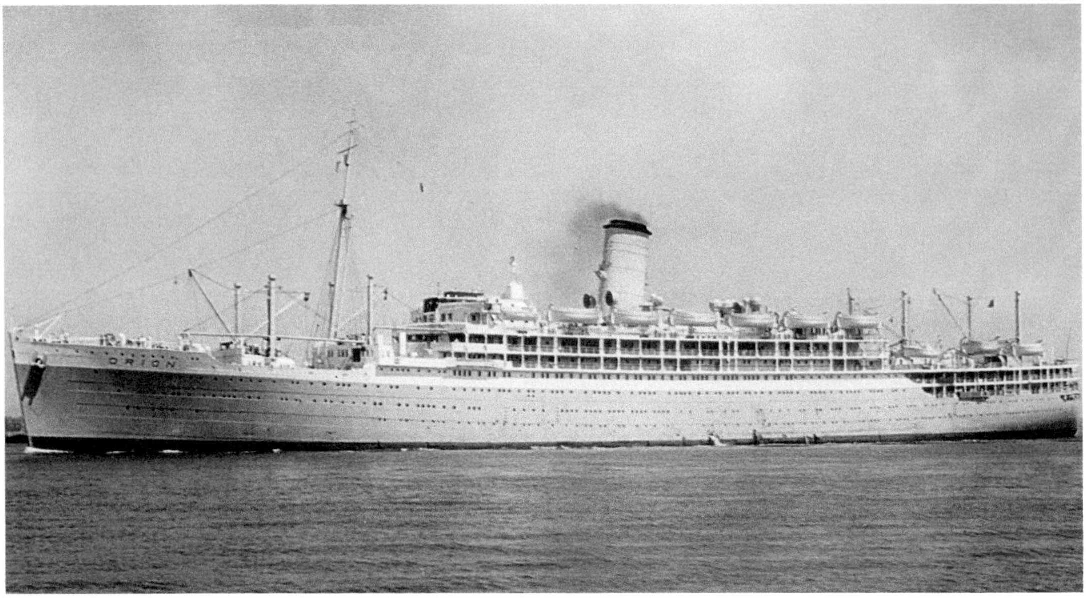

Orion, 23,696 grt, sails sedately up the Thames to Tilbury Landing Stage. Built in 1935 for Orient Line's Australian trade, she was the first of the company's ships to re-enter commercial service after the Second World War, carrying First and Tourist Class passengers.

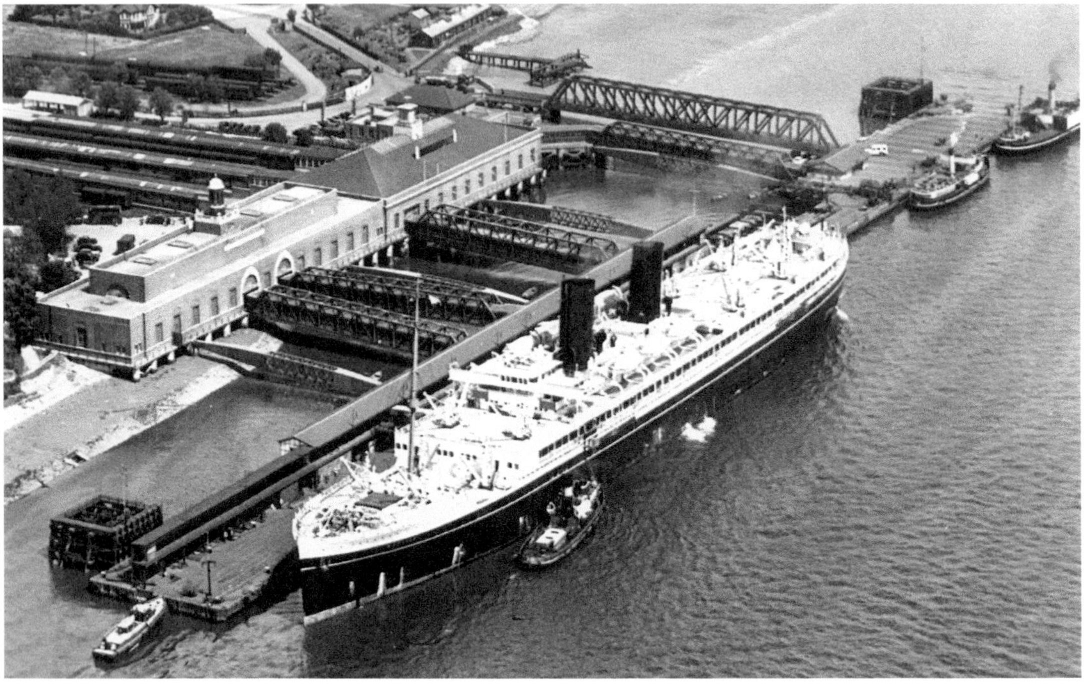

A lady in black: the P&O liner *Mooltan*, 1923/21,039 grt, arrives at Tilbury Landing Stage from Australia. Like her sister *Maloja*, she retained her pre-war black livery after the Second World War while operating as a migrant ship. She was broken up in 1953. Note the Tilbury–Gravesend passenger and car ferries immediately behind her.

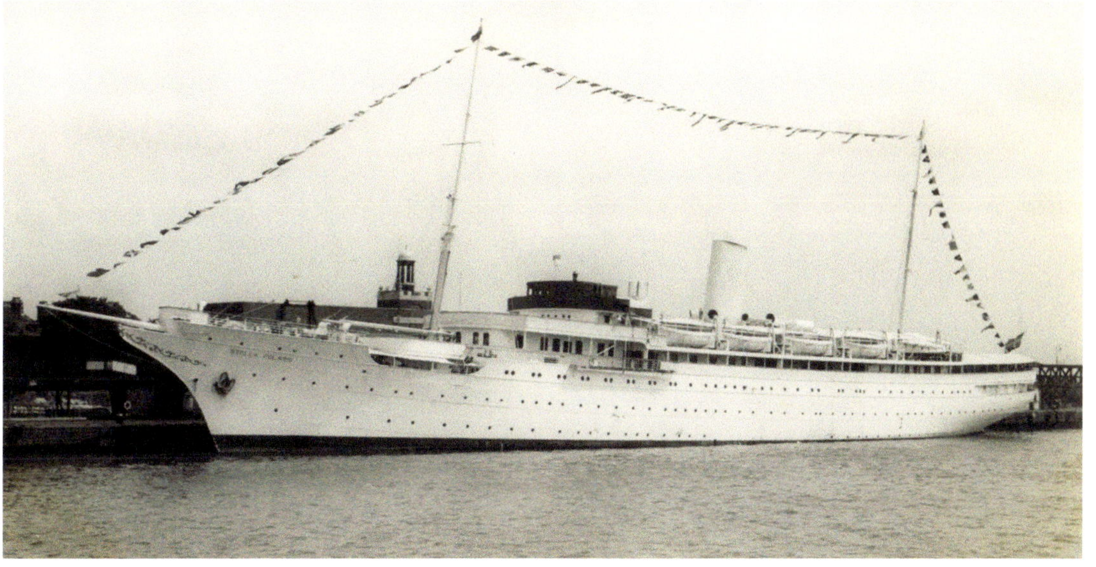

One of the most elegant ships ever to visit the Thames, the 1927-built *Stella Polaris* lies alongside Tilbury Landing Stage. With her yacht-like looks, she was regarded as the 'royal yacht' of cruising, with lavish accommodation for just 200 passengers. Originally owned by Bergen Line, Norway, the 5,209 grt vessel was sold to Clipper Line of Sweden in 1952. In 1969 her cruising career ended and she moved to Japan as a floating hotel. In 2006 she was acquired by a Swedish company but sadly, while under tow to a nearby shipyard, she took on water and sank south-east of Japan.

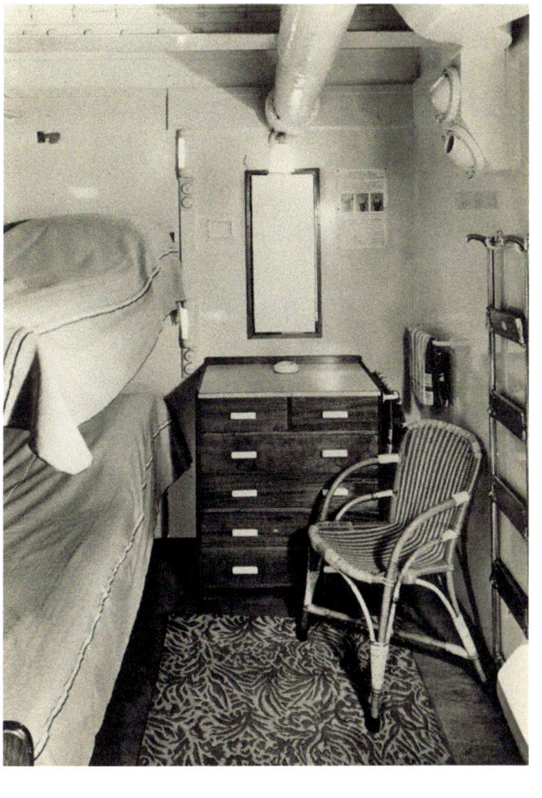

A typically functional two-berth Tourist Class cabin that would be occupied by migrants as well as full-fare paying passengers to Australia.

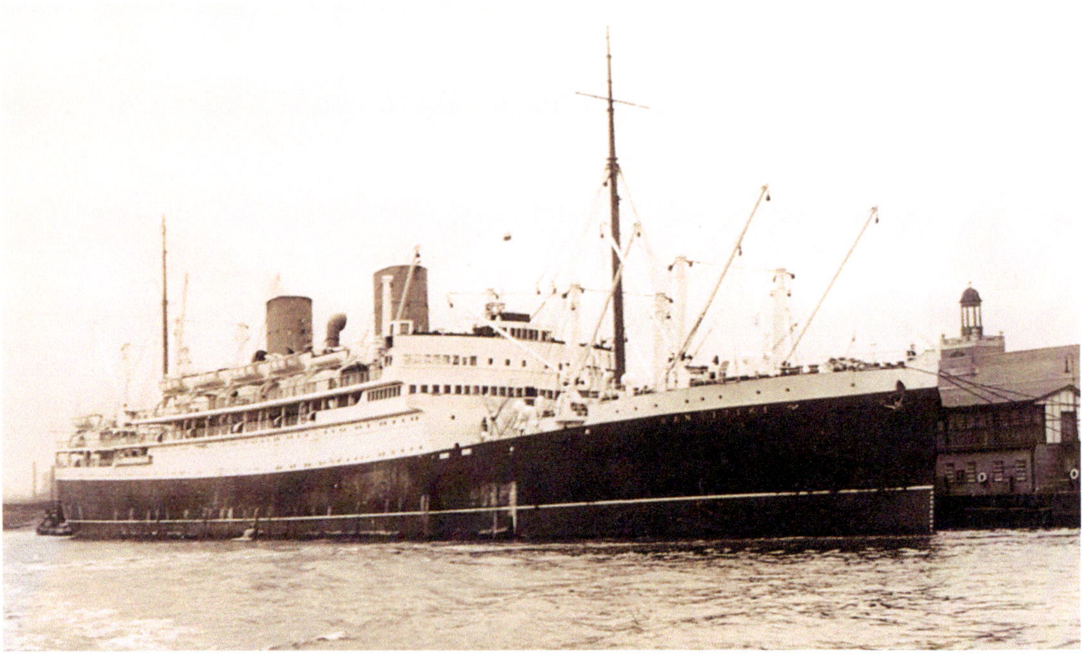

The 16,755 grt motorship *Rangitiki* at Tilbury Landing Stage prior to sailing for New Zealand. Completed in 1929, she was one of the popular 'Rangi-Boats' owned by the New Zealand Shipping Company. After war service she was refitted to carry 405 passengers until being sent for scrapping in 1962, having made eighty-seven round voyages to New Zealand.

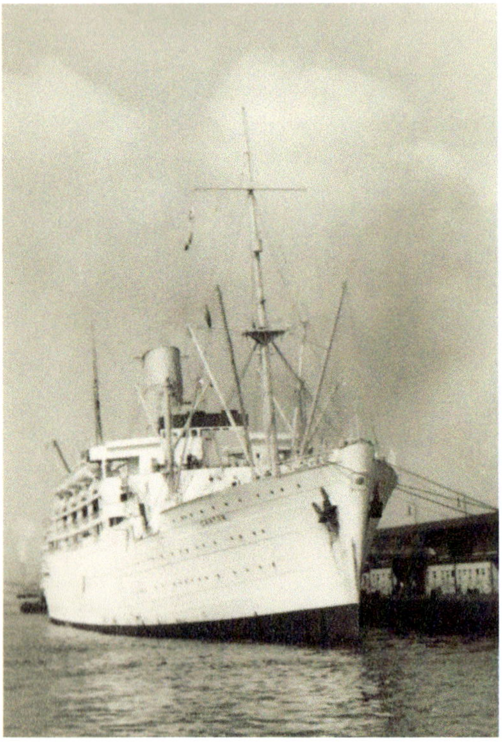

The P&O passenger-cargo liner *Canton,* 16,033 grt, at Tilbury Landing Stage probably during the 1950s. Built in 1938, the vessel operated on P&O's Far East service to Hong Kong and Yokohama. She acted as an armed merchant cruiser and a troopship during the Second World War, after which she was repainted white. She was broken up in 1962.

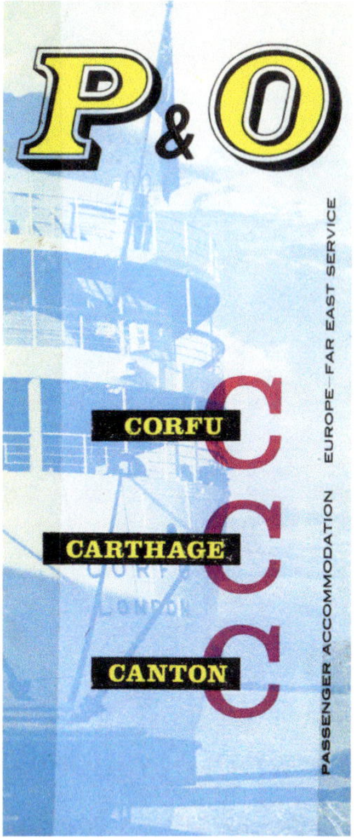

A brochure issued by P&O to promote its Far East service undertaken by *Canton* and the smaller sisters *Corfu* and *Carthage*.

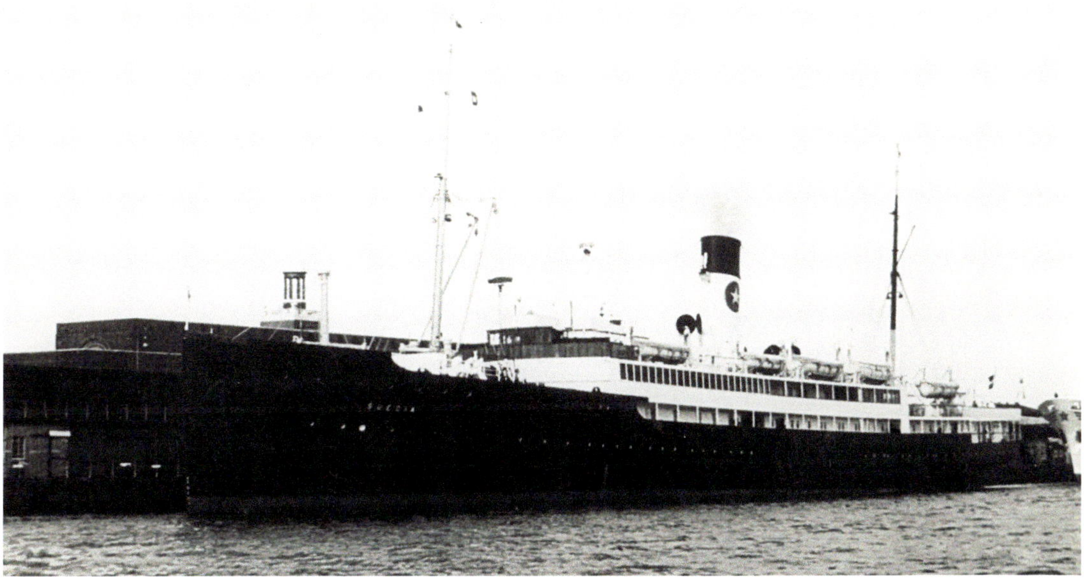

Suecia, 4,661 grt, berthed at Tilbury Landing Stage after another voyage from Gothenburg. In 1937 she sank after being hit by a tanker but, incredibly, she was raised and back in service in three months. Like her sister *Britannia*, she was sold to Greek interests in 1966 and she became the *Istria*. In 1970 she passed on to Turkish shipowners and was scrapped in 1972.

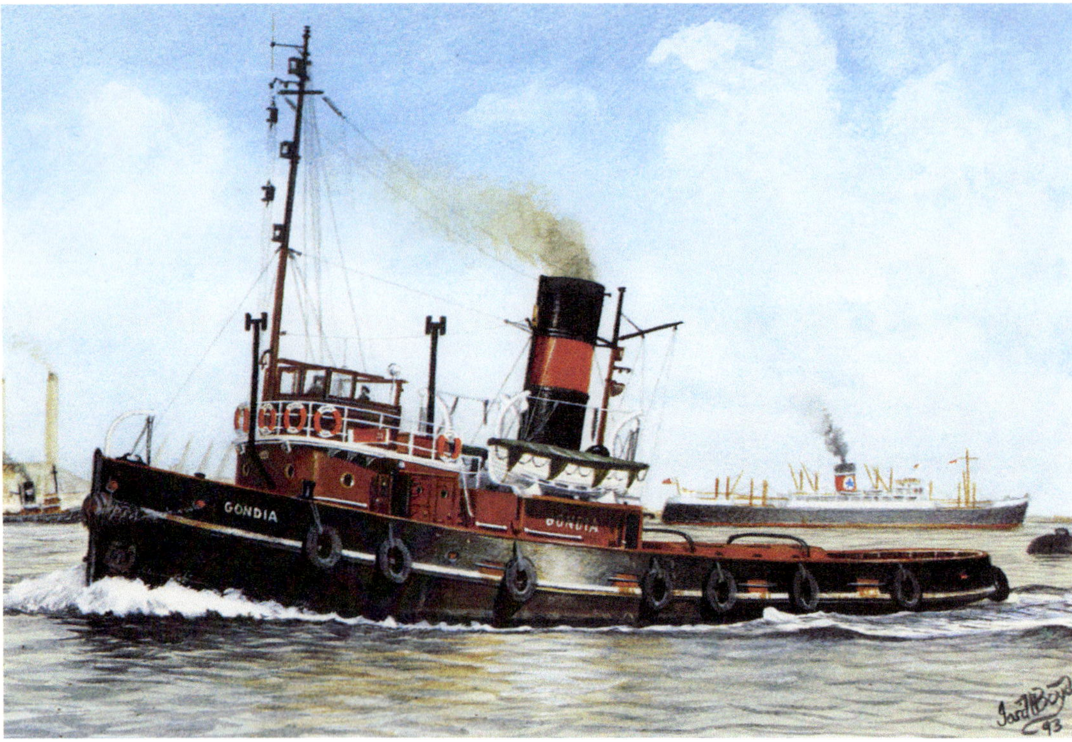

Before the days of giant cruise liners and container ships that require the assistance of ultra-powerful tugs, steam tugs such as the 1927-built *Gondia* would be based at Gravesend's Royal Terrace Pier and various other river locations, ready to handle shipping at Tilbury and upriver docks. Note the outgoing Blue Star Line cargo ship in the background.

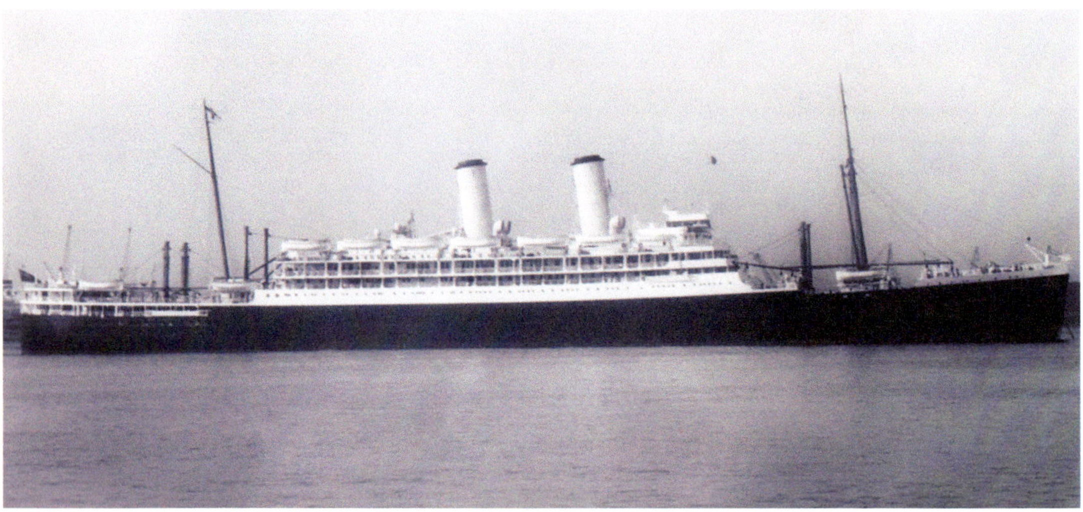

Moored off Tilbury, the Orient Line passenger liner *Orontes* was a familiar sight at Tilbury Landing Stage for many years. Built in 1929, she saw war service as a troopship and was afterwards employed in the carriage of migrants to Australia, being converted into a one-class ship in 1953. She left Tilbury for the final time on 25 November 1961, to be broken up in Spain.

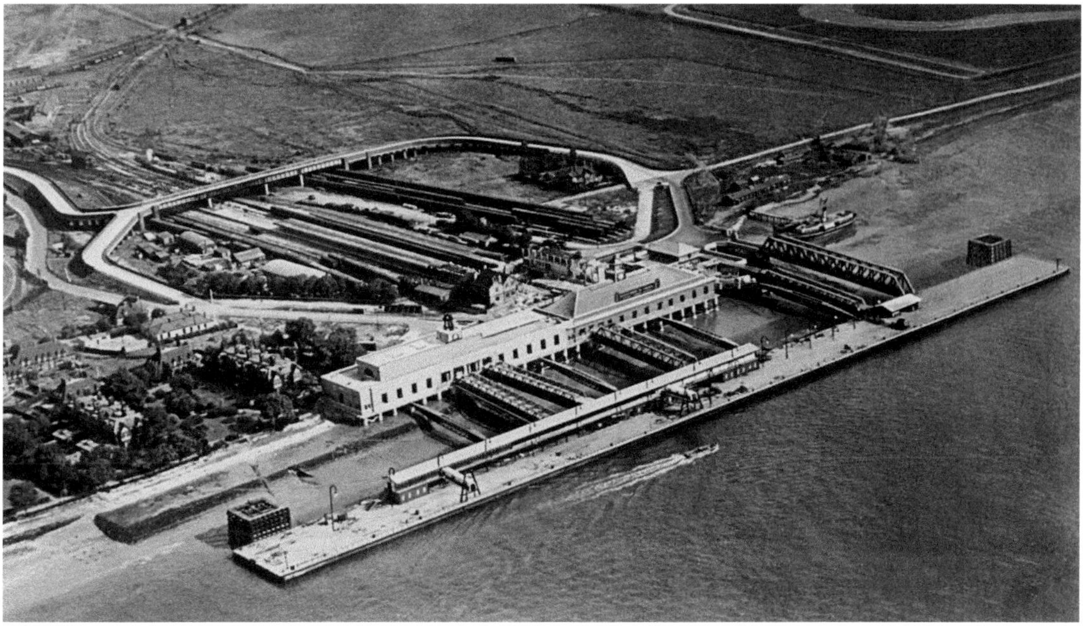

A post-war aerial study of Tilbury Landing Stage, showing the large baggage hall to the left, next to the Tilbury Riverside station building. Platforms, railway lines and approach roads can be seen behind.

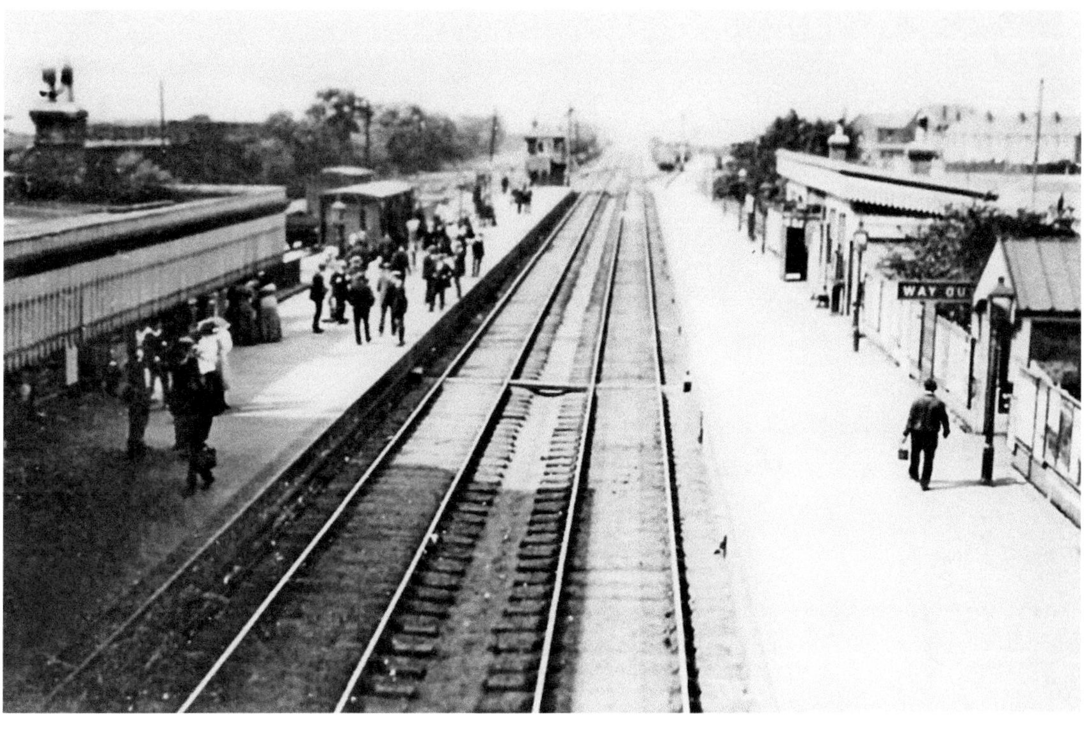

Passengers, probably from the Tilbury–Gravesend ferry, wait on one of the platforms at Tilbury Riverside station for the next train to London or Southend.

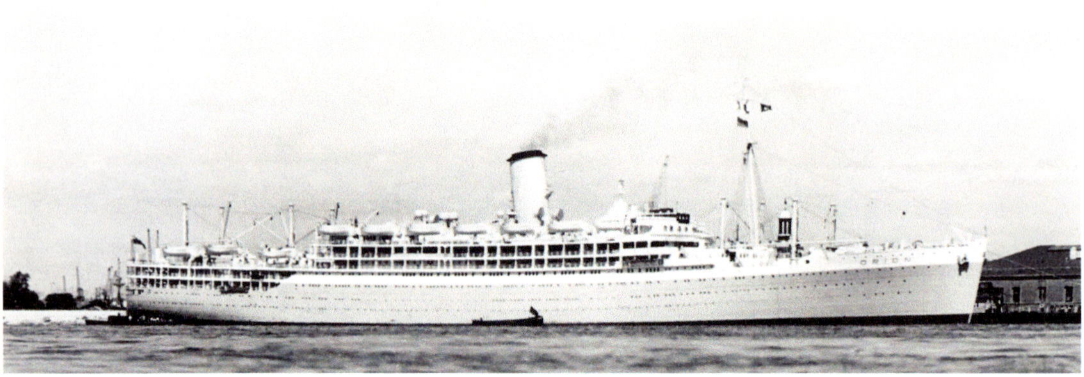

A view of *Orion* embarking passengers for Australia during her later years. In 1958 she was converted to a one-class ship, accommodating up to 1,691 passengers, to cater for the migrant trade. She carried thousands of 'Ten Pound Poms' from Tilbury Landing Stage until her withdrawal from service in May 1963. She was broken up at Antwerp later that year.

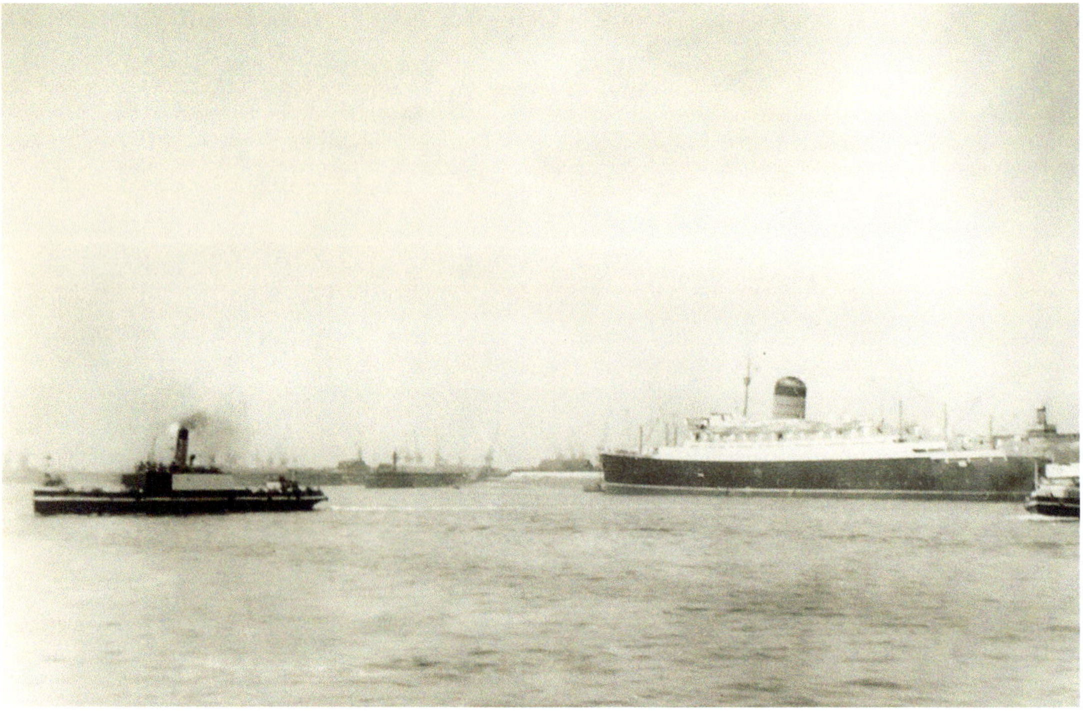

Car and passenger ferries make their way from Tilbury to Gravesend with the 21,717 grt Cunard passenger-cargo liner *Ivernia* berthed at the landing stage. With *Saxonia*, one of her three sisters, *Ivernia* sailed between the UK and Canada in the summer months. In 1962 she was extensively refitted and re-entered service as *Franconia*. In 1971 she was laid up at Southampton and then in the River Fal, awaiting sale.

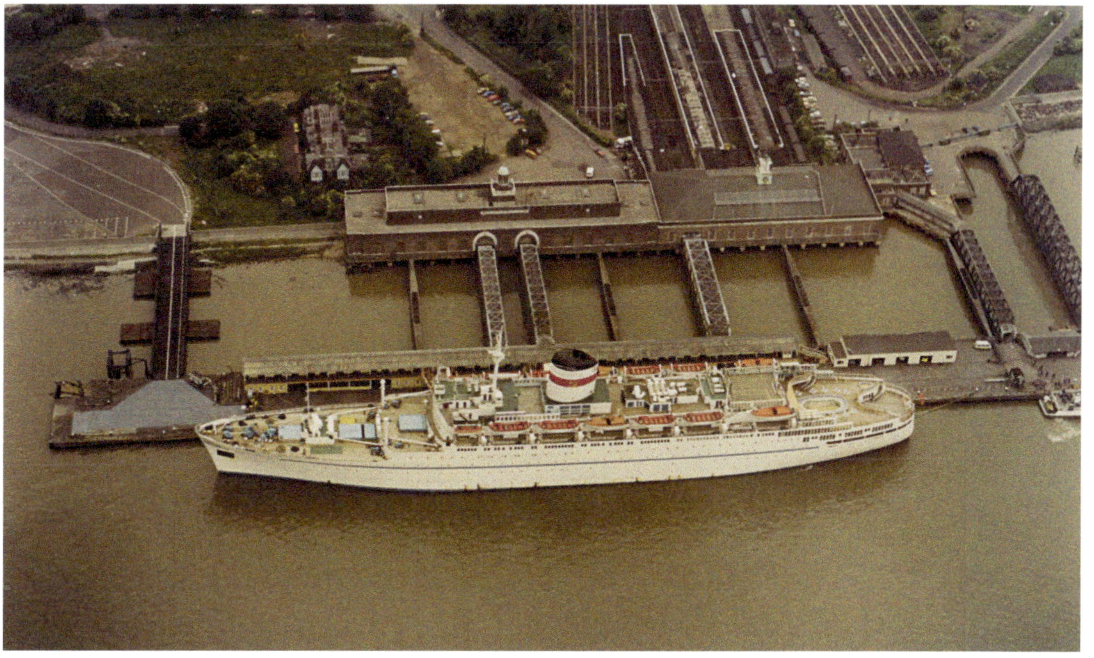

Looking down on the Soviet passenger vessel *Fedor Shalyapin* at Tilbury Landing Stage. Formerly the Cunarder *Franconia*, she was purchased by the Far East Shipping Company in 1963 and taken on charter by CTC Lines for voyages to Australia. Later she was employed in cruising and passed to the Ukraine in 1992, following the breakup of the Soviet Union.

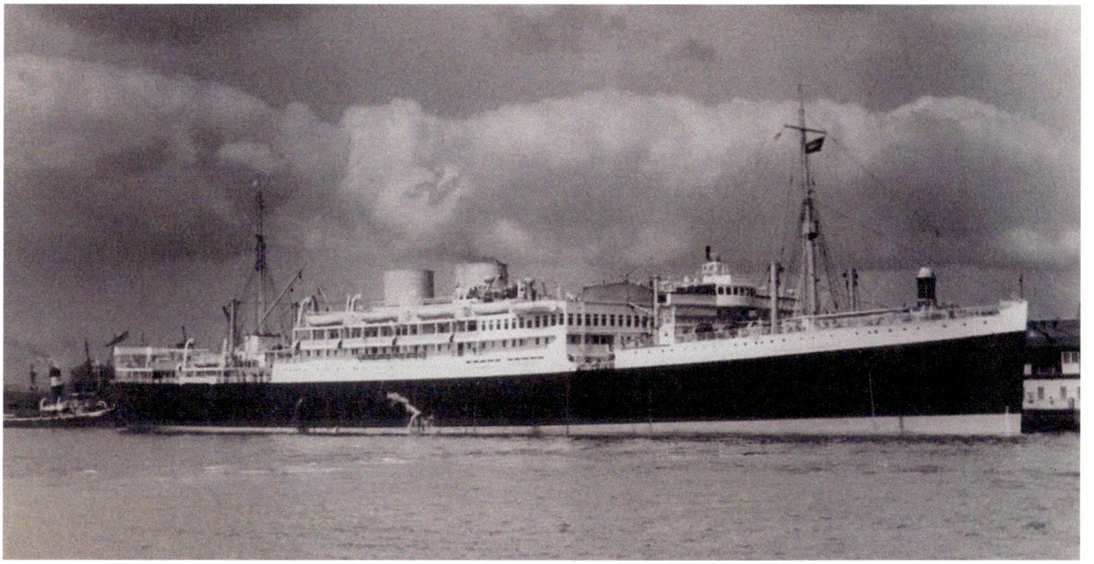

One of the four Highland sisters with their characteristically short funnels, *Highland Princess*, 14,128 grt, entered South American service with the Nelson Line in 1932 but almost immediately passed to Royal Mail Lines following a company merger. She would unload her refrigerated produce in London's Royal Docks before embarking passengers at Tilbury Landing Stage for another voyage to Buenos Aires.

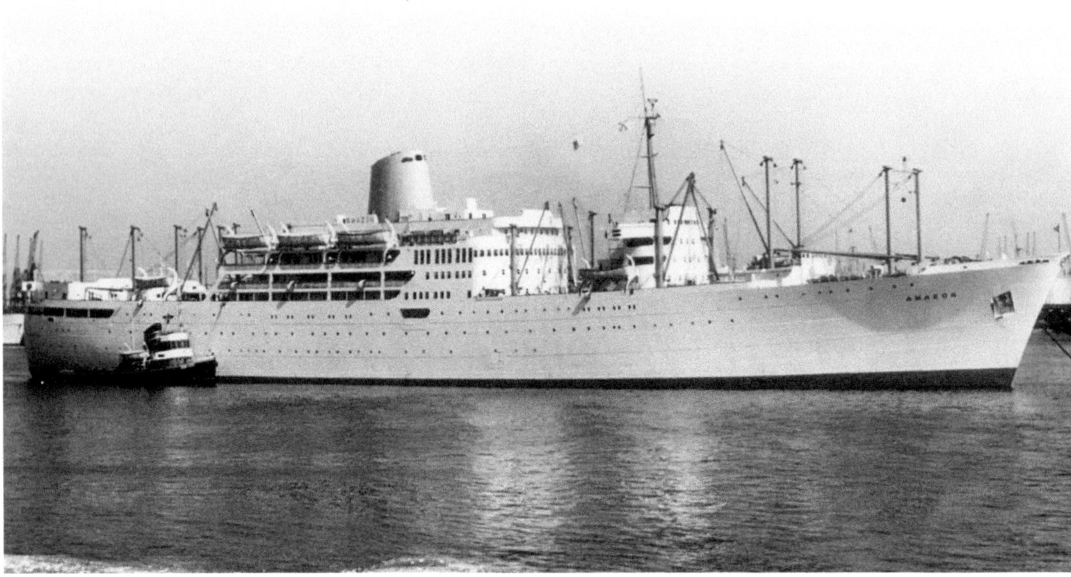

By the early 1960s the quartet had been replaced by three larger, handsome-looking sisters, *Amazon*, pictured above, *Aragon* and *Arlanza*, which would be employed on the route for fewer than ten years.

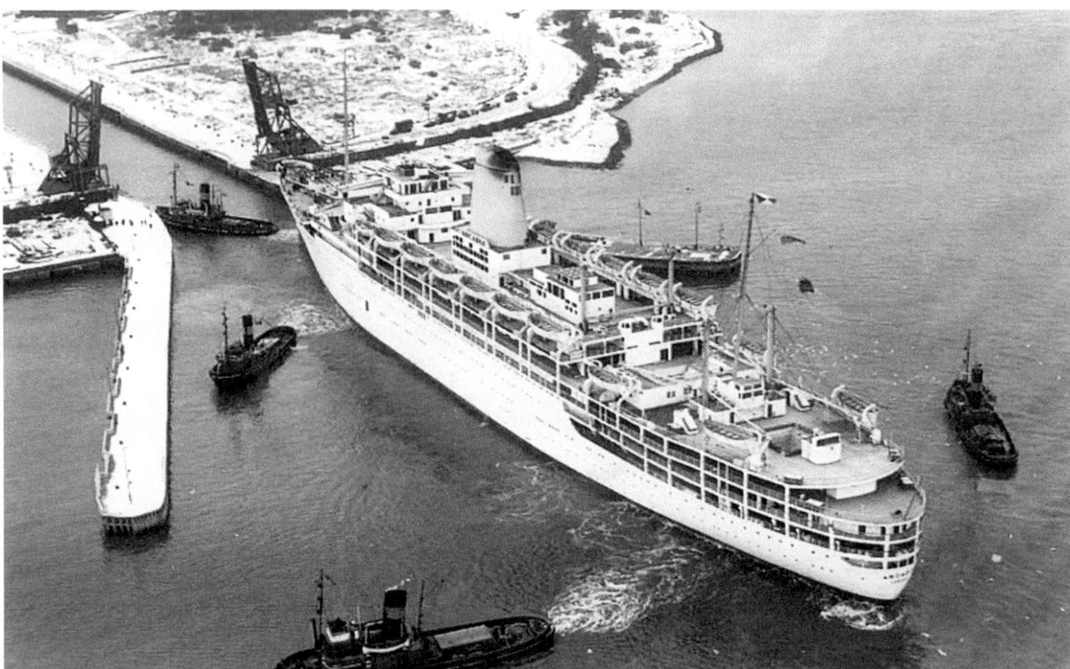

A superb view of the P&O liner *Arcadia* being manoeuvred into the entrance lock of Tilbury Docks, having discharged her passengers at Tilbury Landing Stage. At 29,871 grt she was the largest passenger ship on Australian service to use Tilbury. After a few years of cruising she was broken up in 1979, at just twenty-five years old.

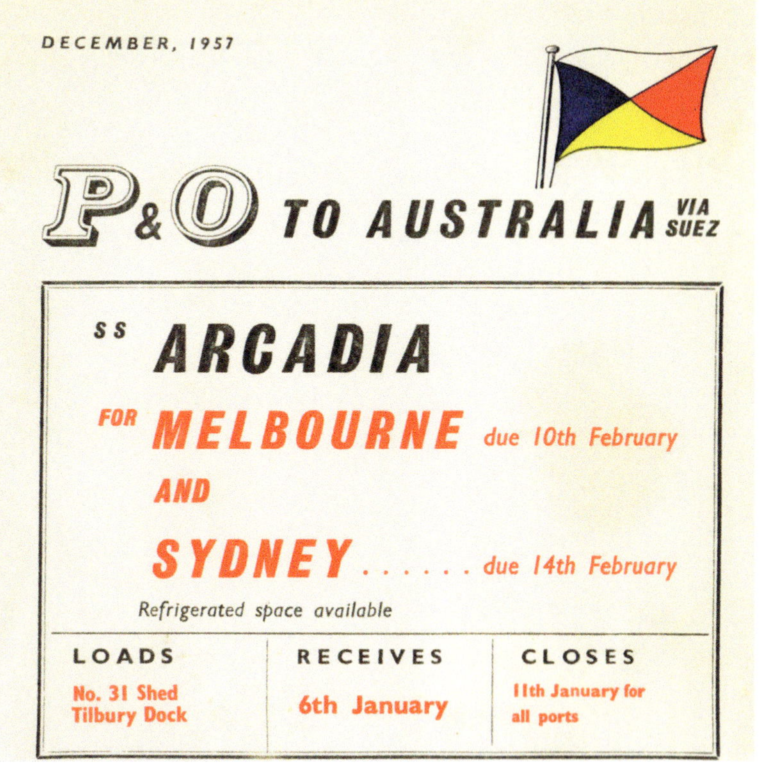
DECEMBER, 1957

P&O TO AUSTRALIA VIA SUEZ

SS ARCADIA

FOR MELBOURNE due 10th February

AND

SYDNEY . . . . . . due 14th February

Refrigerated space available

LOADS	RECEIVES	CLOSES
No. 31 Shed Tilbury Dock	6th January	11th January for all ports

Like other P&O passenger ships of the day, *Arcadia* could carry copious amounts of cargo, which would be handled at No. 31 Shed in Tilbury Docks, as this loading broker's card from 1957 shows.

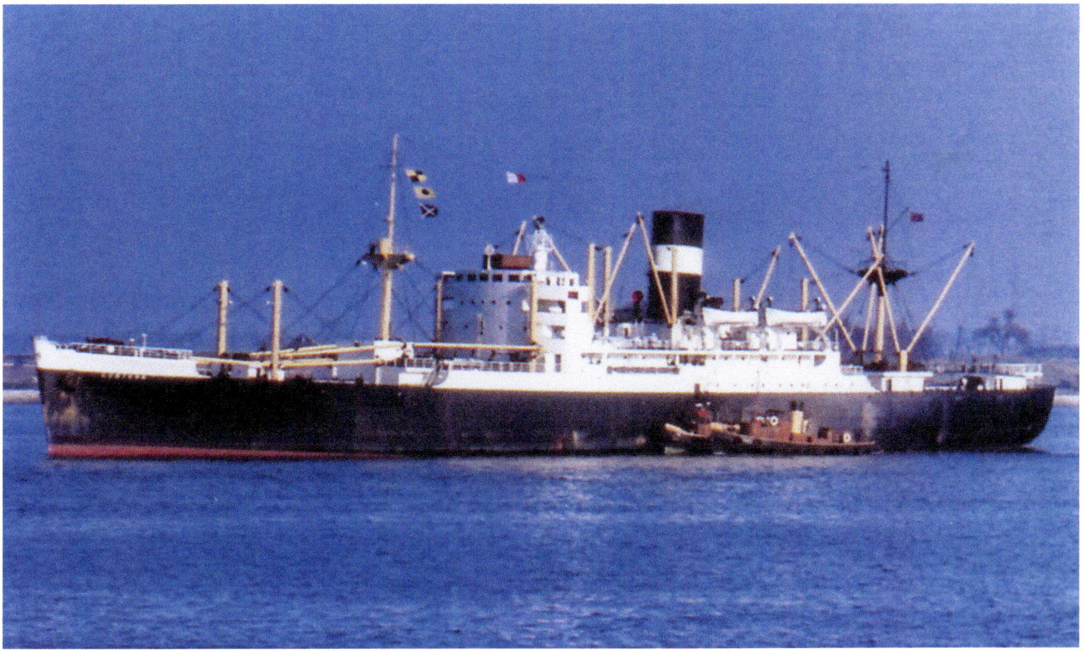

Owned by Glasgow company the Donaldson Line, the cargo ship *Cortona*, 1947/8,289 grt, makes a rare appearance in Gravesend Reach while on River Plate service. Sold to Greek owners in 1967, she was broken up in 1980.

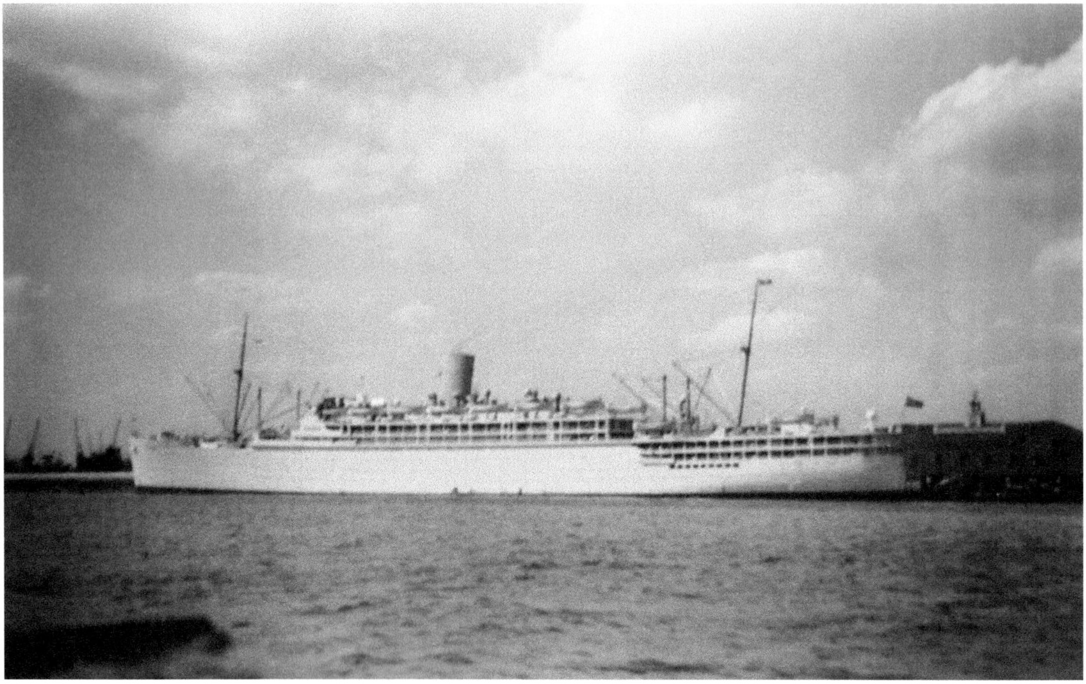

The 23,580 grt passenger liner *Strathmore* at Tilbury Landing Stage in 1958. She was delivered to P&O Line in 1935 for the company's voyages to India and Australia. After wartime troopship duties, she re-entered the Australian service in 1949.

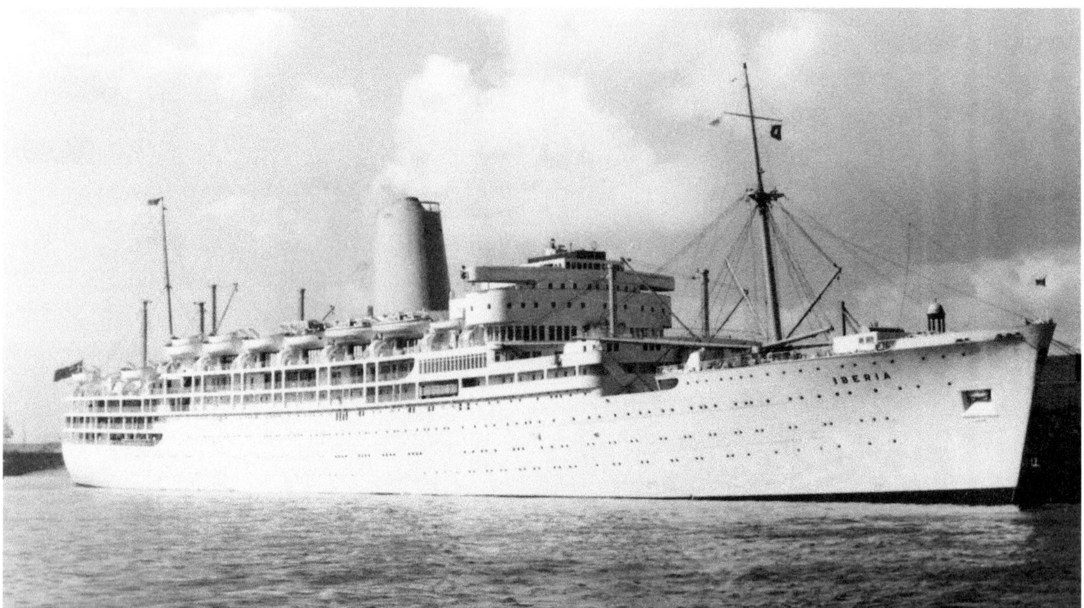

A near-sister to P&O's *Arcadia*, the liner *Iberia*, 1954/29,614 grt, boards passengers for Australia at Tilbury Landing Stage. Unfortunately, this handsome vessel was plagued by mechanical problems throughout her life and was sent for breaking in 1972.

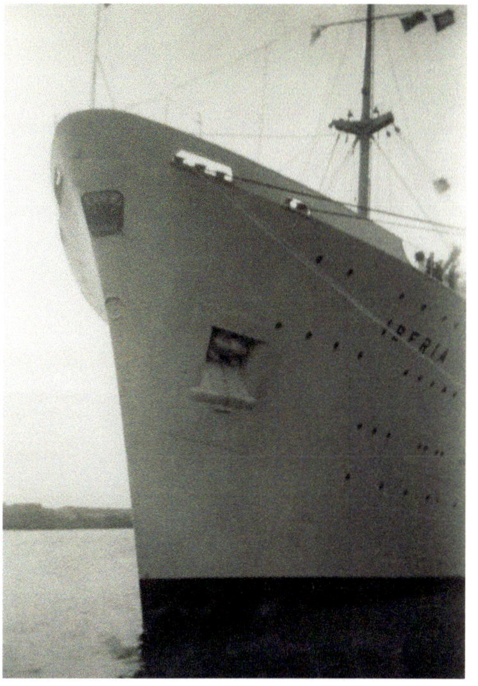

A bow view of *Iberia* as she prepares to leave Tilbury for Australia in late autumn 1958. On board were members of the touring England cricket team.

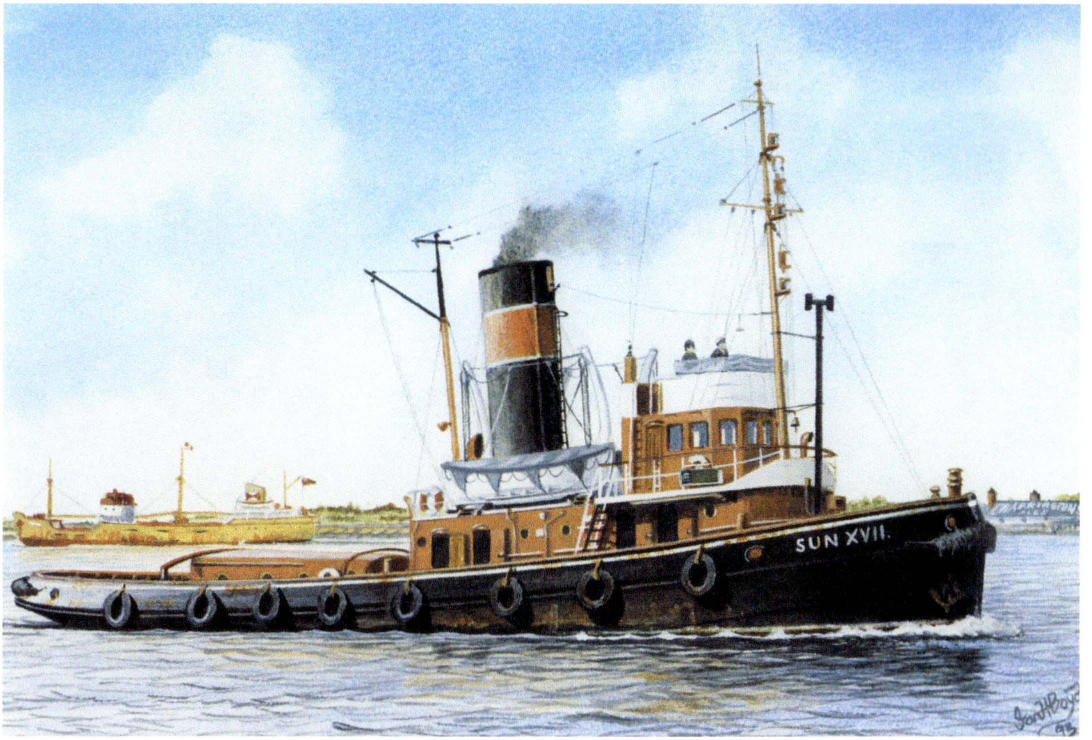

The fleet of 'Sun Tugs', owned by W. H. J. Alexander Ltd, was a familiar sight on the Thames for many decades. *Sun XVII*, seen off Tilbury, dated from 1946 and was sold to Italian owners in 1968 and renamed *Rania G.* She was scrapped in Palermo in 1983.

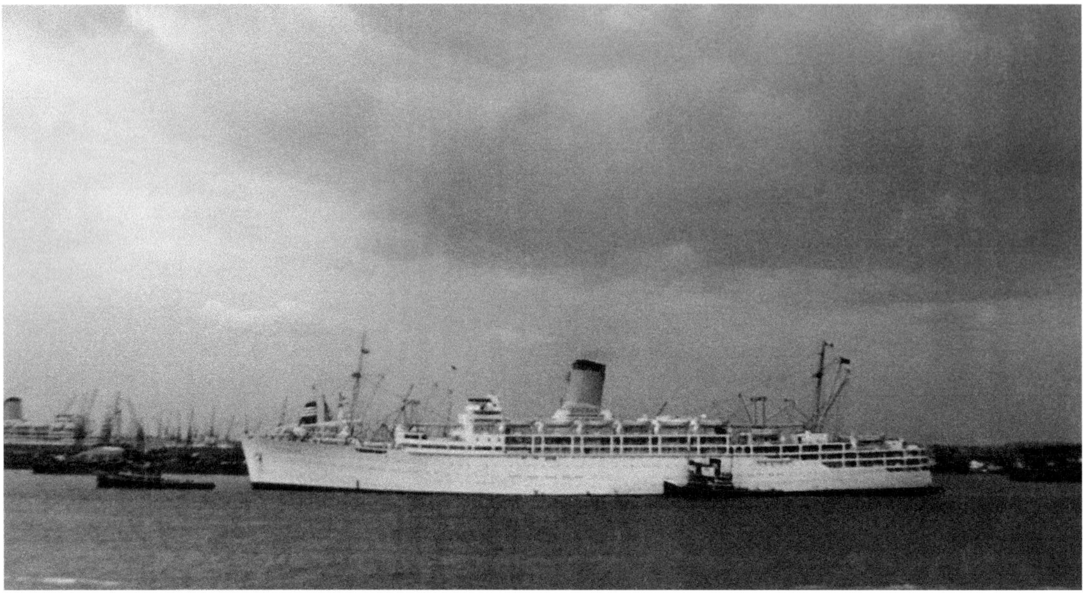

The P&O liner *Chusan* moves upriver to Tilbury Docks from the landing stage. Built in 1950, the 24,215 grt vessel could accommodate 988 passengers and sailed between London, Bombay (Mumbai) and Japan until 1963, after which she was placed on Australian service. She was broken up in 1973.

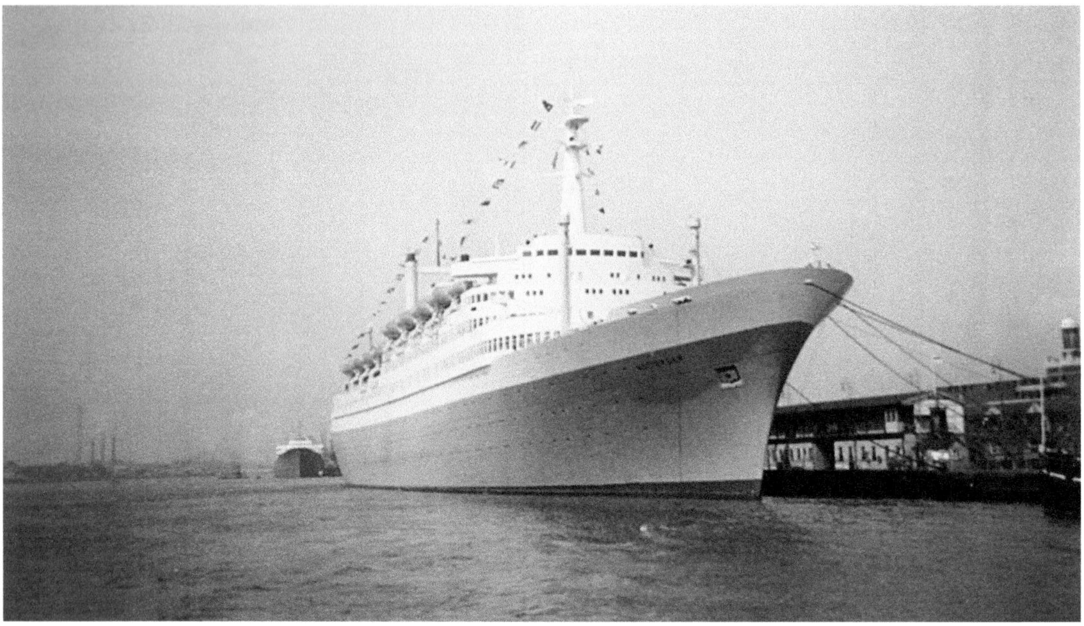

The legendary Dutch liner *Rotterdam*, 1959/37,783 grt, berthed at Tilbury Landing Stage in 1960, her one and only visit to the Thames. The flagship of the Holland-America Line, she was extremely popular as both a transatlantic liner and cruise ship before being sold in 1997 to Premier Cruise Lines as the *Rembrandt*. On retirement from service she was refitted and towed to her home city of Rotterdam, where she opened as a floating hotel.

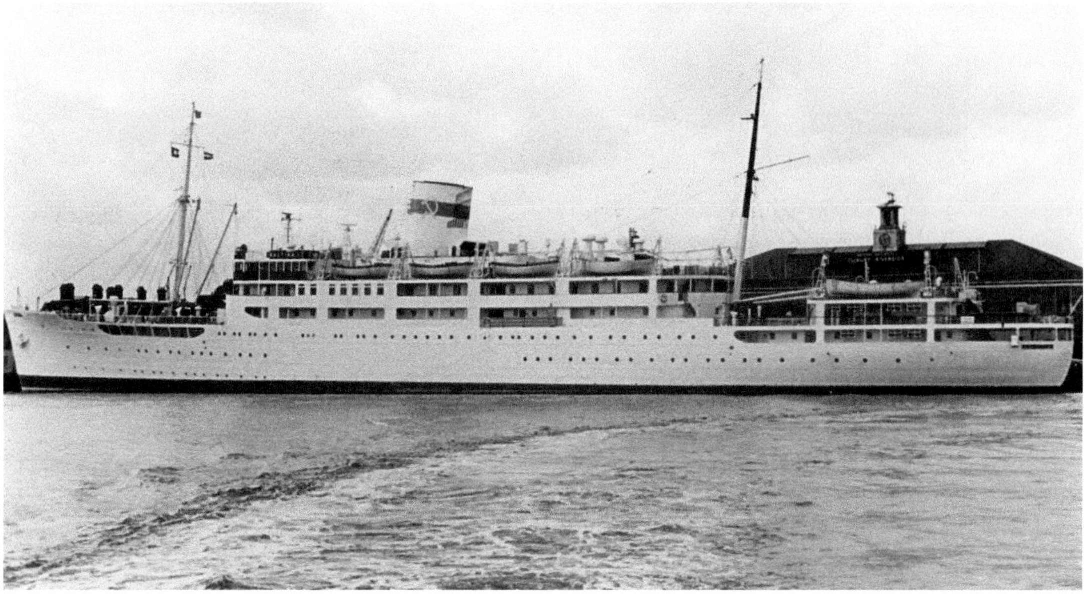

Built for the Soviet Union, the 7,494 grt passenger ship *Baltika* was christened *Vyacheslav Molotov* in 1940. After the Second World War she ran regularly between Leningrad (St Petersburg) and Tilbury Landing Stage, changing her name to *Baltika* in 1957. Her claim to fame was the transporting of Soviet Premier Nikita Khrushchev to New York in 1960.

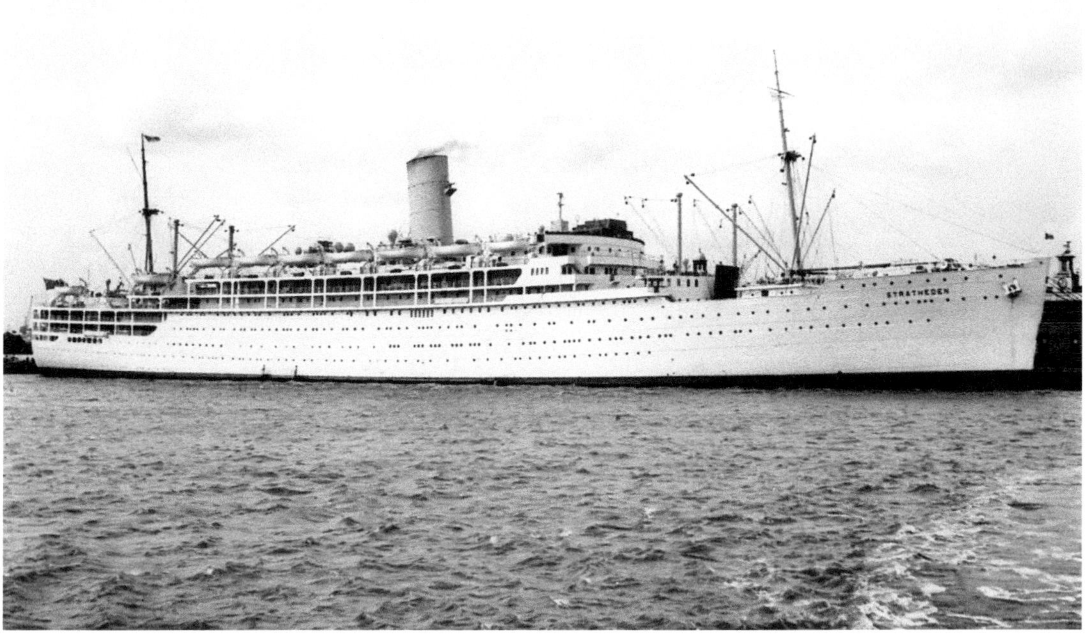

Stratheden, 23,732 grt, was launched in 1937 and could carry 1,011 passengers. During the war she steamed almost a half a million nautical miles as a troopship. In May 1947 she re-opened the India and Australia service for P&O, becoming a familiar visitor to Tilbury Landing Stage. Together with her sister *Strathmore*, she was sold to Latsis Lines of Greece in 1963.

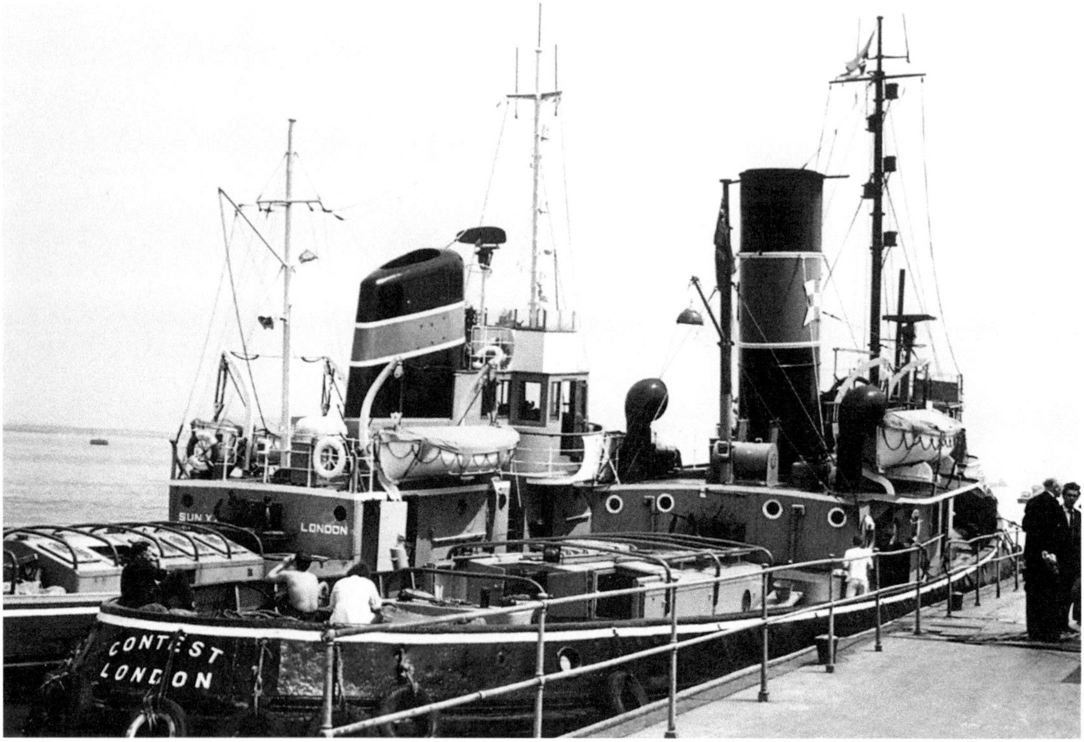

Two tugs taking a rest at Tilbury Landing Stage some time during the 1960s. *Contest*, 213 grt, was built in 1933 for Elliot Steam Tugs and worked on the Thames all her life, apart from during wartime, when she took part in the Dunkirk evacuation. The 'Sun' tug on her left appears to be the 1957-built *Sun XX*.

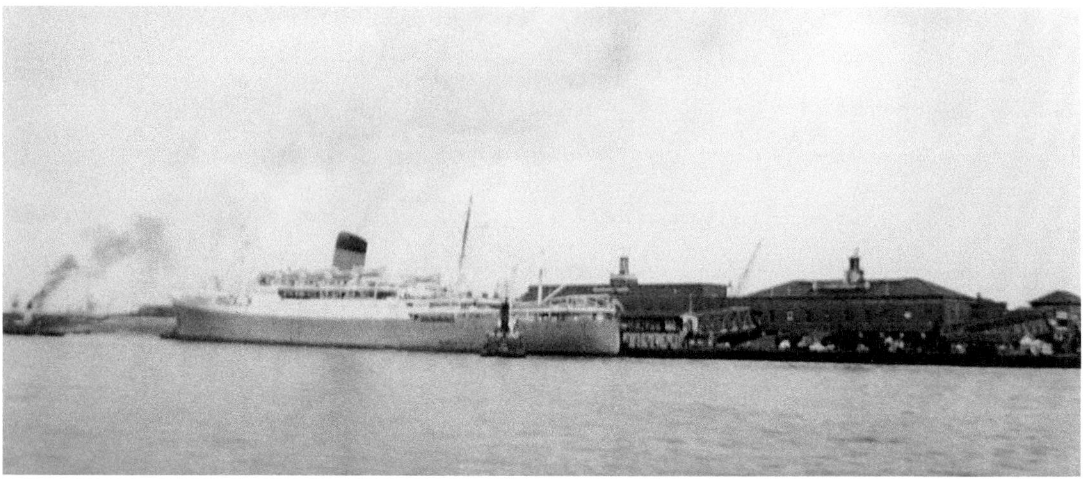

The liner *Braemar Castle*, 17,029 grt, at Tilbury Landing Stage in the early 1960s. Built in 1952, she later undertook a refit when a dome top was added to her funnel and her passenger capacity was amended to 459. Employed on Union-Castle's round-Africa service, her career lasted fewer than fourteen years due to competition from air travel and the independence of former African colonies.

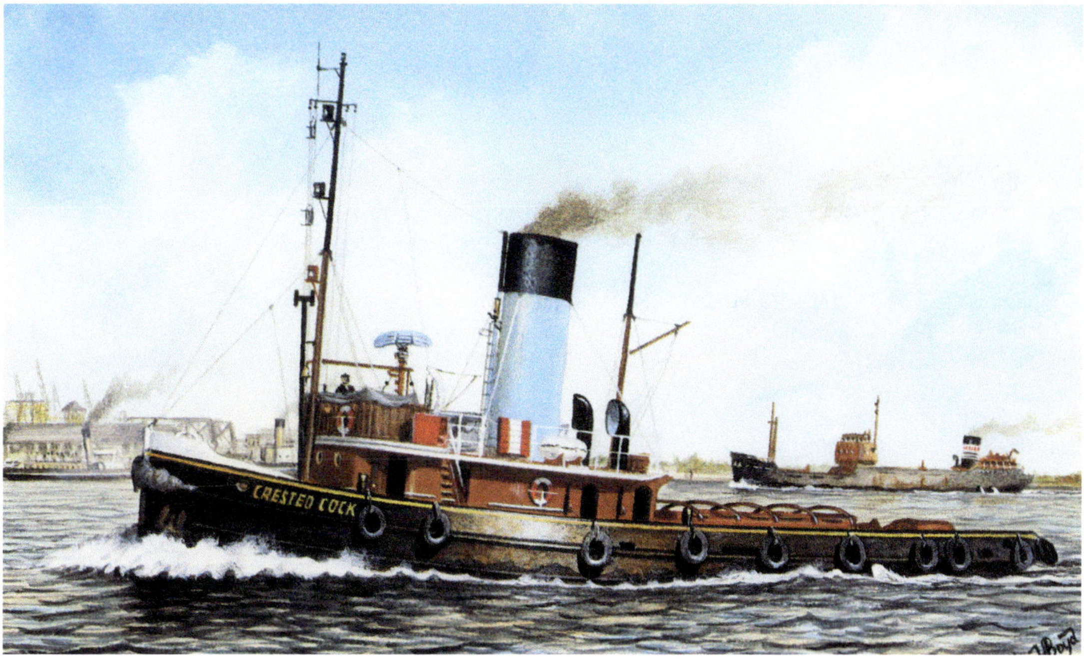

The 177 grt steam tug *Crested Cock* passes Tilbury Landing Stage followed by a collier. Built in 1935 for the Gamecock Steam Towing Company, she was involved in the Dunkirk evacuation during the Second World War. Transferred to Ship Towage (London) in 1964 and then William Watkins Ltd in 1969, she was broken up the following year.

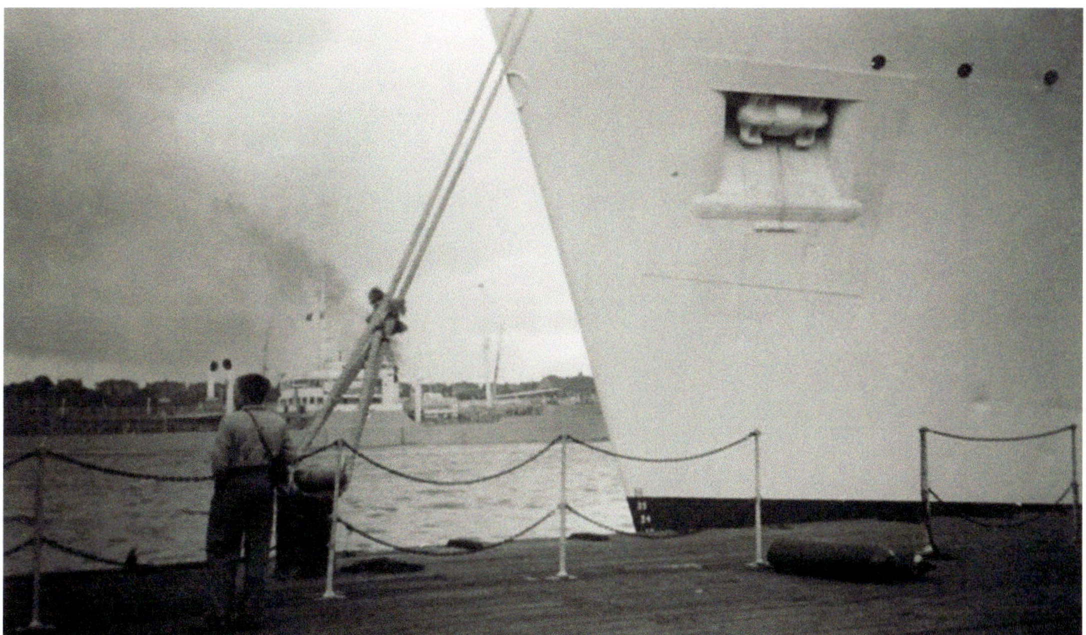

Under the bows of *Iberia*: a ship enthusiast watches an incoming vessel pass the liner at the landing stage.

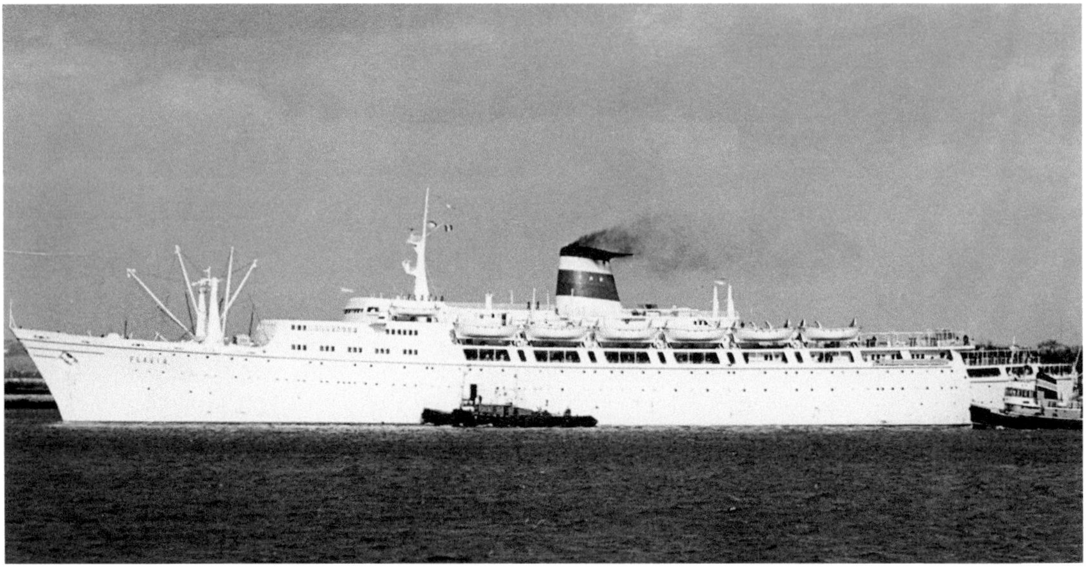

Moving up the Thames towards Tilbury Landing Stage, the 15,468 grt passenger liner *Flavia* began life as Cunard's passenger-cargo ship *Media*. Built in 1947, she sailed between Liverpool and New York. In 1961 she was completely rebuilt to carry 1,320 Tourist Class passengers and under the ownership of Costa Armatori Spa, Italy, she sailed from Bremerhaven to Australian ports via Tilbury.

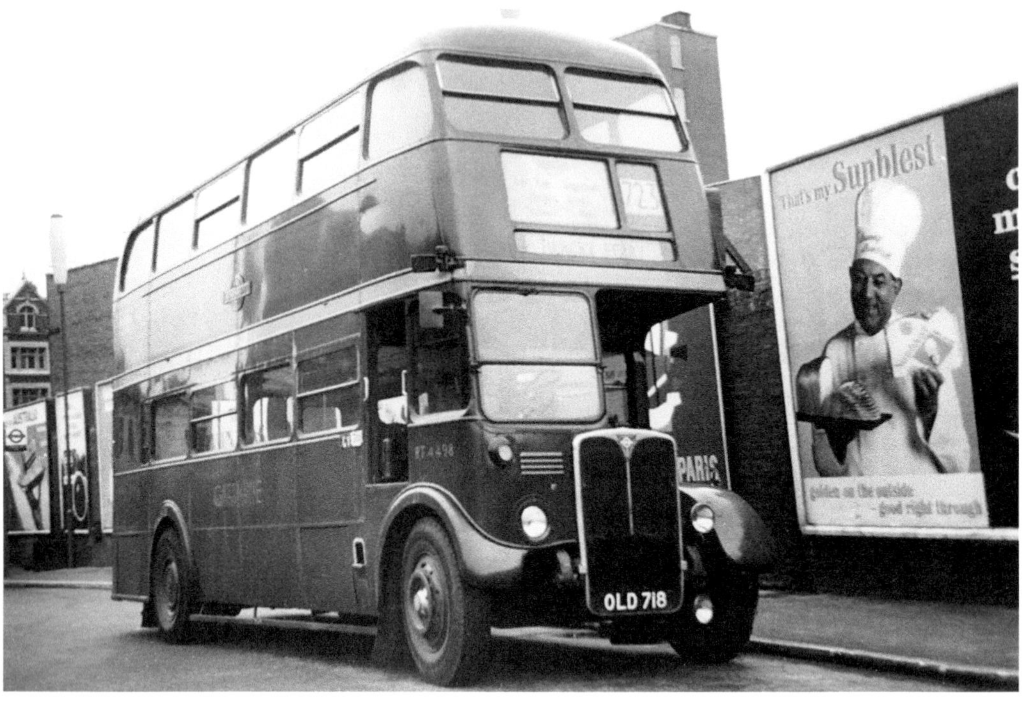

Green Line RT-type bus RT 4498 on its way to drop off and pick up passengers at Tilbury Ferry. RT buses were built for London Transport during the 1950s and were still prevalent a decade later.

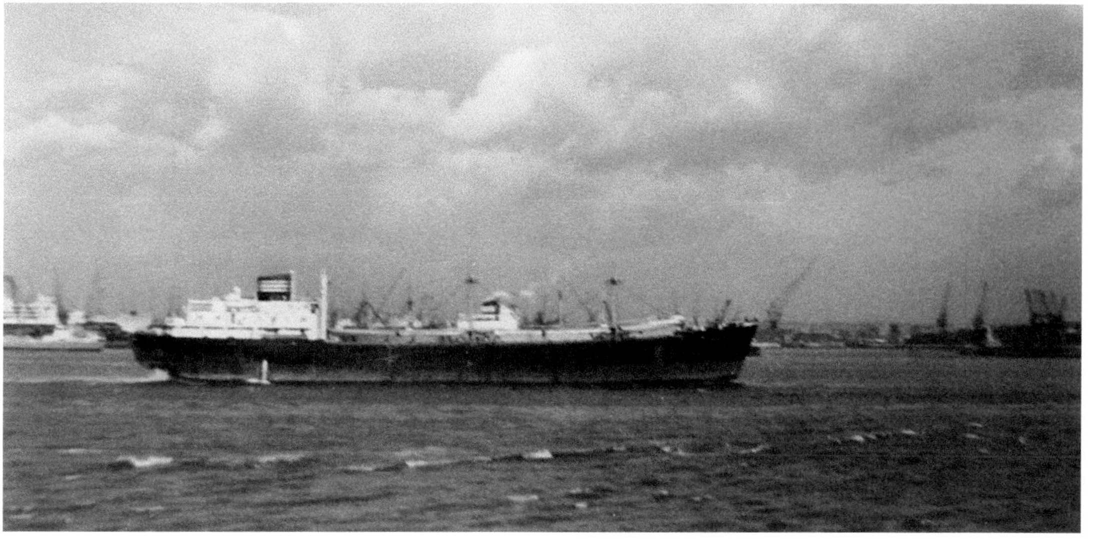

The 6,358 grt bulk carrier *Sugar Carrier* passes Tilbury outward bound from Tate & Lyle's refinery at Silvertown. Built in 1960, she remained in the Sugar Line fleet until 1969, when she was sold to Finnish owners and renamed *Vallila*. Three further name changes followed before she was broken up in 1985.

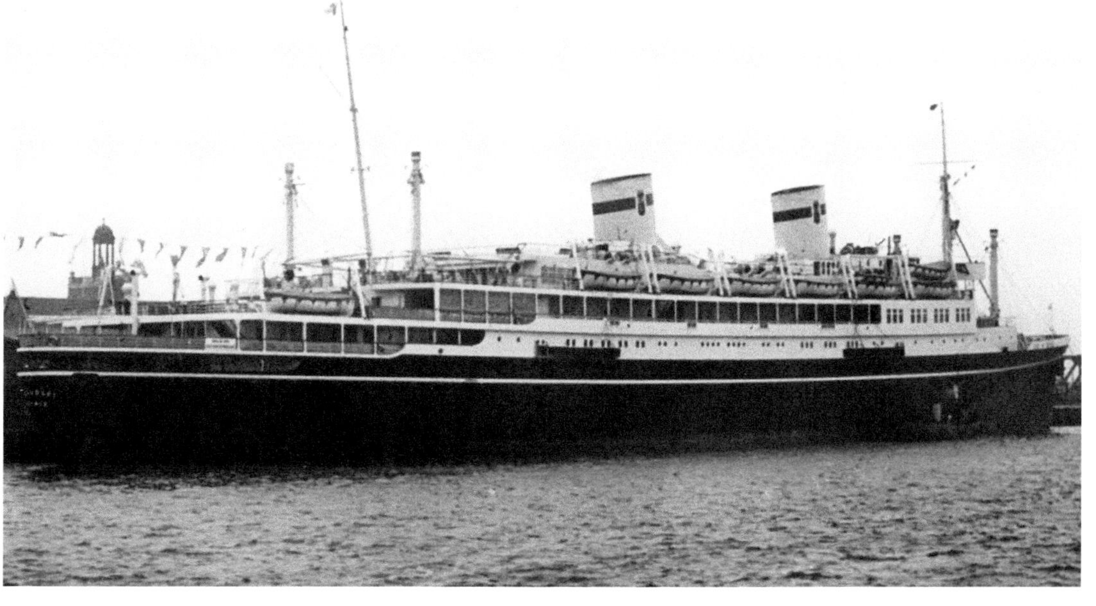

The classic Polish liner *Batory* pays a visit to Tilbury Landing Stage. The 14,287 grt ship was delivered to Gdynia-America Line in 1936 and during the Second World War survived so many military actions she was known as the 'Lucky Ship'. In 1951 her owners became Polish Ocean Lines after a merger and by the time *Batory* was withdrawn from service in 1969 she had made 222 round voyages, mostly transatlantic, and seventy-five cruises. She was broken up in 1971 after two years as a floating hotel at Gydnia.

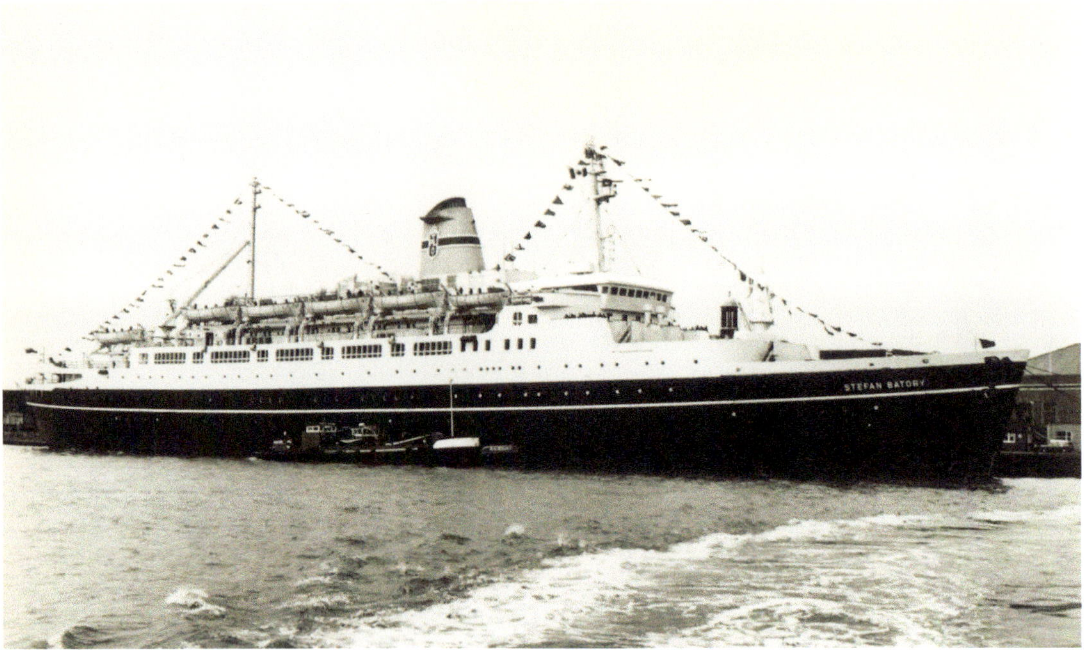

As a replacement for the *Batory*, Polish Ocean Lines purchased the 1951-built *Maasdam* from Holland-America Line, renaming her *Stefan Batory*. She sailed as the company's flagship between Gdynia and Montreal via Southampton and Tilbury (as pictured) until 1988, when she was sold to Stena Line. Laid up from 1992, she was eventually scrapped in 2000.

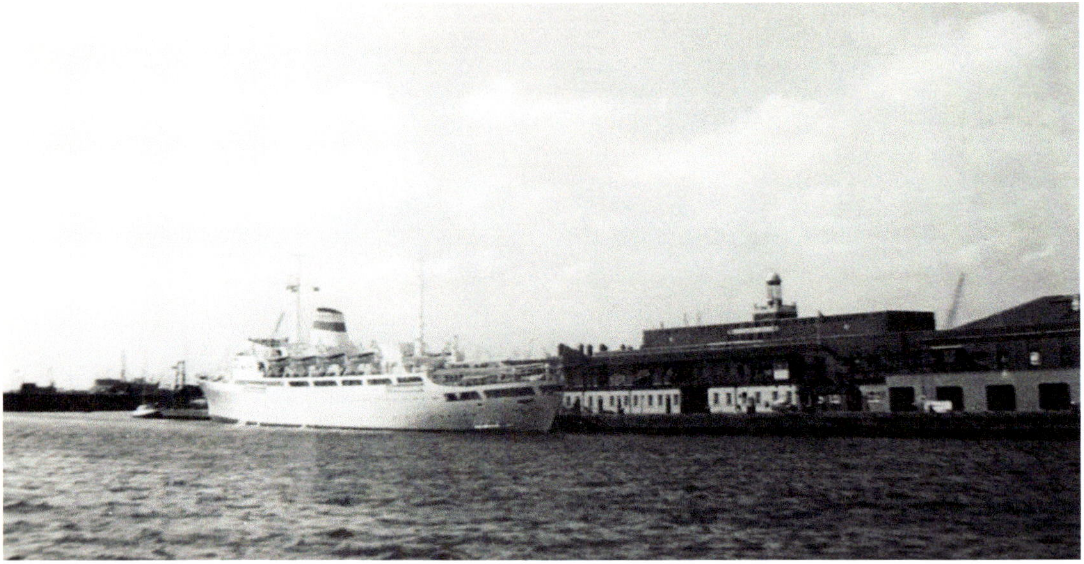

Making one of her regular visits to Tilbury Landing Stage in the 1960s, the 5,261 grt *Nadeshda Krupskaya* linked the Thames with Leningrad (St Petersburg) as well as doing some cruising. One of a class of nineteen vessels built for the Soviet Union, another of which was the *Estonia*, she entered service in 1963 and could carry around 330 passengers. In 1975 she became *Kuben*, then *Susana* in 1994 before being broken up in 1998.

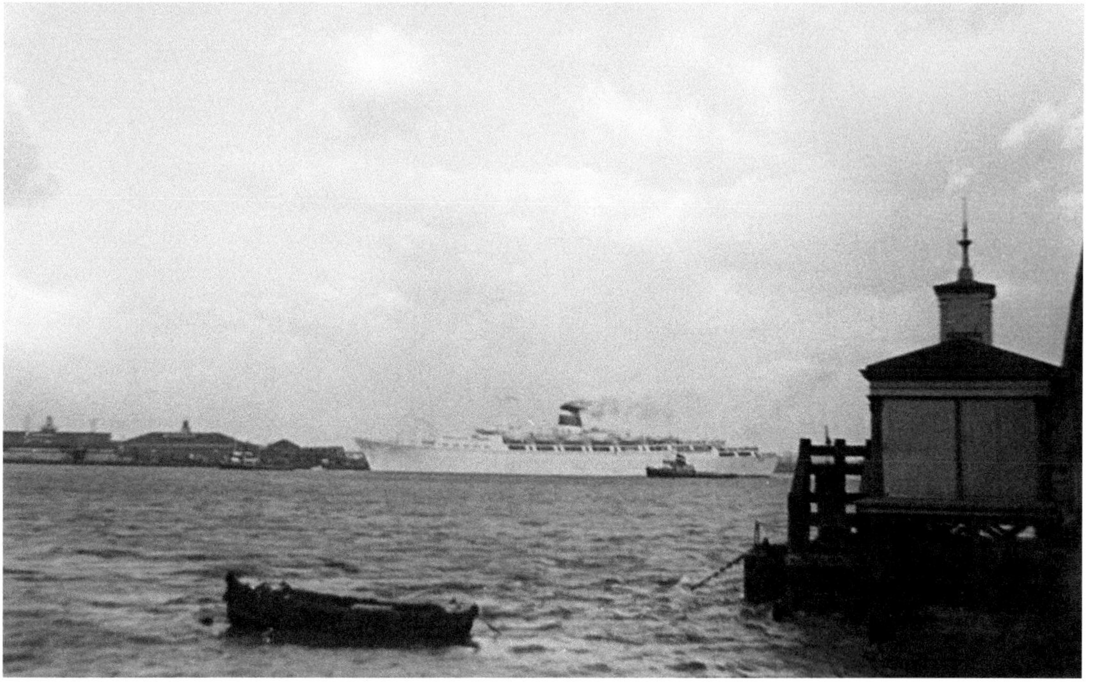

Flavia approaches Tilbury Landing Stage during the early 1960s. In 1969 she was refitted as a cruise ship and renamed *Flavian*. In 1982 she was sold to Panama to become *Lavia*, but while in the shipyard she caught fire and had to be broken up.

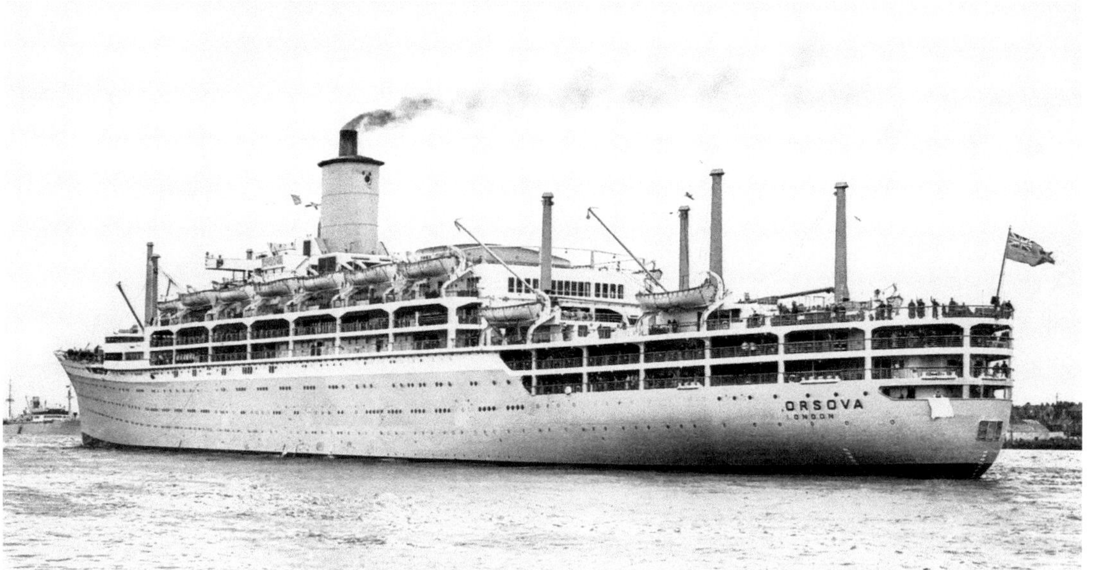

The Orient Line passenger ship *Orsova*, 1954/28,790 grt, departs Tilbury Landing Stage for Australia. She accommodated 681 First and 813 Tourist Class passengers and was later adapted for cruising. However, her career was cut short in 1974 when she was broken up in Kaohsiung.

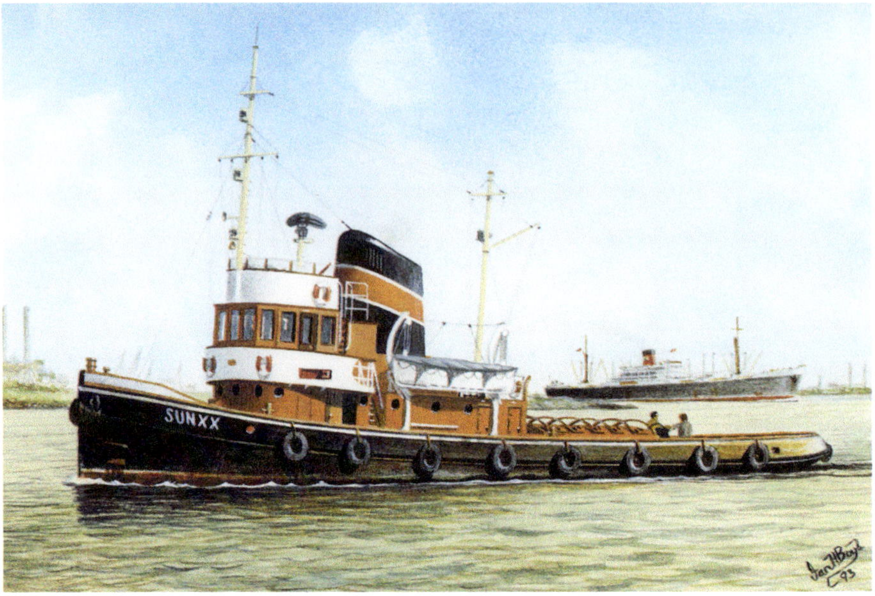

The diesel-driven tug *Sun XX*, 192 grt, one of the last members of the 'Sun Tugs' fleet, was built in 1957. Seen here passing Tilbury power station and followed by a Federal Line cargo ship, she worked on London's river until 1979, when she was sold to Italy and renamed *Sole Secondo*. She was scrapped in 1996.

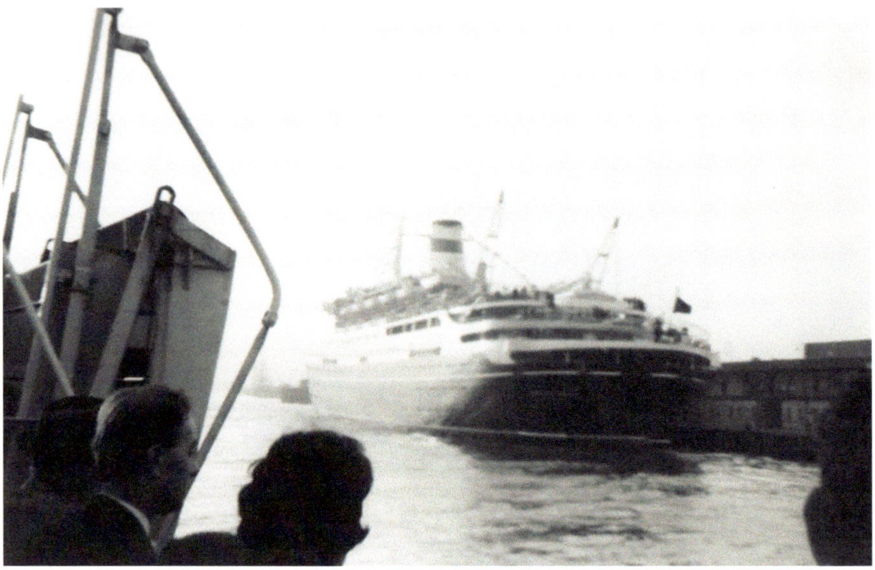

Passengers on the Tilbury ferry observe the Soviet liner *Alexandr Pushkin* berthed at Tilbury Landing Stage during her maiden voyage in August 1965. In her early years the 19,860 grt ship was employed on transatlantic service, sailing between Leningrad (St Petersburg) and Canadian ports via Tilbury, with some winter cruising. *Alexandr Pushkin* was the second of five Ivan Franko-class sisters and was extensively refitted in the 1970s. In 1985 she was chartered to UK-based CTC Lines and thereafter cruised extensively, especially from Australia, until 1989 when she left Soviet ownership.

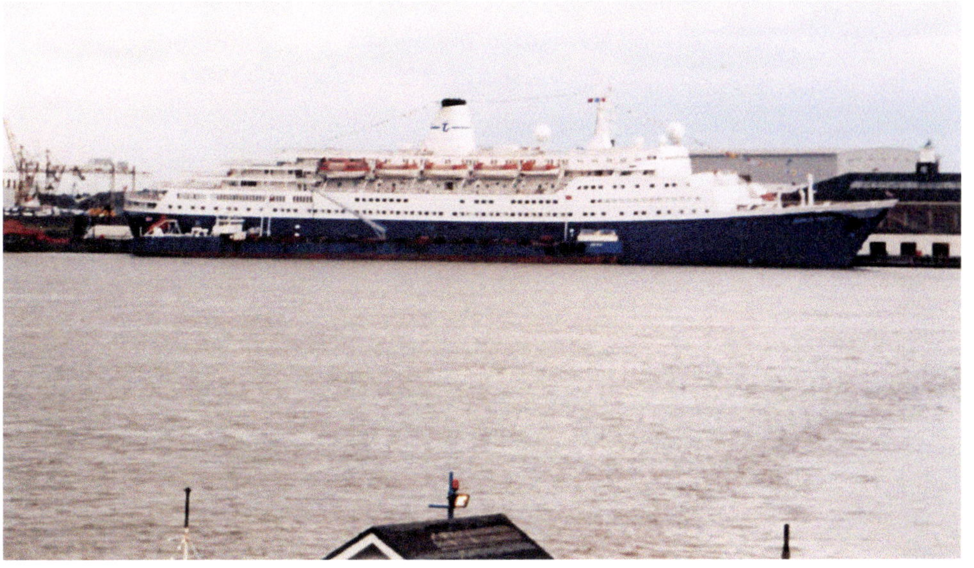

The former *Alexandr Pushkin* makes a welcome return to Tilbury Landing Stage as the cruise ship *Marco Polo*. In 1991 she was acquired by Orient Lines, a new one-ship venture set up by cruise and hotel entrepreneur Gerry Herrod, and following a lengthy refit she began worldwide cruising. In March 2008 *Marco Polo* was sold to Greek-owned Global Maritime Group, who chartered her to the German holiday company Transocean Tours, for whom she undertook cruises out of the UK (as pictured here) and Germany.

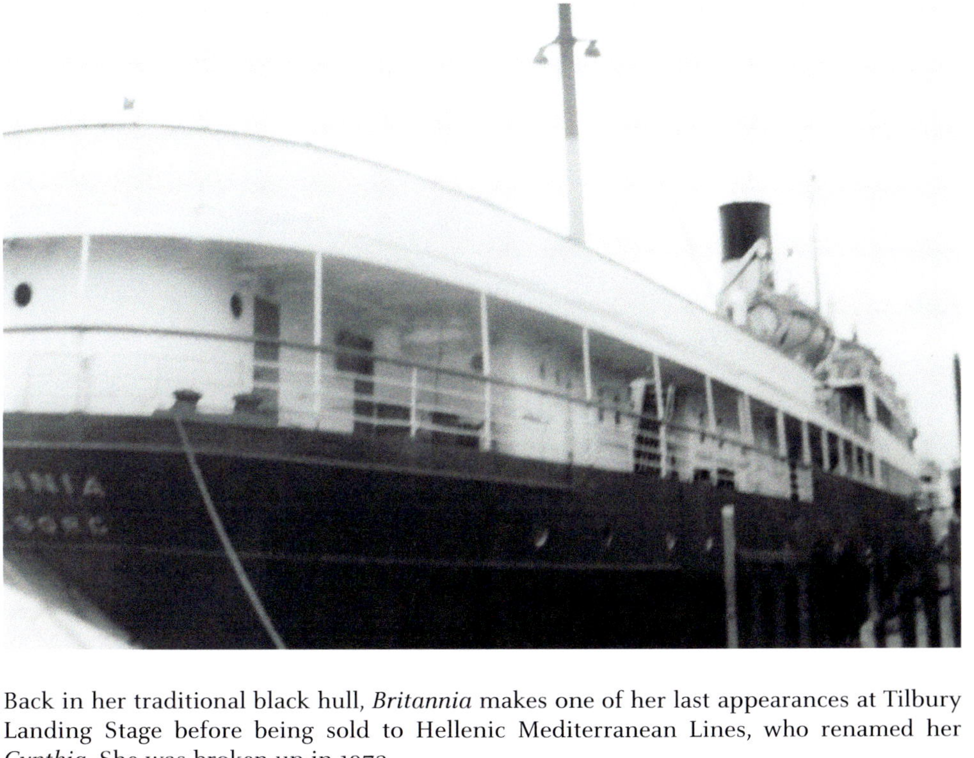

Back in her traditional black hull, *Britannia* makes one of her last appearances at Tilbury Landing Stage before being sold to Hellenic Mediterranean Lines, who renamed her *Cynthia*. She was broken up in 1973.

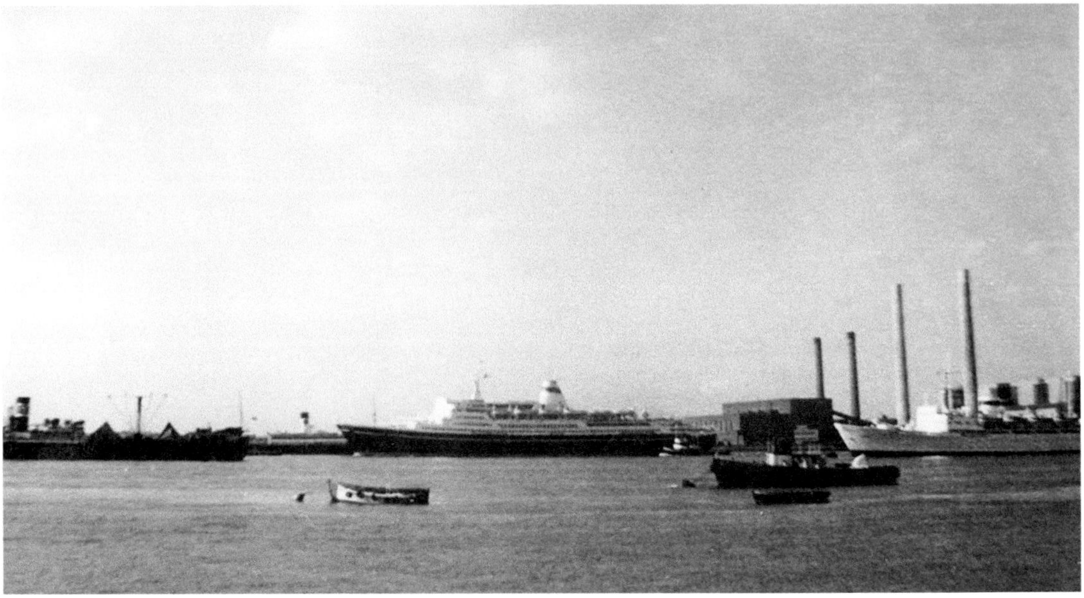

Rush hour in Gravesend Reach: the 19,872 grt Soviet liner *Ivan Franko* (centre) heads for Tilbury Landing Stage, passing the outgoing *Suecia*. Far left is the wartime freighter *Free Trader*, while to the right the Soviet mini-liner *Estonia* awaits a berth at the landing stage.

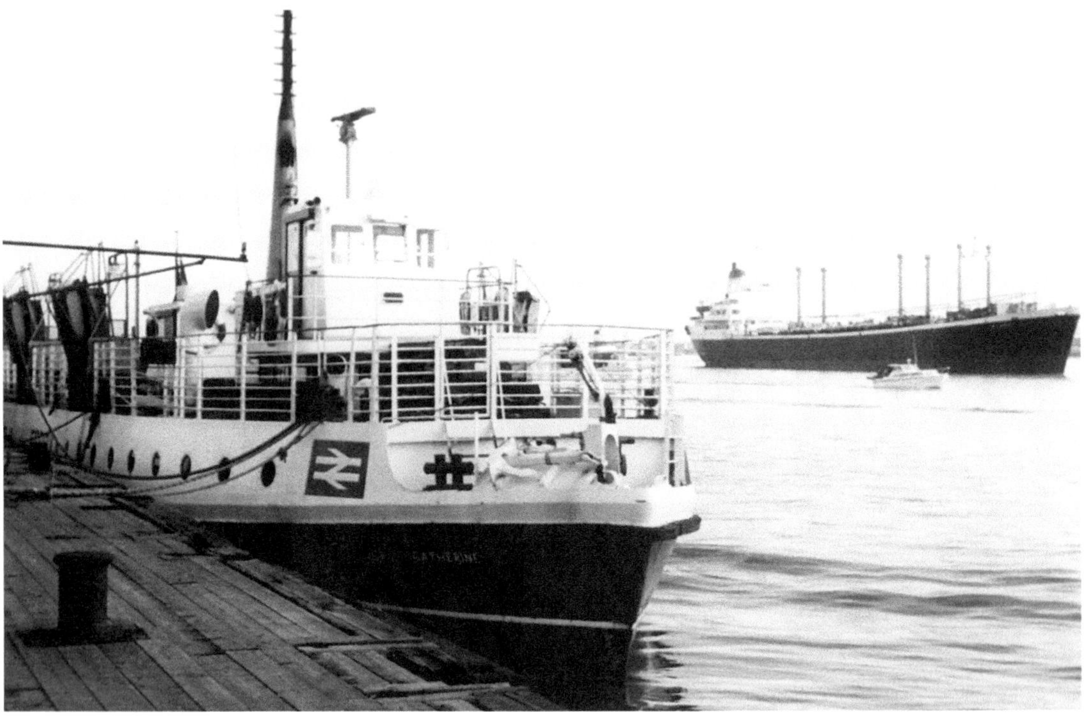

In 1961 diesel vessels replaced the old steam passenger ferries on the Tilbury–Gravesend service. Here, the new *Catherine* is tied up at the eastern end of Tilbury Landing Stage. An incoming cargo ship can be seen behind.

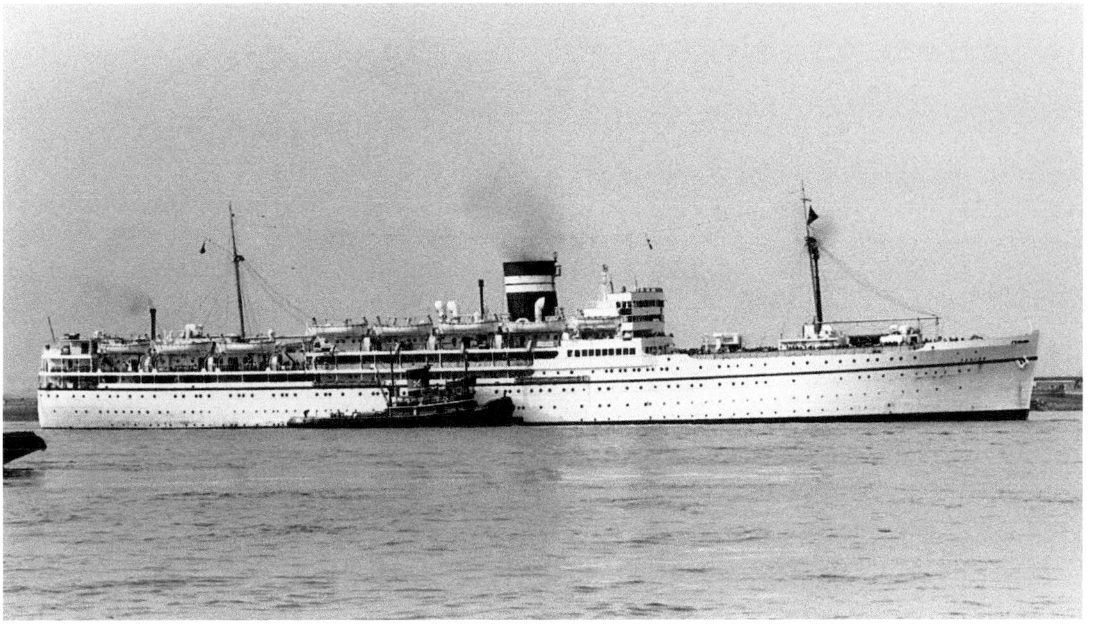

An educational cruise ship owned by British India Steam Navigation, the 12,620 grt *Dunera* is seen here in Gravesend Reach. Built in 1937 as a passenger liner, she became a wartime troopship. After her trooping charter ended in 1960 *Dunera* was refitted to carry 187 cabin passengers and 834 children. She was scrapped in 1967.

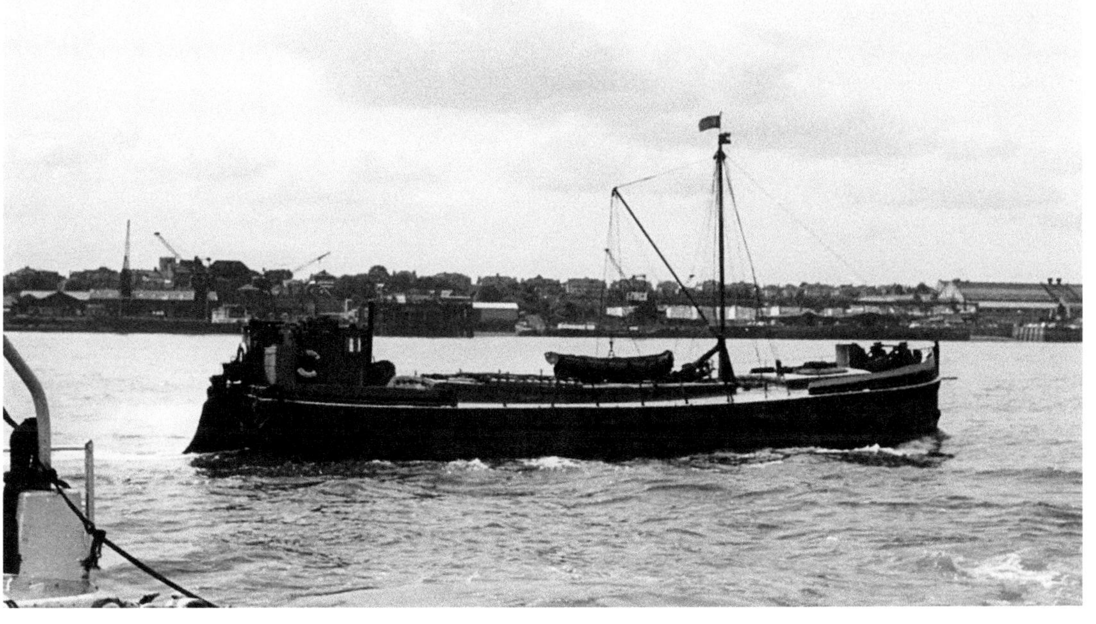

The 76-ton barge *Cabby*, built at Rochester in 1928, passing Tilbury Landing Stage in 1967. For many years she transported grain, animal feeds, timber and other cargoes between the London Docks, Colchester and Whitstable. After conveying her last load in the late 1960s, she was converted into a passenger-carrying sailing barge.

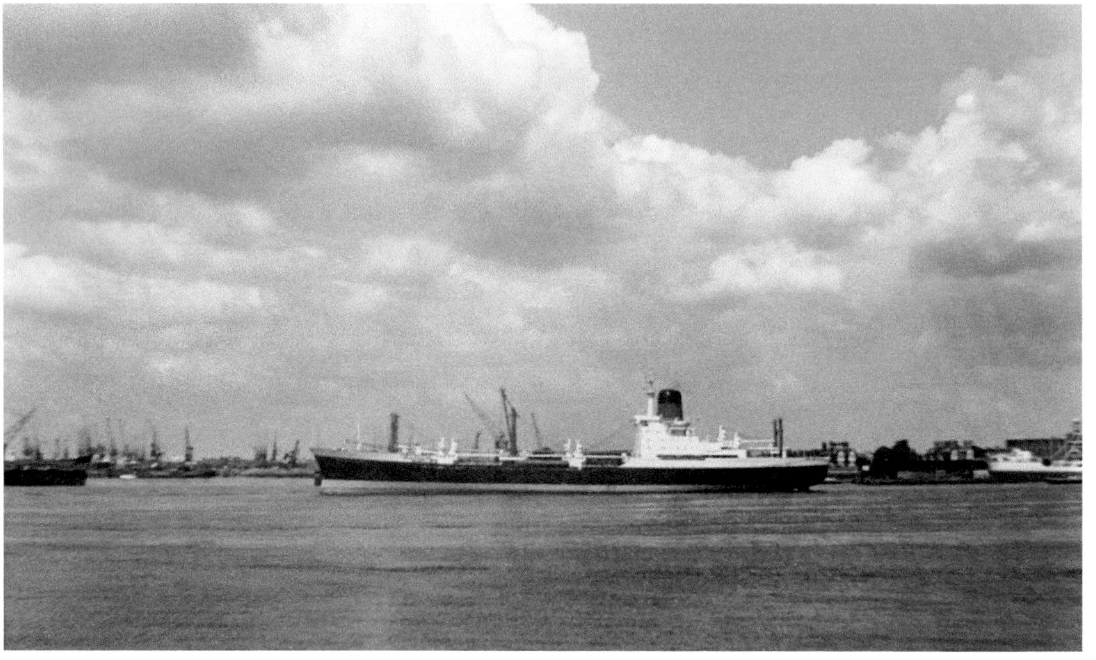

A handsome cargo liner of her day, the 12,294 grt *Pembrokeshire* passes Tilbury Landing Stage on her way to the Royal Docks. Built in 1967 for Glen Line, she became a victim of the container ship revolution and was sold in 1972. After several name changes she was broken up in 1995.

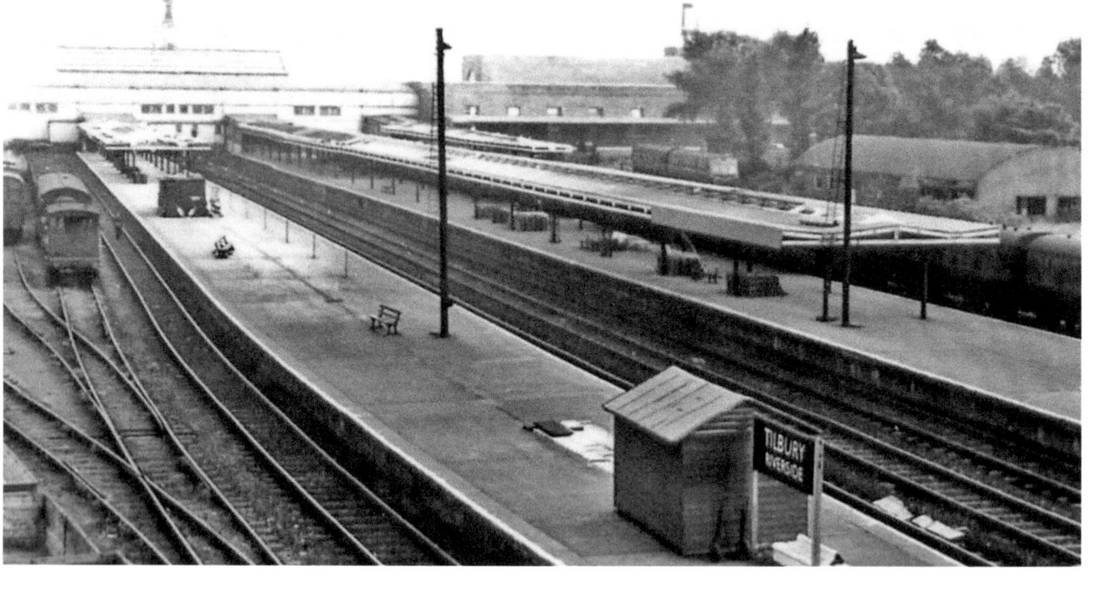

A quiet moment: looking along deserted platforms of Tilbury Riverside station towards the station building on the left and the landing stage's passenger baggage hall to the right.

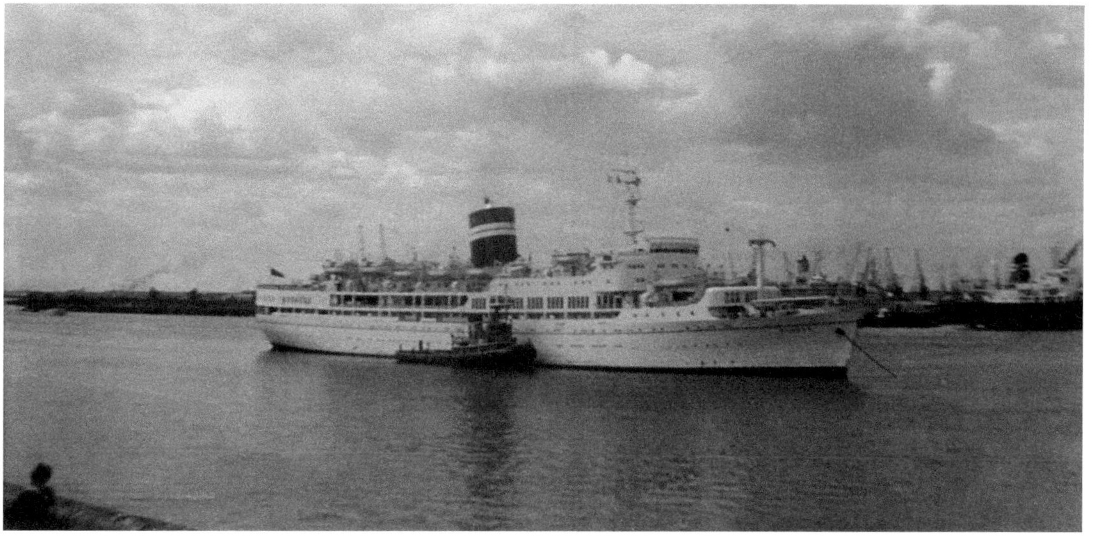

In her role as an educational cruise ship, SS *Uganda* waits off Gravesend for her turn at Tilbury Landing Stage. Built in 1952 for British India Line's East Africa service, she was refitted in 1968 to offer cruises specifically for schoolchildren, a venture that proved very successful. Originally designed to carry 300 passengers, her accommodation was altered to provide 920 dormitory berths out of a total capacity of 1,226 passengers. Her gross tonnage was consequently increased from 14,420 to 16,907. In 1982 she participated in the Falklands War as a hospital ship. In 1986 she was sent for breaking in the Far East but a typhoon drove her ashore and dismantling did not begin until 1992.

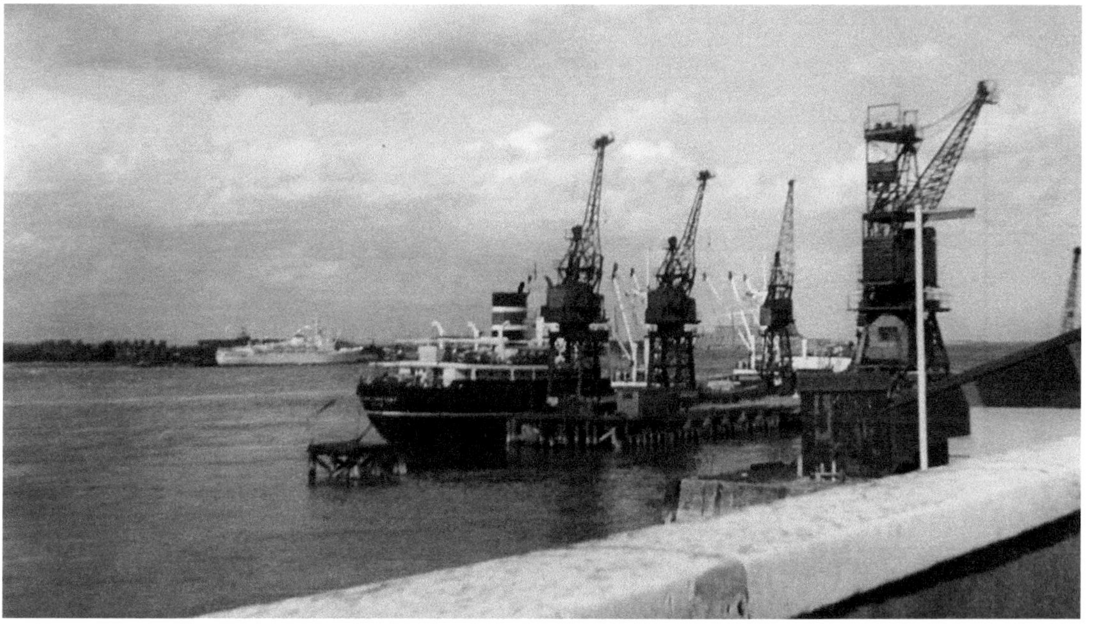

Looking across Gravesend Reach from the Kent side. In the foreground is the cargo vessel *Lottinge*, 1956/4,215 grt, while in the distance the small Soviet passenger ship *Estonia* lies at Tilbury Landing Stage.

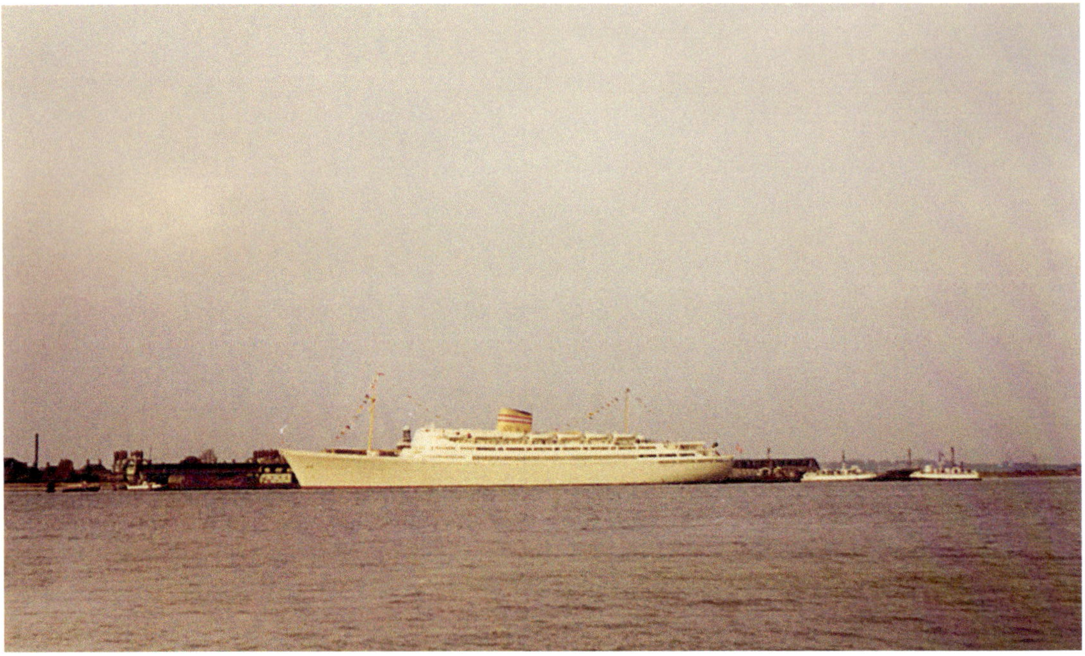

A rare colour picture of the classically designed passenger ship *Bergensfjord* at Tilbury Landing Stage in October 1971, just a month before her sale to the French Line as *De Grasse*. Built in 1956 for the Norwegian America Line, she offered high-class facilities for her 420 passengers. Sadly, she caught fire, capsized and sank during a refit in 1980.

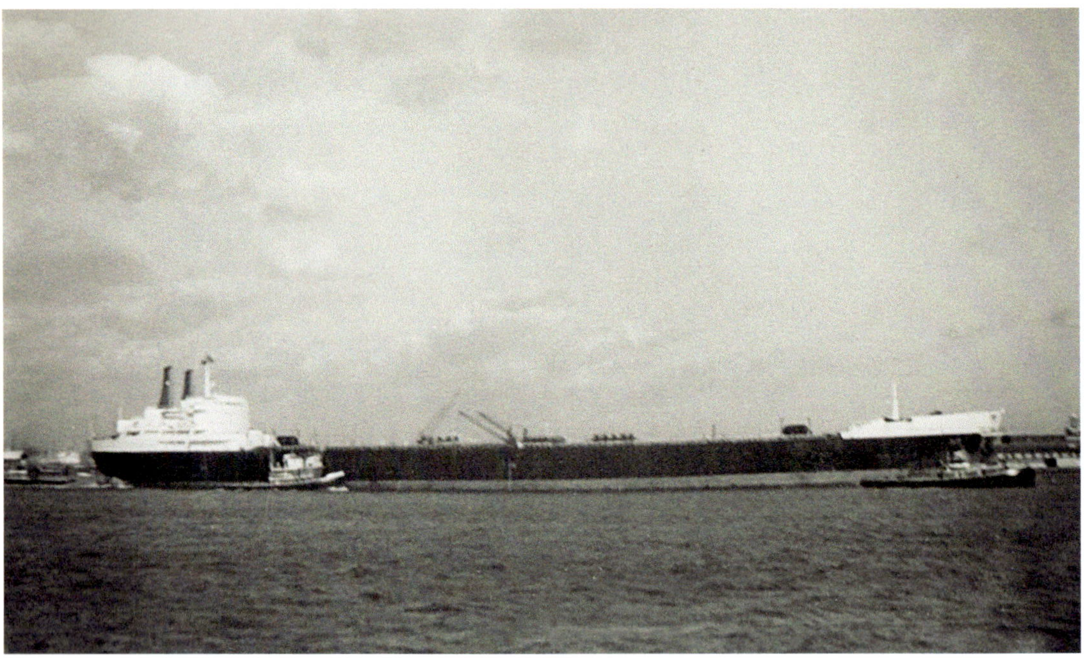

The Shell tanker *Drupa*, 39,796 grt, leaves the Tilbury Tanker Repair Jetty, just upriver from the landing stage. Built in 1966, she was scrapped at Alang in 1993.

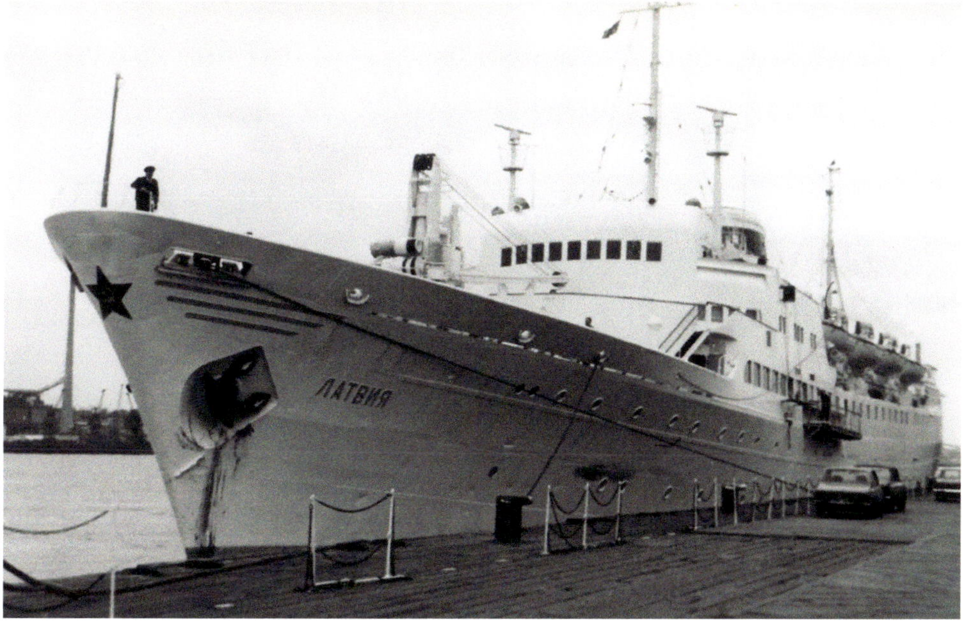

A sister to the small Soviet passenger ships *Nadeshda Krupskaya* and *Estonia*, the 1960-built *Latvia*, 5.035 grt, is pictured at Tilbury Landing Stage in April 1975.

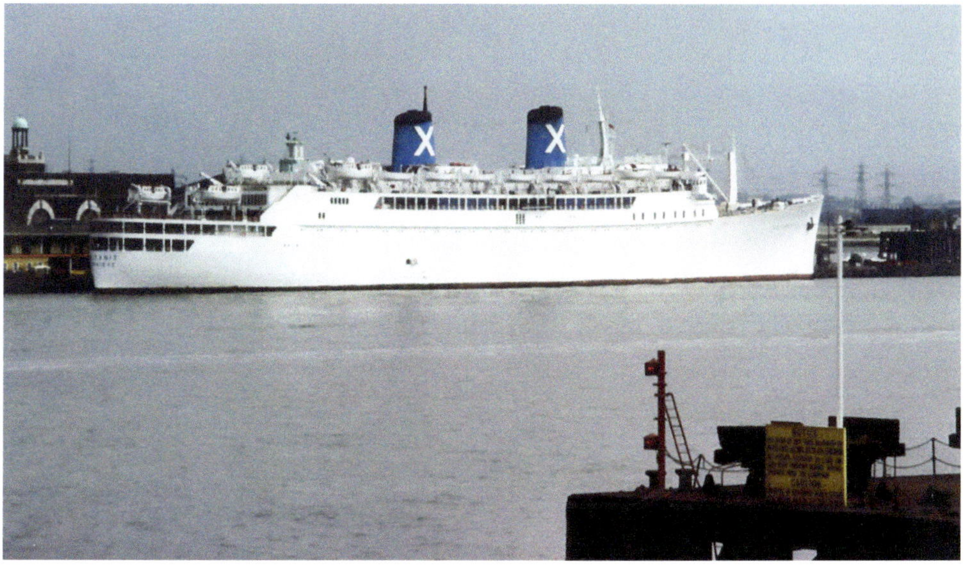

A cruise ship with a fascinating history, the 18,655 grt *Britanis* makes a rare visit to Tilbury Landing Stage. Completed in 1932 as SS *Monterey* for American shipowners Matson Lines as a luxury liner for Pacific Ocean service, she acted as a fast troop carrier during the Second World War. Following a five-year lay-up after the war, she was purchased by the US Government in 1952 but was repurchased by Matson Lines in 1956, becoming *Matsonia*. In 1963 she was re-christened *Lurline* to replace a previous ship of the same name, but in 1970 she was sold to Chandris Lines to operate as the 1,655-passenger *Britanis*. In October 2000, while being towed for breaking, she capsized and sank off Cape Town.

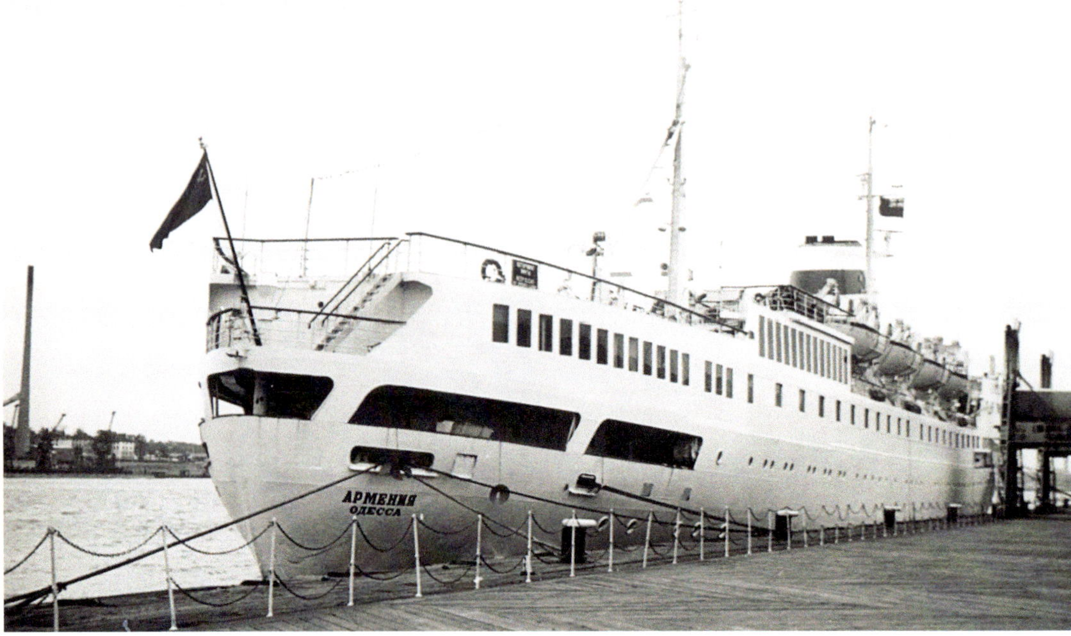

Another of the nineteen-strong class of Soviet mini-liners, *Armeniya*, 1963/5,169 grt, called at Tilbury Landing Stage in May 1977. She was broken up in Turkey in 1995.

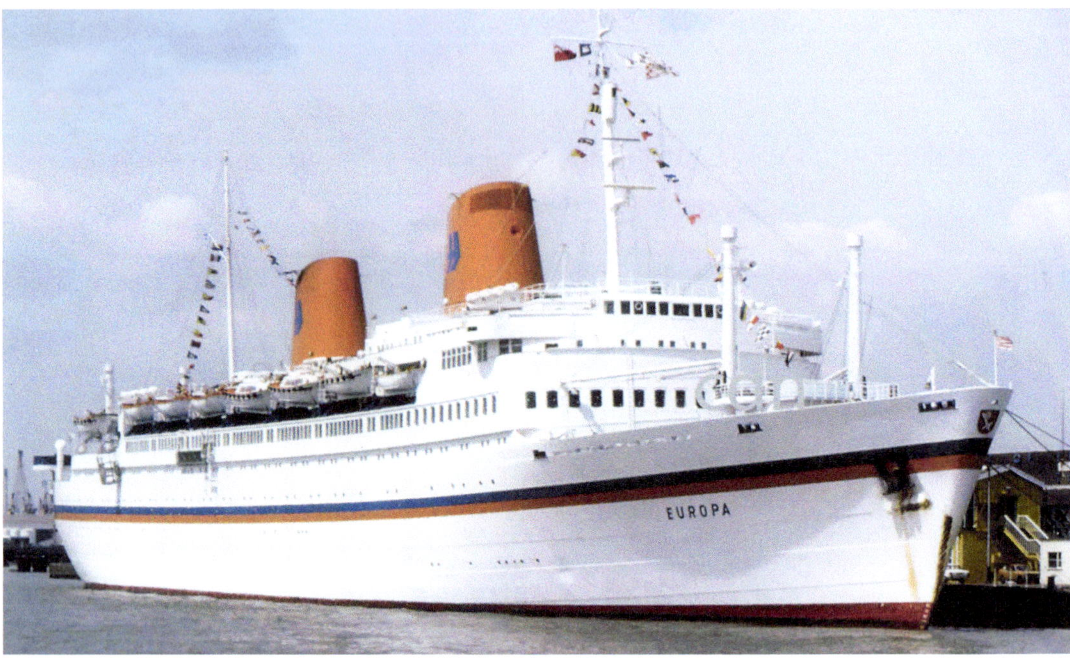

Berthed alongside Tilbury Landing Stage, the German cruise ship *Europa*, the second ship of that name, was originally a transatlantic liner. She was built as *Kungsholm* for the Swedish America Line in 1953, but after twelve years the 21,164 grt liner was sold to North German Lloyd, later known as Hapag-Lloyd, where she became *Europa*.

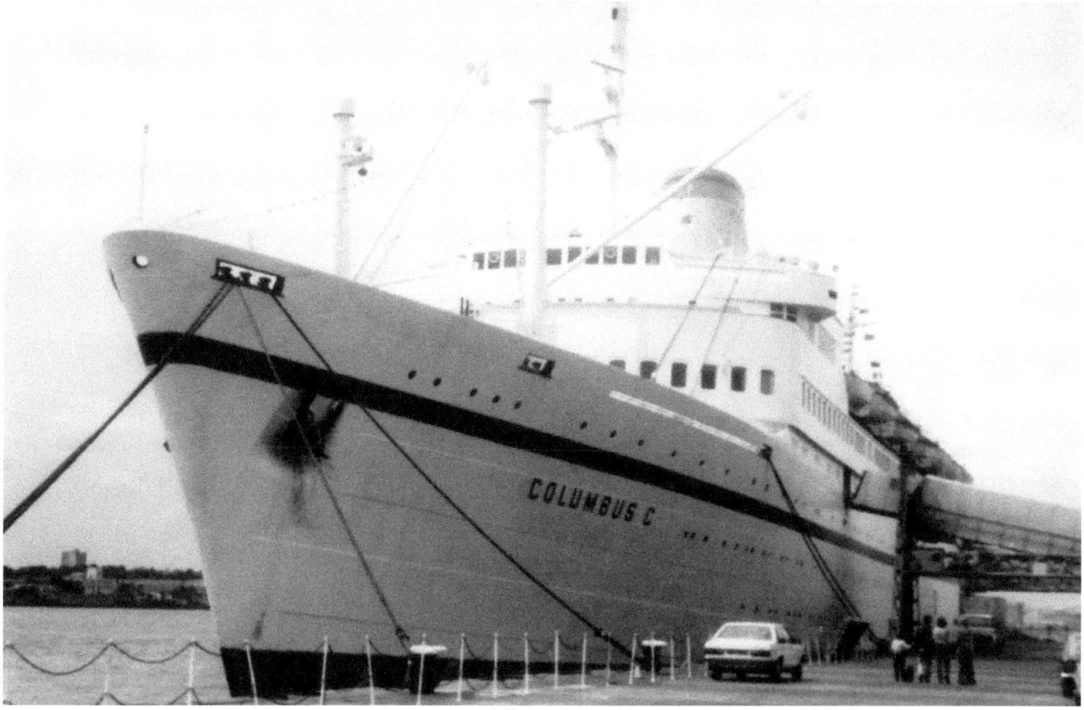

In 1981 *Europa* was bought by the Italian cruise company Costa Cruises and renamed *Columbus C.* She returned to the landing stage before meeting her fate in 1984, when she sank after ramming a breakwater at Cadiz. Although refloated, she was broken up at Barcelona the following year.

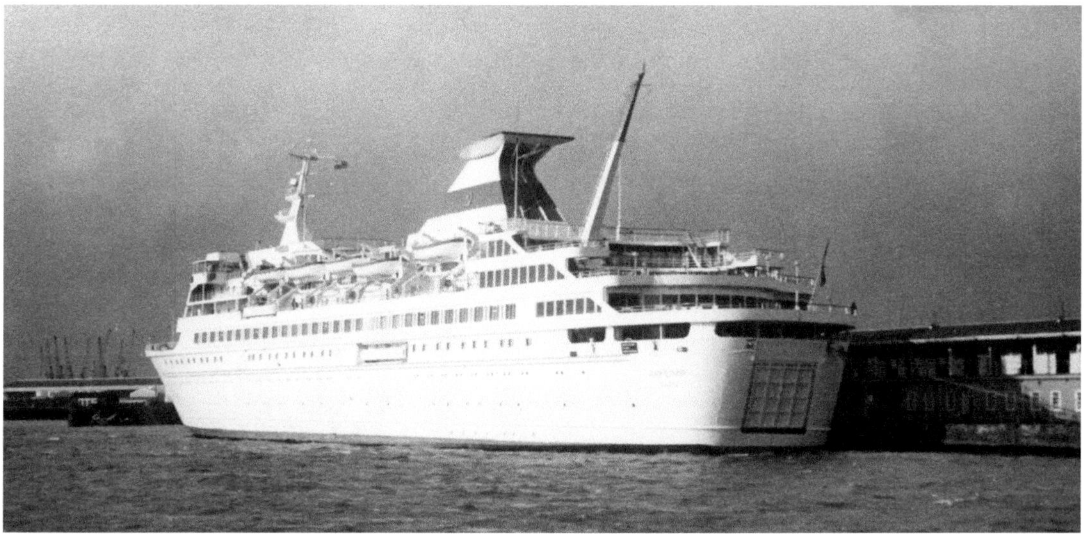

Pictured at Tilbury Landing Stage in 1978, two years after her completion, *Kareliya* was one of five Soviet sister ships built for passenger-car ferry service in the Black Sea as well as occasional cruising. As a ferry she carried 504 cabin passengers and 505 passengers on deck plus 256 cars, but her cruising capacity was reduced to 350 one-class passengers.

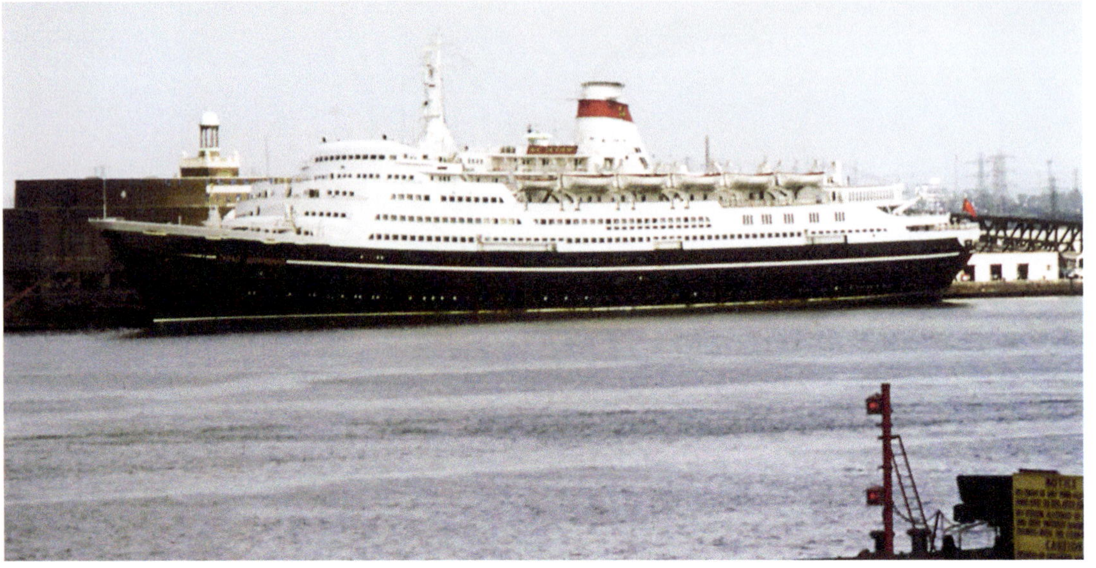

The third of the Ivan Franko-class ships to be delivered, the Soviet liner *Taras Schevchenko* joined the Black Sea Shipping Company fleet in April 1967. She was chartered by CTC Lines in 1973, making a voyage to Australia and cruising down under before returning to the UK the following year. Pictured at Tilbury Landing Stage, the vessel continued cruising but was laid up in 1998. An unsuccessful return to cruising in 2003 led to a long voyage to Alang in 2005 to be broken up.

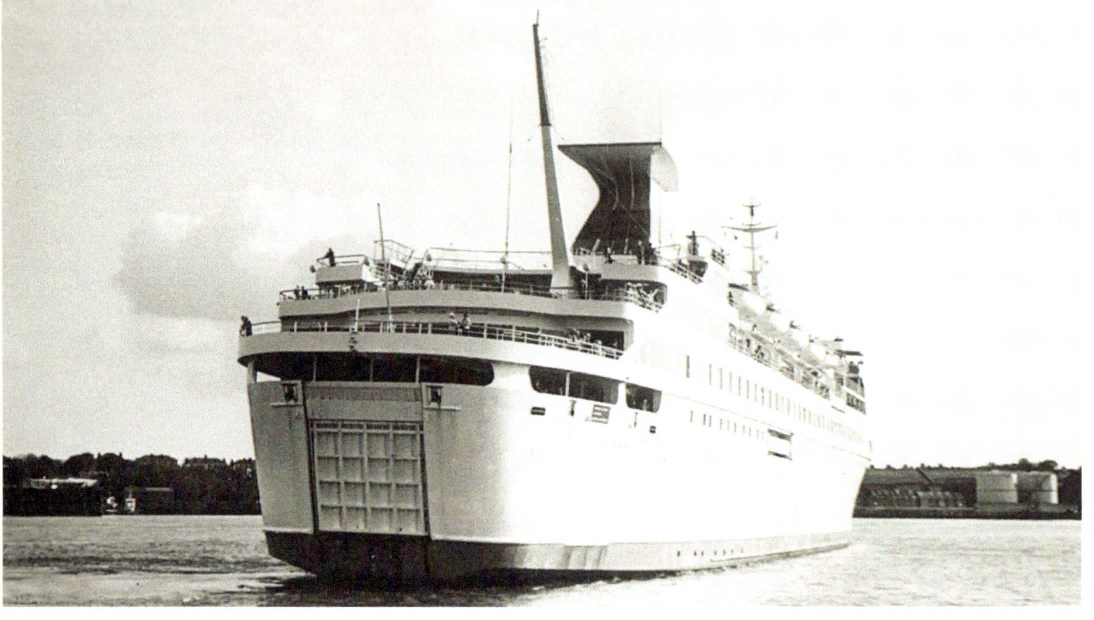

Kareliya approaching Tilbury in May 1981. Within weeks she ran aground close to Arricife, Canary Islands, suffering extensive damage, and was subsequently converted into a 650-passenger cruise ship at a Tyne shipyard. In December 1982 she was renamed *Leonid Brezhnev* but reverted to the name *Kareliya* in 1989. She cruised almost exclusively from Tilbury for CTC Lines (later CTC Cruise Lines) until 1994.

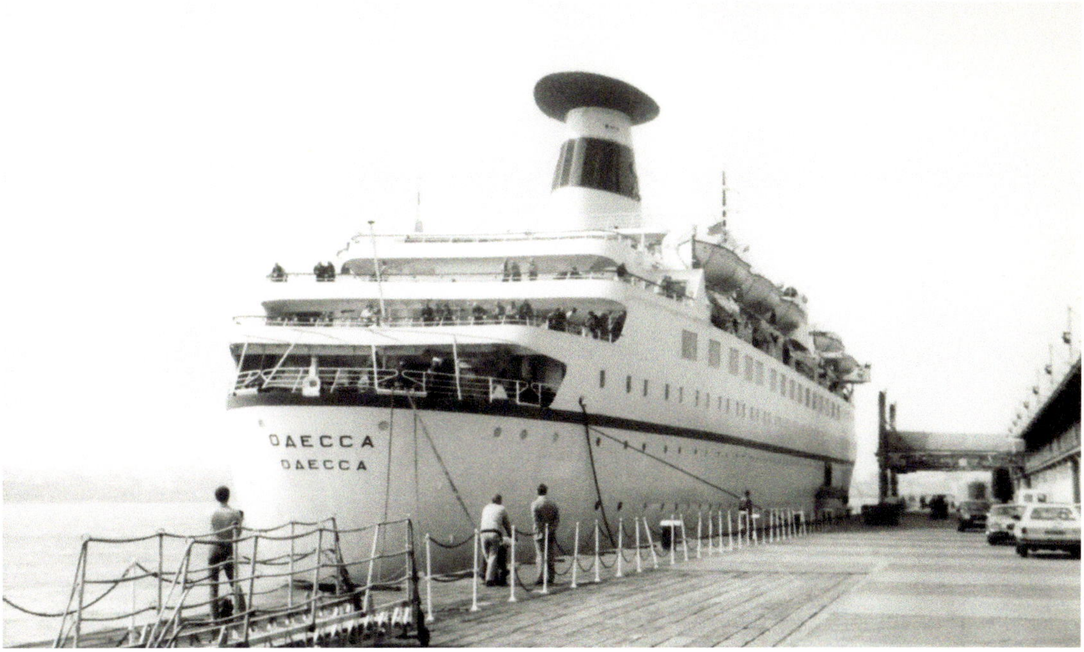

Seen at Tilbury Landing Stage in April 1982, the Soviet passenger ship *Odessa*, 11,889 grt, was completed in the UK in 1974 as MS *Copenhagen* for Danish owners, but within a year she was purchased by the Soviet Union's Black Sea Shipping Company. In 1996 she was arrested and laid up but plans to refurbish the ship came to nothing and she was broken up in 2007.

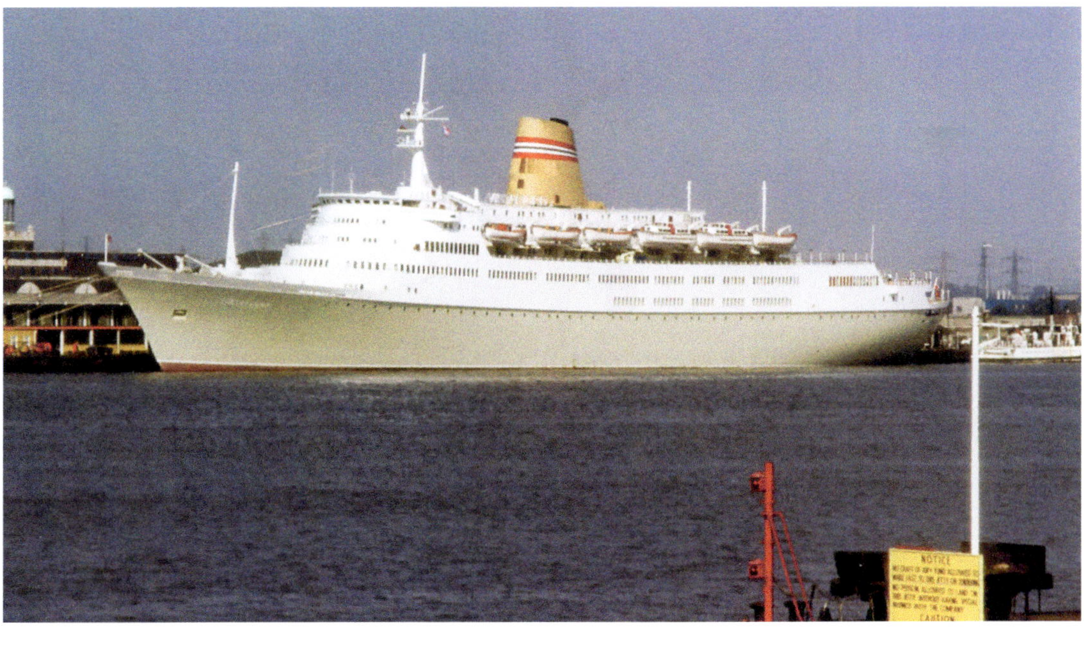

The attractive profile of the 24,292 grt passenger liner *Vistafjord* is in evidence here as she lies alongside Tilbury Landing Stage in the early 1980s. Built in 1973 for the Norwegian America Line, she was a near-sister to the 1965-built *Sagafjord*.

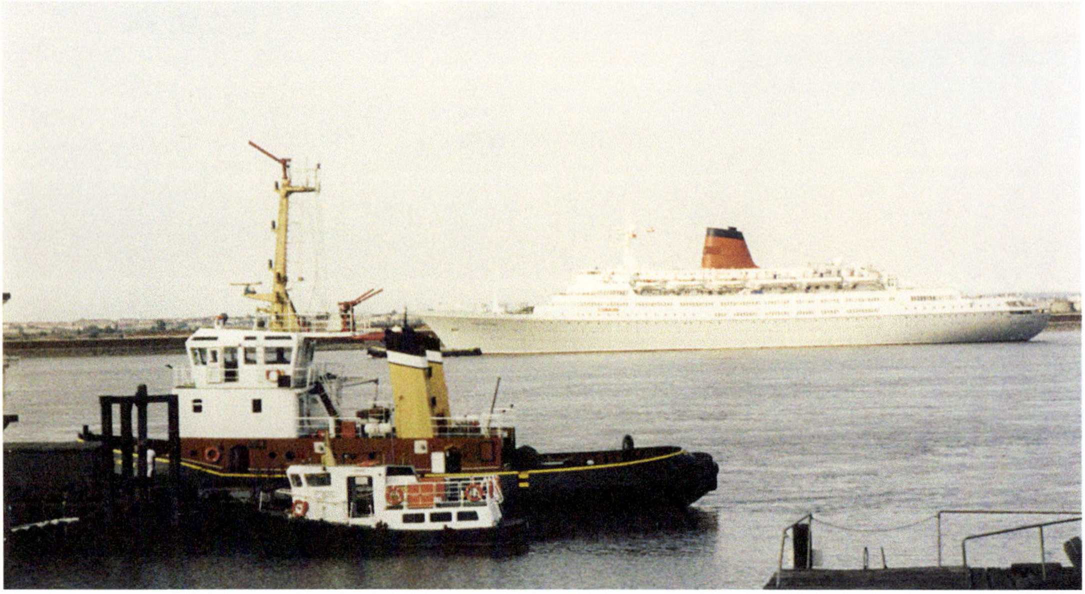

A few years later, *Vistafjord* heads up the Thames to the landing stage having been sold to Cunard Line in 1983. In 1999 Cunard renamed her *Caronia,* but five years later she was bought by Saga Cruises, becoming *Saga Ruby*. In 2014 she was sold for use as a floating hotel but unfortunately her new owners went bankrupt and this fine ship was broken up in 2017.

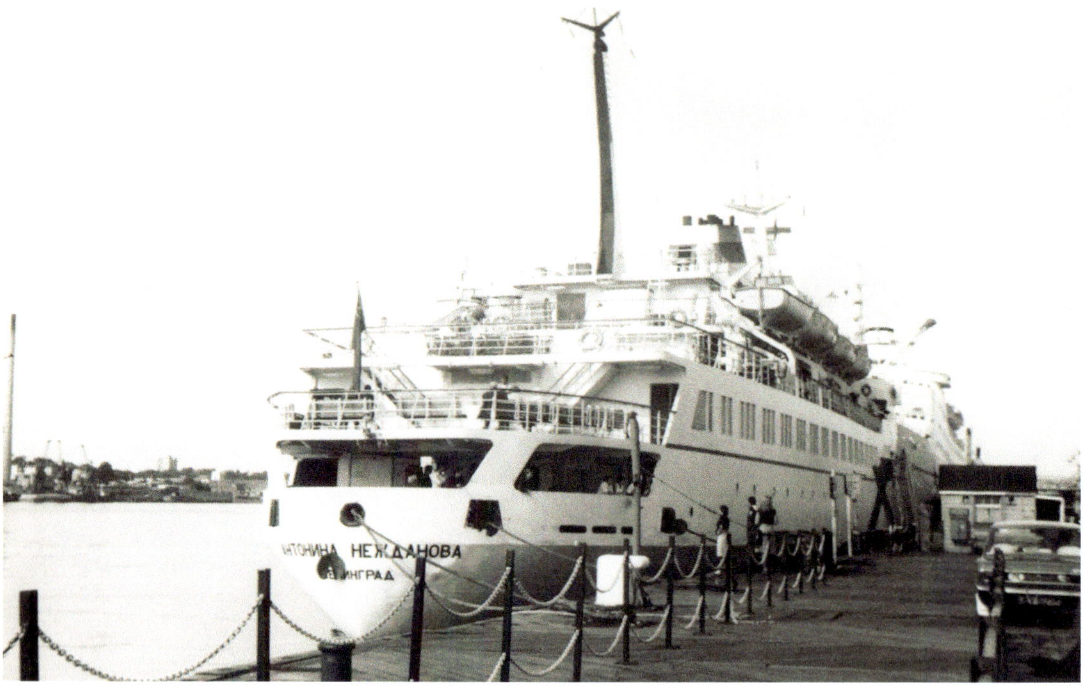

Eighth of a class of small passenger vessels built in Yugoslavia for the USSR, the 3,923 grt *Antonina Nezhdanova* is seen berthed at Tilbury Landing Stage in August 1982. She was struck by a Japanese storm wave in 2004 and had to be scrapped.

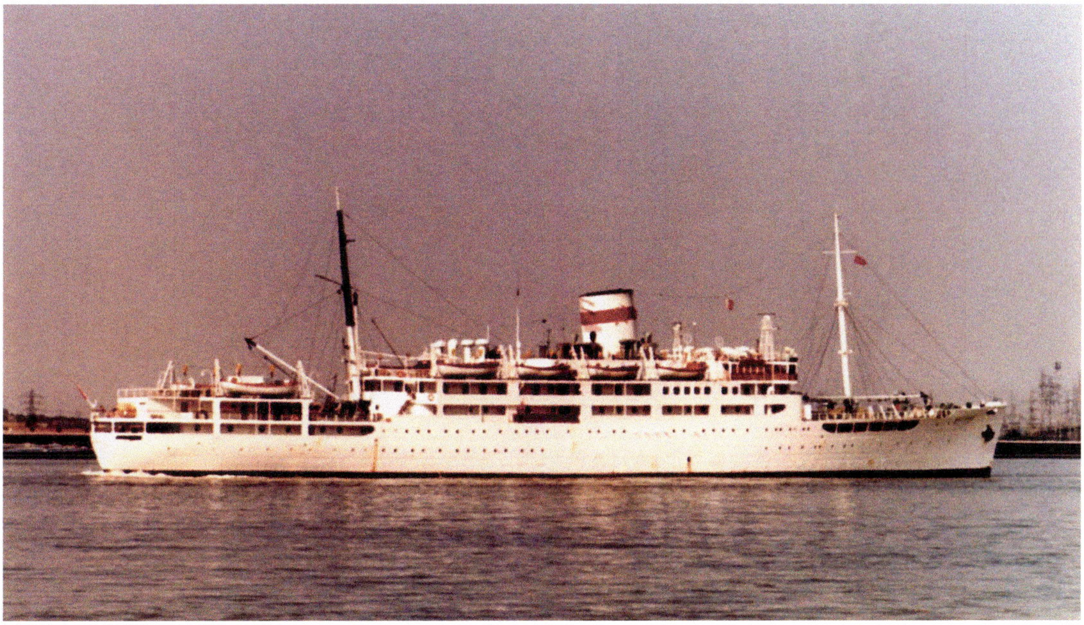

Nearing the end of her days the Soviet liner *Baltika* still cuts a handsome figure as she sails down the Thames from Tilbury Landing Stage. Despite her rather spartan accommodation, she combined cruising with line voyages from Russia in her later years. She was broken up in Pakistan in 1987.

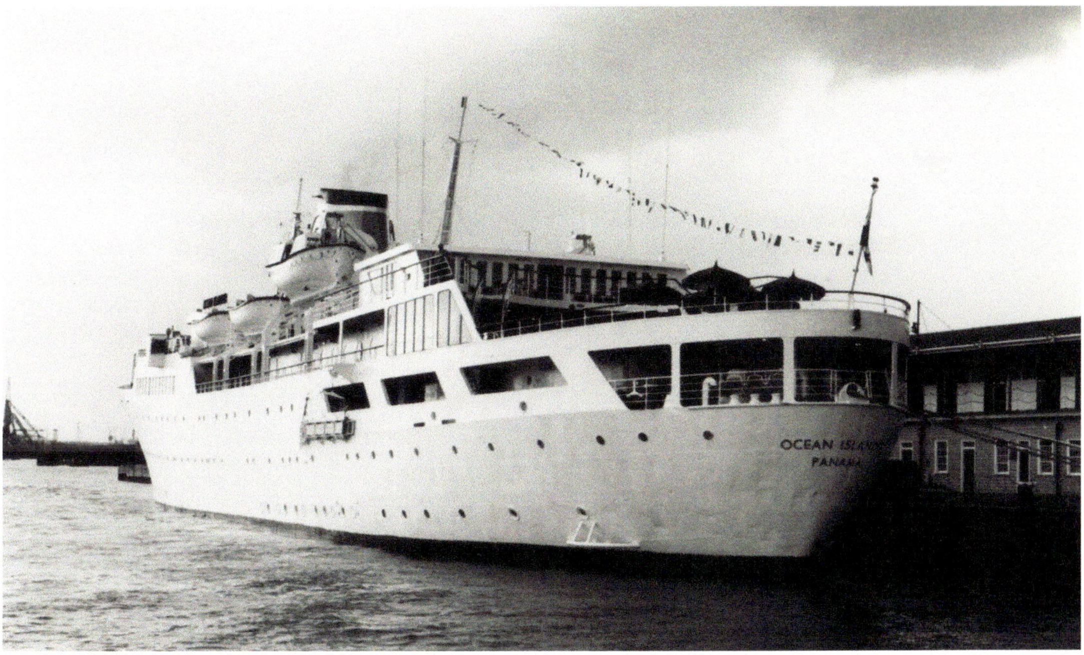

Converted into a luxury cruise ship, the 5,263 grt *Ocean Islander* was originally a small Italian liner dating from 1956. Seen at Tilbury Landing Stage in May 1986, she was sold to the Swiss-owned African Safari Club in 1990 to become *Royal Star*. She was broken up in 2012.

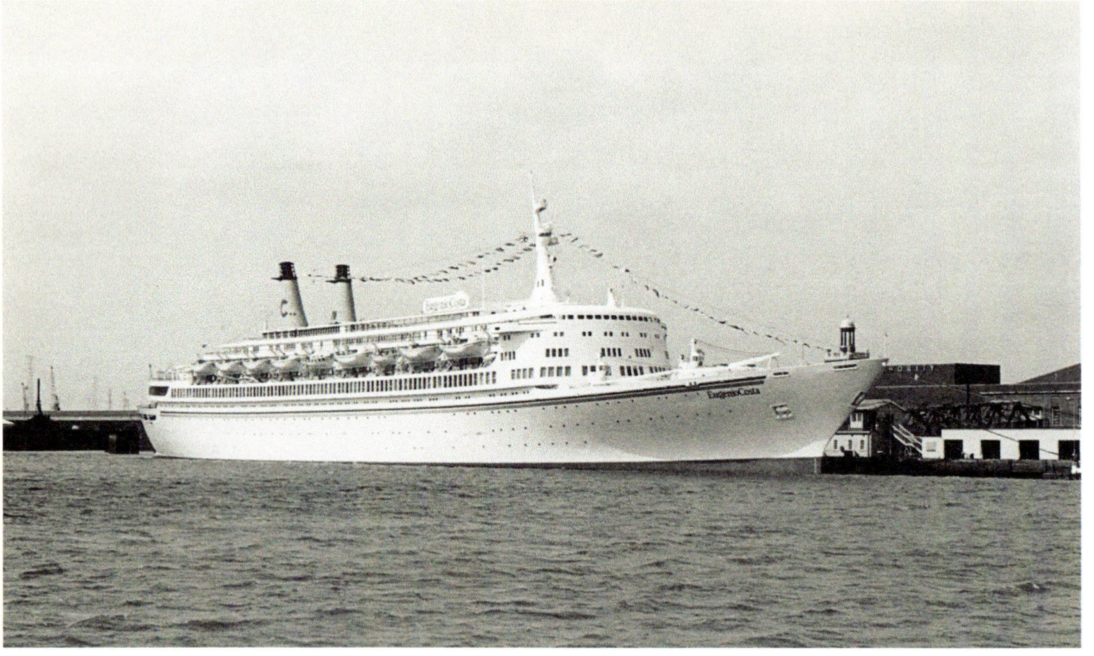

On 9 August 1989 an unfamiliar visitor arrived at Tilbury Landing Stage in the distinctive shape of the 32,753 grt Italian cruise ship *Eugenio Costa*. Built in 1966 for Costa Line's South American service, she was converted for cruising in the late 1970s. She was broken up at Alang in 2005.

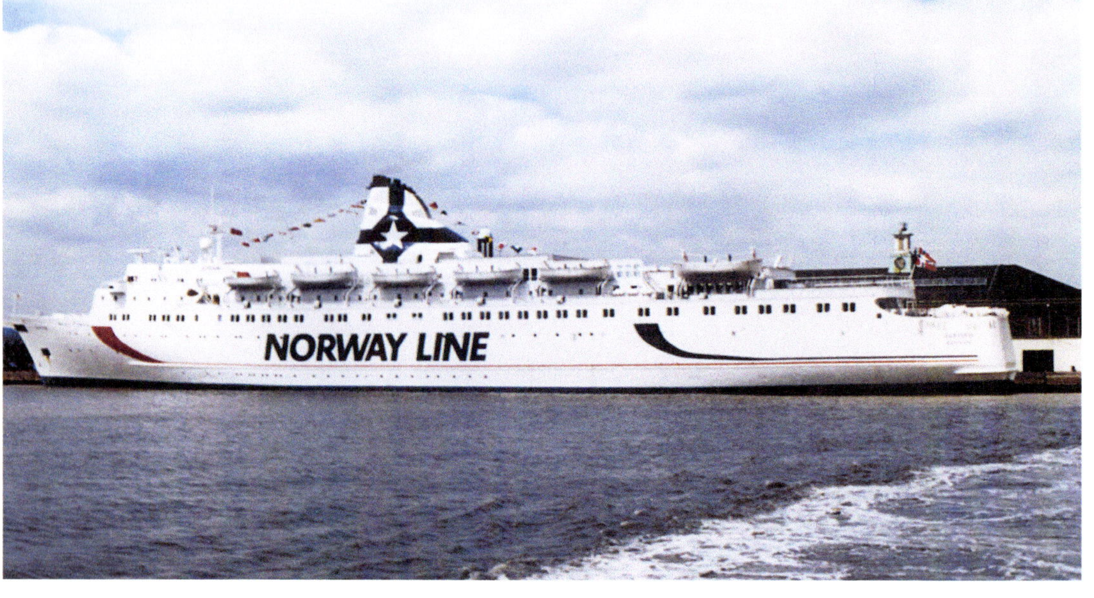

Dressed overall, the pristine-looking ferry *Jupiter* visits Tilbury Landing Stage in the late 1980s. Built in 1966, she led a double life for many years, sailing between Newcastle and Bergen in the summer months and from London to the Canary Islands as Fred Olsen's *Black Watch* during the winter. Acquired by Norway Line in 1986, she was sold in 1990 for eastern Mediterranean service and was later laid up.

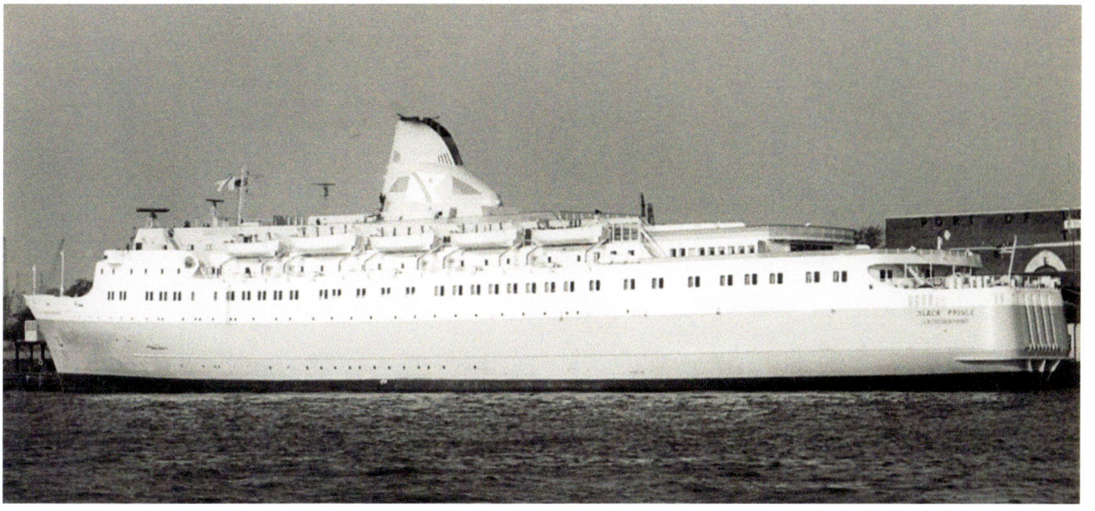

Sister to *Jupiter/Black Watch*, the 9,499 grt Fred Olsen ferry *Black Prince* disembarks passengers at Tilbury Landing Stage having arrived from the Canary Islands. Like her sister she transformed into a Norwegian ferry each summer, under the name *Venus*. In 1985 she was converted into a very successful fully fledged cruise ship.

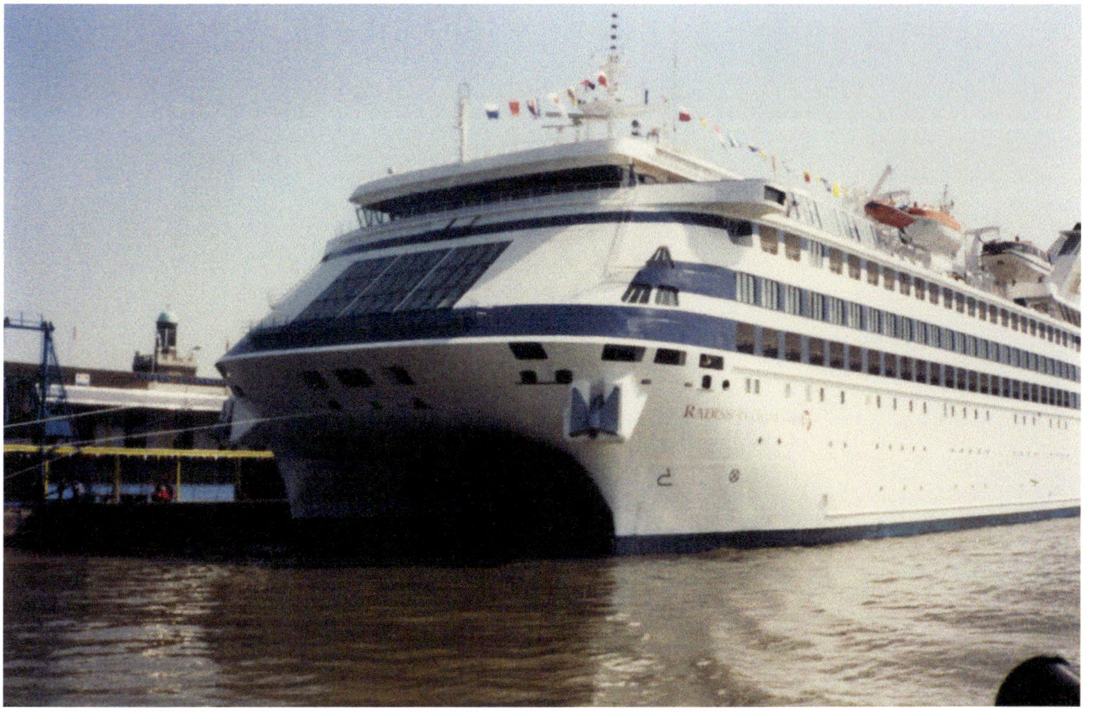

The only twin-hulled cruise ship ever built, *Radisson Diamond* called briefly at Tilbury Landing Stage in May 1992 prior to her christening at Greenwich. Designed to carry 354 passengers, the 20,295 grt vessel was sold in 2005 by her owners Diamond Cruise Inc. to become a Hong Kong gambling ship, *Asia Star*. However, she moved again in 2012 to the China Cruise Company and was renamed *China Star*.

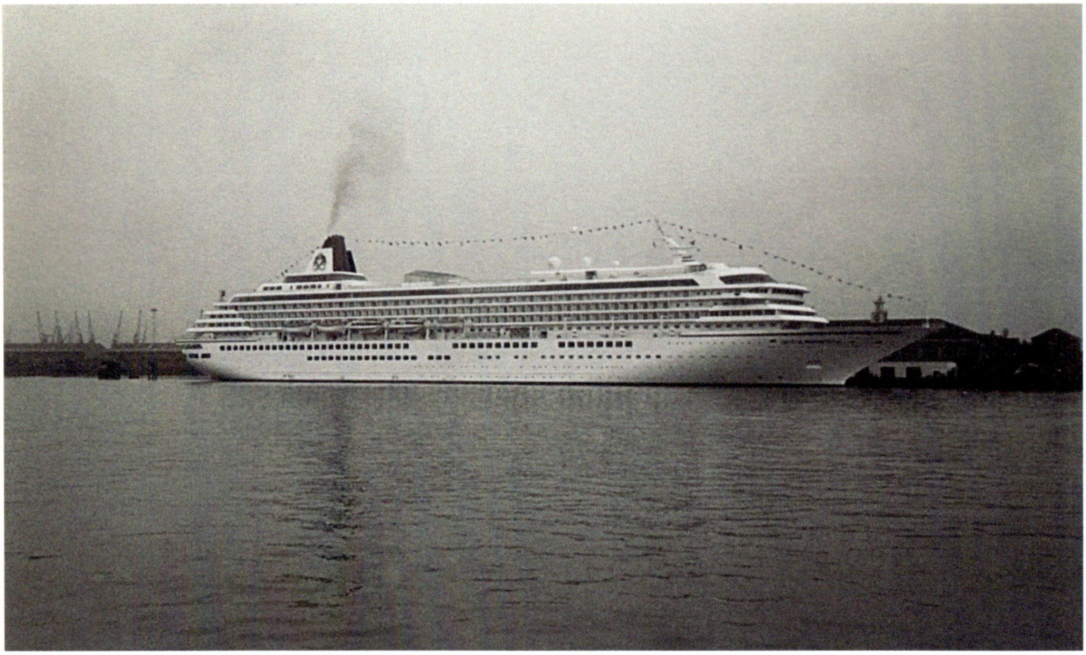

Crystal Cruises is an American luxury cruise line established in 1988. Its first ship, *Crystal Harmony*, 48,621 grt, was making her first visit to Britain in May 1992 when she arrived at Tilbury Landing Stage. In 2005 she transferred to Crystal's parent company NYK of Japan, and was renamed *Asuka II*, a name she retains to this day.

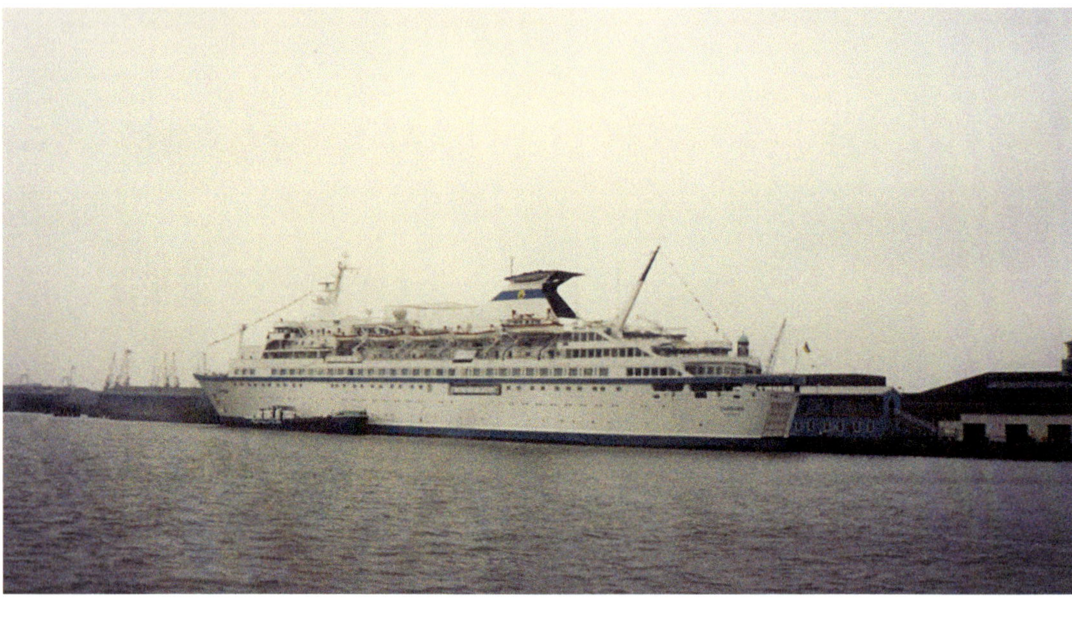

Now displaying the colours of the Ukraine on her funnel, *Kareliya*, 15,065 grt, takes on passengers for another cruise from Tilbury Landing Stage in 1993. By this time she had become one of the most popular cruise ships to be based at Tilbury, sailing in tandem with her sister *Azerbaydzhan* in the summer season.

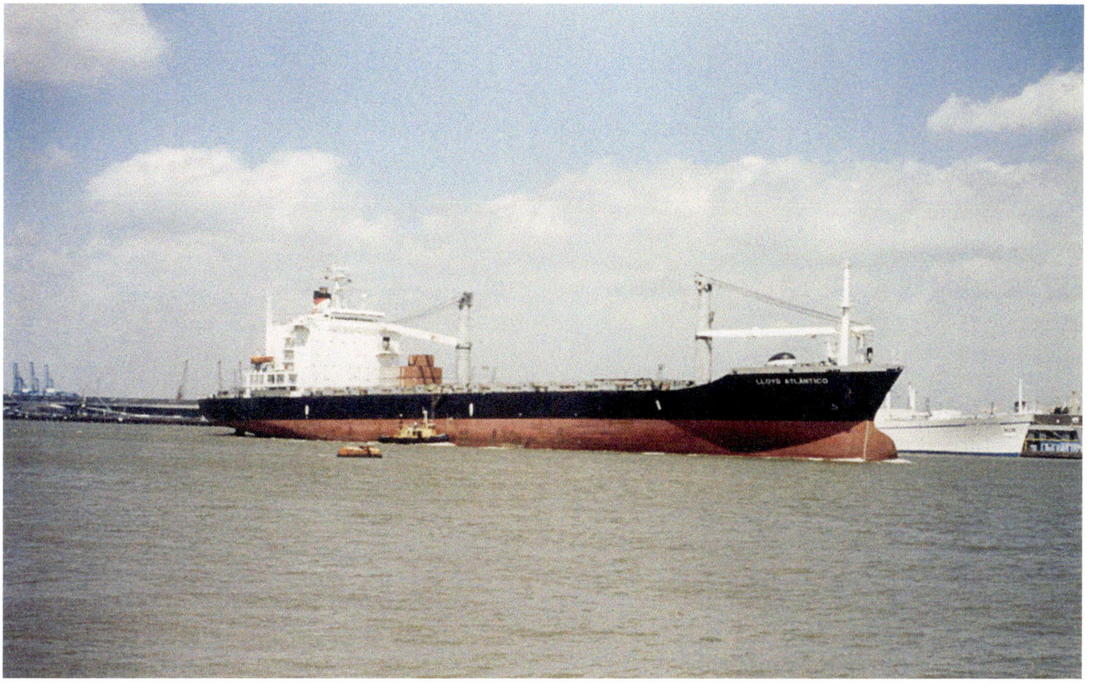

Having discharged most of her cargo, the Brazilian container ship *Lloyd Atlantico*, 22,201 grt, passes Tilbury Landing Stage.

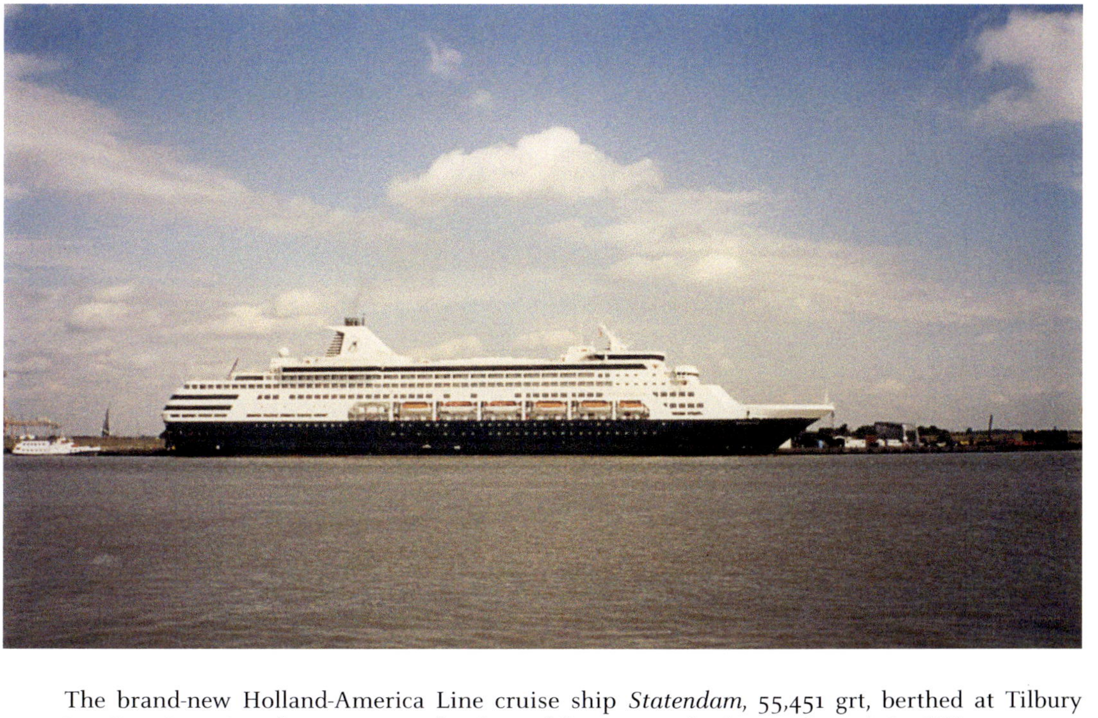

The brand-new Holland-America Line cruise ship *Statendam*, 55,451 grt, berthed at Tilbury Landing Stage in July 1993. One of a class of four sisters built in Italy and the fifth passenger vessel to bear the name, she was designed to accommodate 1,629 passengers in 633 staterooms.

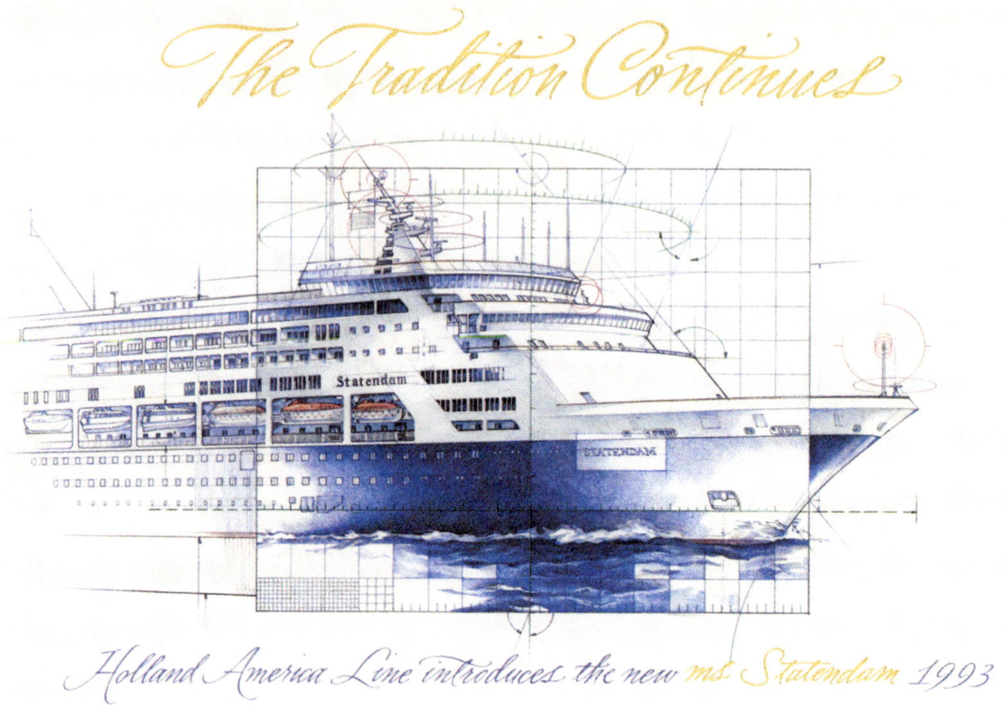

The author had the privilege of being invited on board *Statendam*, which at the time was one of the largest and most luxurious cruise ships to have called at Tilbury.

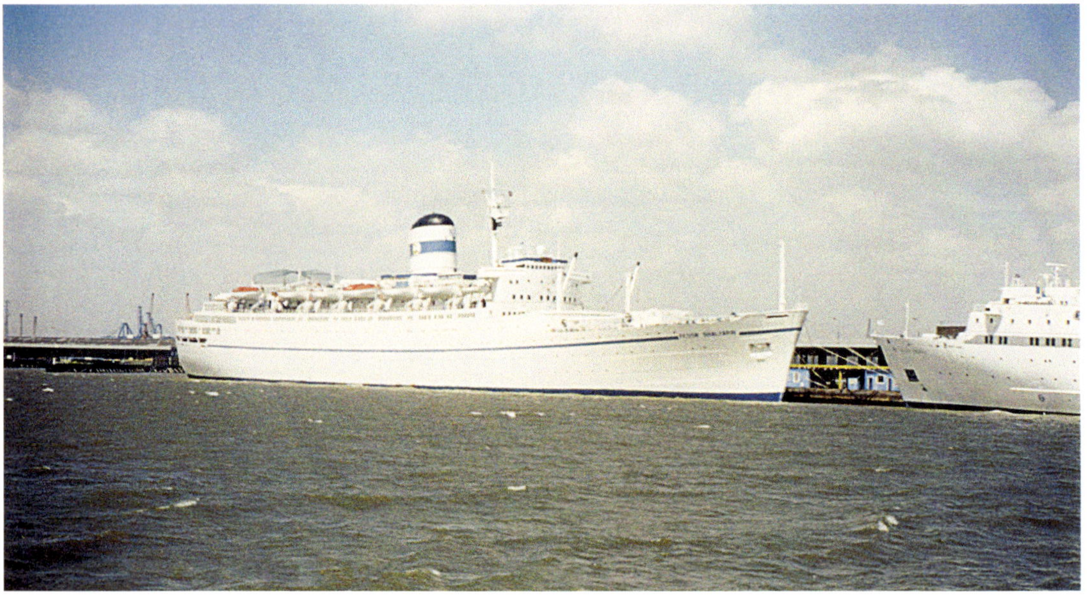

On a hot August day in 1994, the Ukrainian cruise ship *Fedor Shalyapin* makes her penultimate visit to Tilbury, tying up at the landing stage. Once owned by Cunard as the *Ivernia* and then *Franconia*, she sailed into Tilbury Docks a few weeks later, prior to leaving for the Ukraine on what proved to be her last ever cruise.

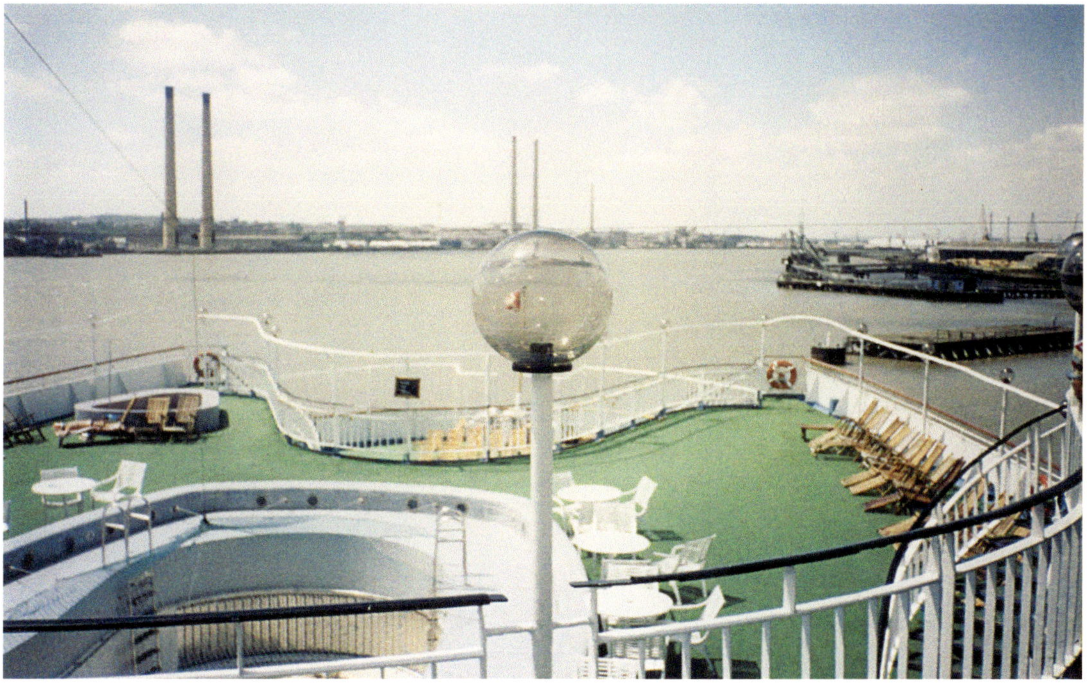

Looking upriver over the stern of *Fedor Shalyapin* while at Tilbury Landing Stage. The swimming pool is surprisingly devoid of water despite the hot weather.

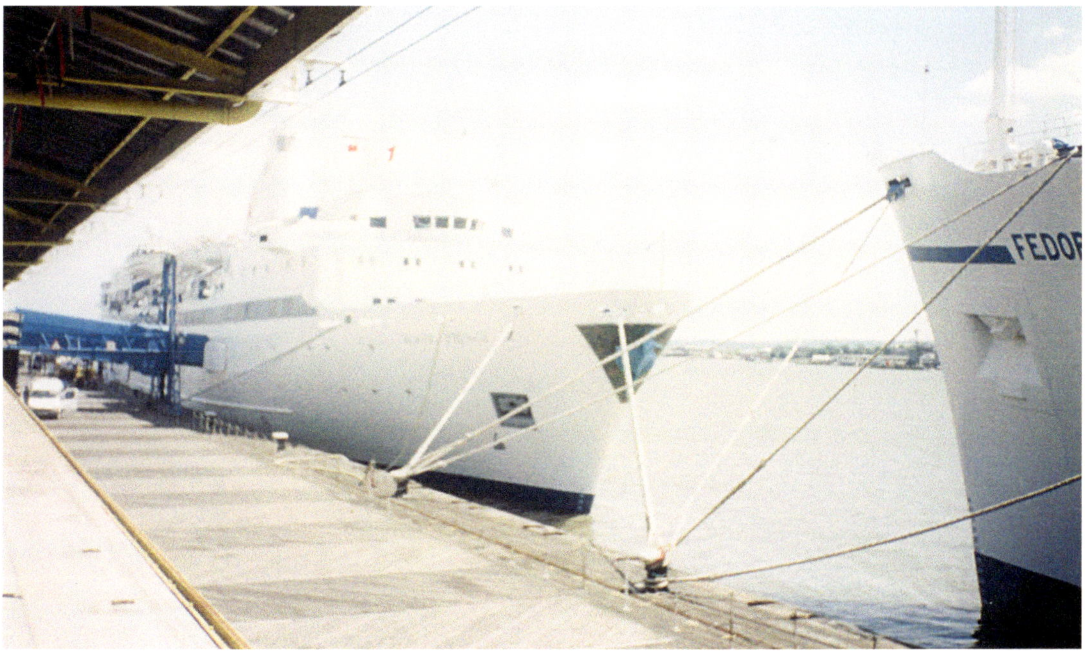

The much-loved cruise ship *Black Prince*, 11,209 grt, lies alongside Tilbury Landing Stage in August 1994. She later changed her home port to Dover but continued to cruise for Fred Olsen Lines until 2009, when she moved to Venezuelan waters. She was broken up in 2012.

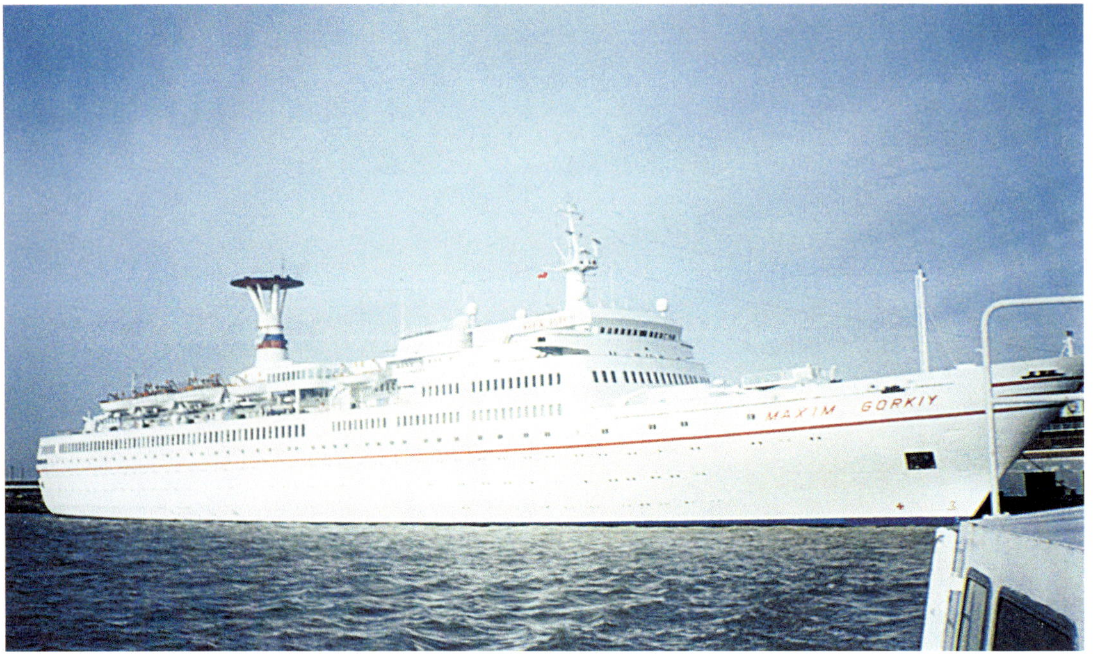

Known as the 'space ship' because of her unusual funnel and spacious interior, the former Soviet cruise ship *Maxim Gorkiy*, 24,981 grt, is seen tied up at Tilbury Landing Stage in November 1994 while on a twenty-year charter to the German tour operator Phoenix Reisen. Built as *Hamburg* for the German Atlantic Line in 1969, she was later renamed *Hanseatic* and laid up for a while before being bought by the Black Sea Shipping Company. She was scrapped in 2009.

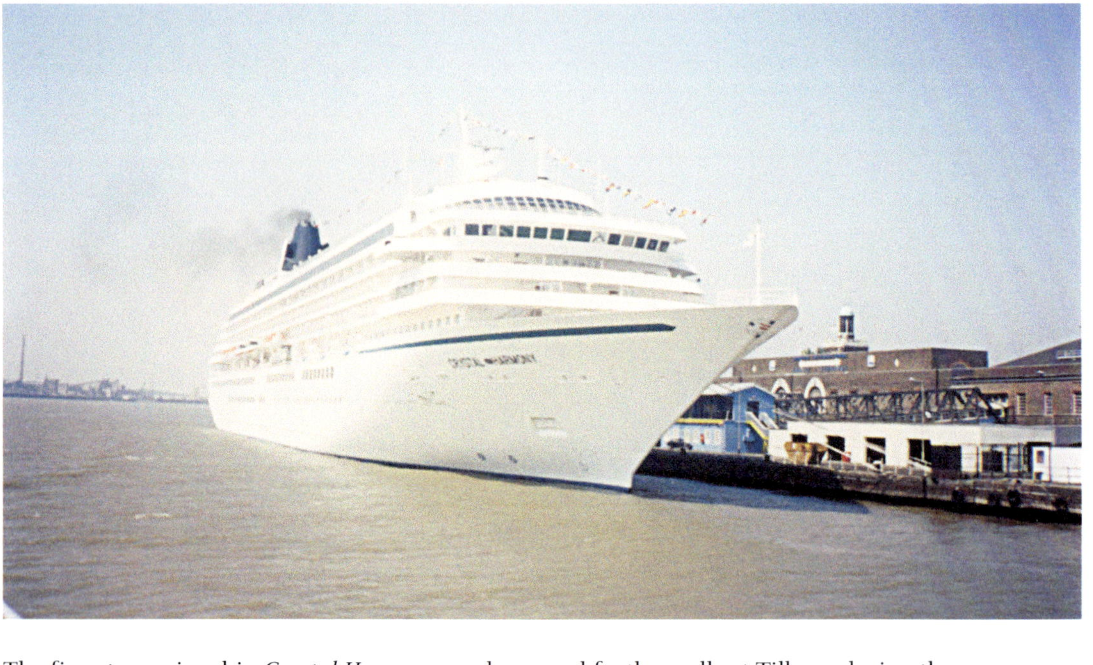

The five-star cruise ship *Crystal Harmony* made several further calls at Tilbury during the 1990s until her cruise schedules took her elsewhere.

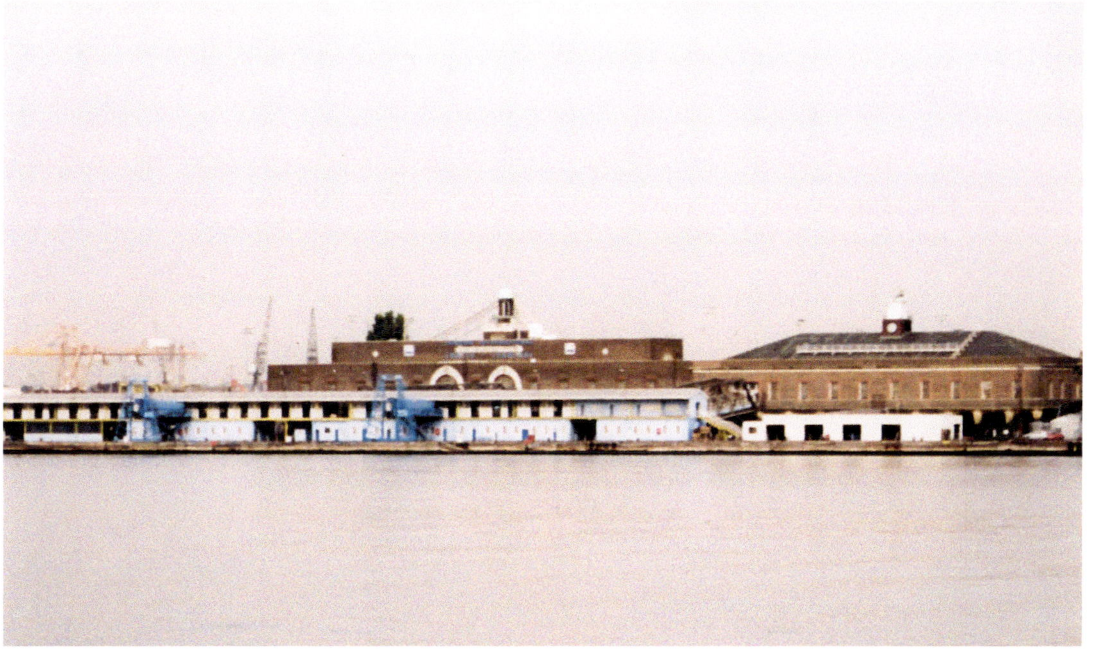

Tilbury Landing Stage was upgraded and reopened as the Tilbury Cruise Terminal in 1995 to meet the demands of modern cruise ships.

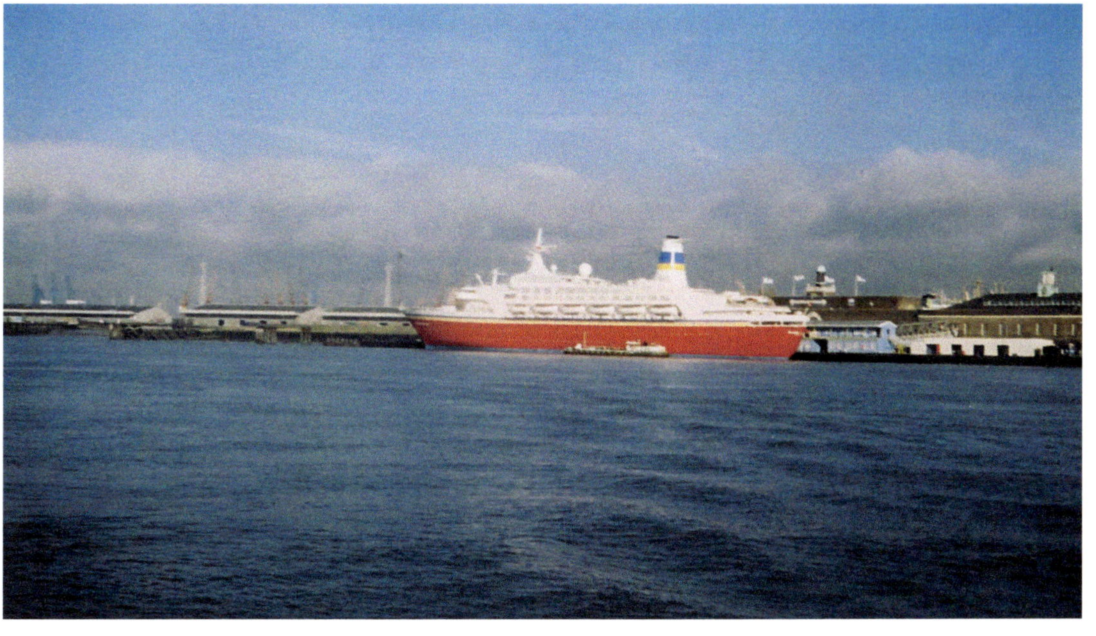

With her bright red hull, CTC Cruise Lines' 17,070 grt *Southern Cross* arrives at Tilbury for her rechristening ceremony at the Cruise Terminal on 7 March 1995. Built in 1972 as *Spirit of London* for P&O, she became *Sun Princess* for Princess Cruises in 1974. She moved to Premier Cruise Line before joining the CTC fleet. With the demise of CTC in 1997, the vessel was sold to Festival Cruises and renamed *Flamenco*. She sank off Thailand in February 2016.

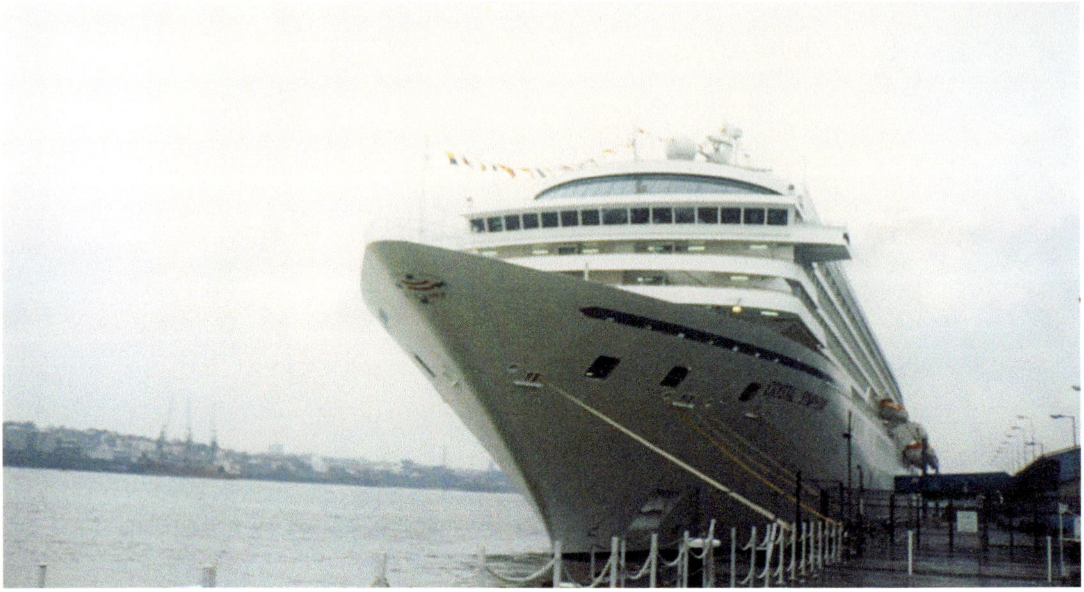

Crystal Cruises' second ship, the 50,202 grt *Crystal Symphony*, dominates Tilbury Landing Stage after sailing in direct from her builders in April 1995. During her stay she was showcased to members of the media and the travel industry.

Crystal Symphony

INAUGURAL

CRYSTAL CRUISES

CORDIALLY INVITES YOU

TO PREVIEW THE LINE'S SECOND LUXURY SHIP

CRYSTAL SYMPHONY

DURING HER INAUGURAL FESTIVITIES IN TILBURY/LONDON

SATURDAY, THE TWENTY-SECOND OF APRIL

NINETEEN HUNDRED AND NINETY-FIVE

NINE-THIRTY IN THE MORNING

PORT OF TILBURY/LONDON

Kindly respond on or before the twelfth of April by using the enclosed RSVP card.

RSVP and picture identification required for boarding.

INVITATION IS FOR YOU AND A GUEST ONLY, AND IS NOT TRANSFERABLE.

Another invitation for the author and a chance to appreciate the high-class accommodation and wide choice of eating places on board the new *Crystal Symphony*.

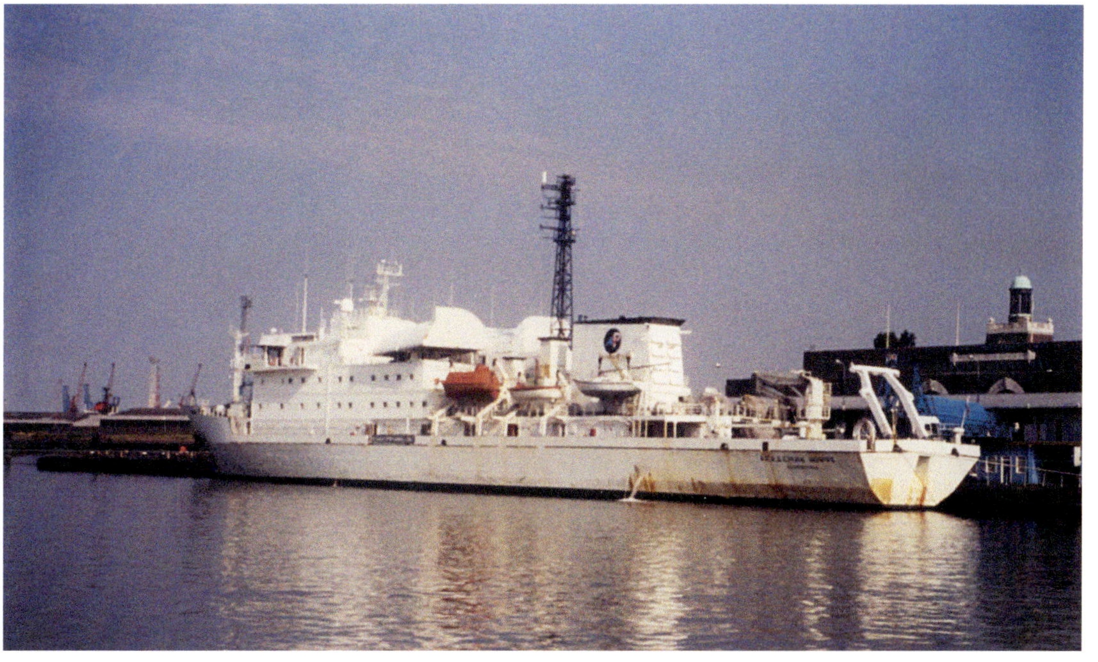

Pole to pole: in July 1995 a Russian polar research ship, the 6,231 grt *Akademik Ioffe*, arrived at Tilbury Landing Stage in her role as an expedition cruise ship. With her three laboratories and underwater surveillance equipment, she also provides comfortable accommodation for up to ninety-six passengers, who have the use of a swimming pool and sauna.

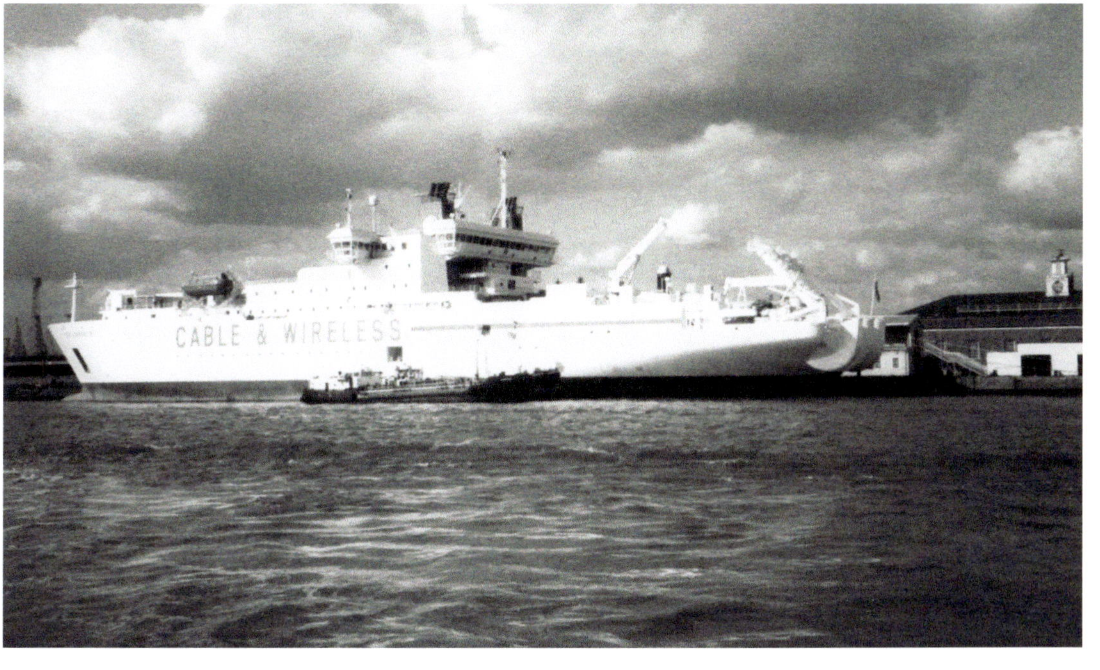

In 1995 the 14,277 grt *Cable Innovator* made a courtesy call at Tilbury Landing Stage, announcing herself as the world's largest cable vessel.

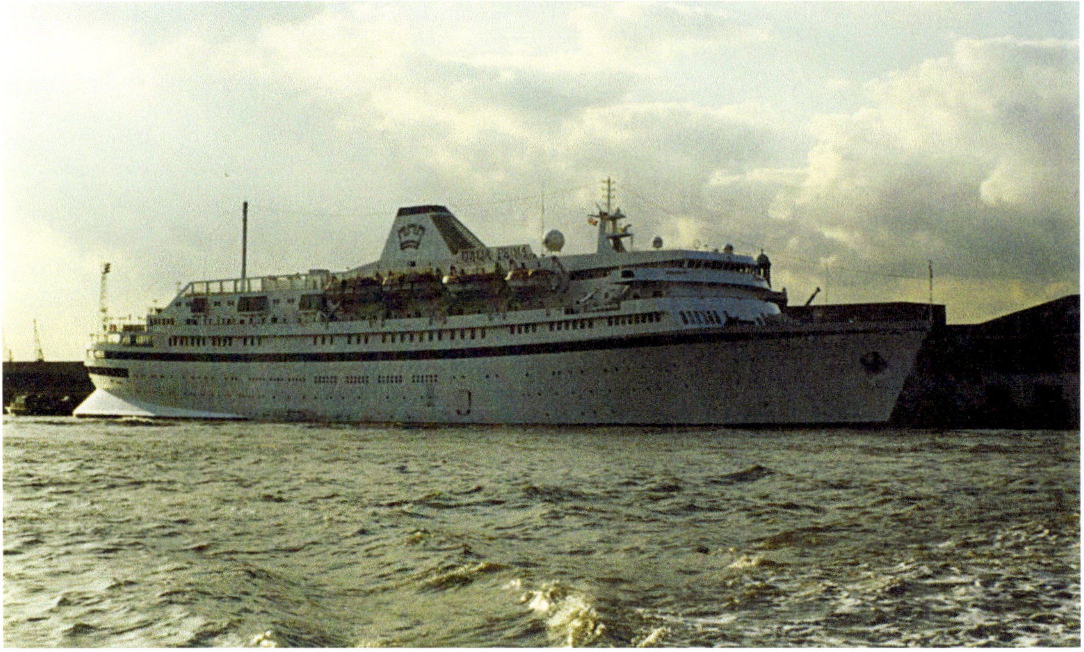

Caught in the evening shadows, the Italian cruise ship *Italia Prima* lies alongside the landing stage at Tilbury in July 1996. A ship with a varied career, she was completely rebuilt on the hull of the 1948-built Swedish liner *Stockholm*, which made the headlines in 1956 for her collision with the liner *Andrea Doria*, which subsequently sank. At the time of her visit to Tilbury *Italia Prima* was under charter to the German tour company Neckerman.

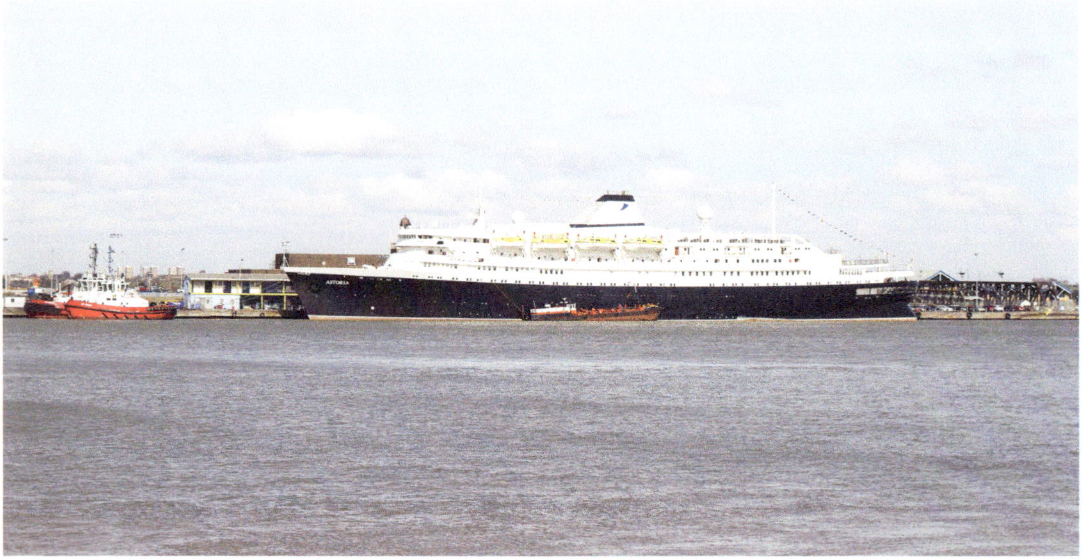

Five name changes later, the former *Italia Prima* is back at Tilbury as *Astoria*. The 12,165 grt vessel, owned by Portuscale Cruises, was chartered to UK-based Cruise & Maritime Voyages (CMV) in 2015 as *Athena*, only to have her name changed again. With CMV she has been sailing from UK regional ports as well as Tilbury.

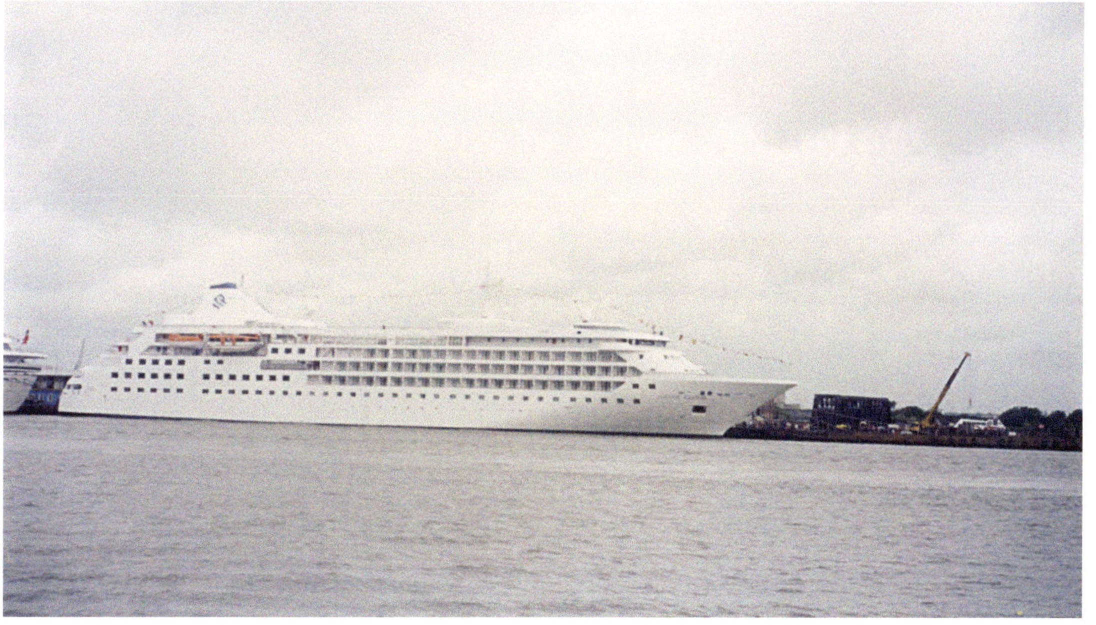

Luxury cruise company Silversea Cruises was founded in 1994, taking delivery of its first ship, the 16,927 grt *Silver Cloud*. With her identical sister *Silver Wind*, she proved popular with clientele seeking top-class service and accommodation and has recently been refitted for expedition cruising.

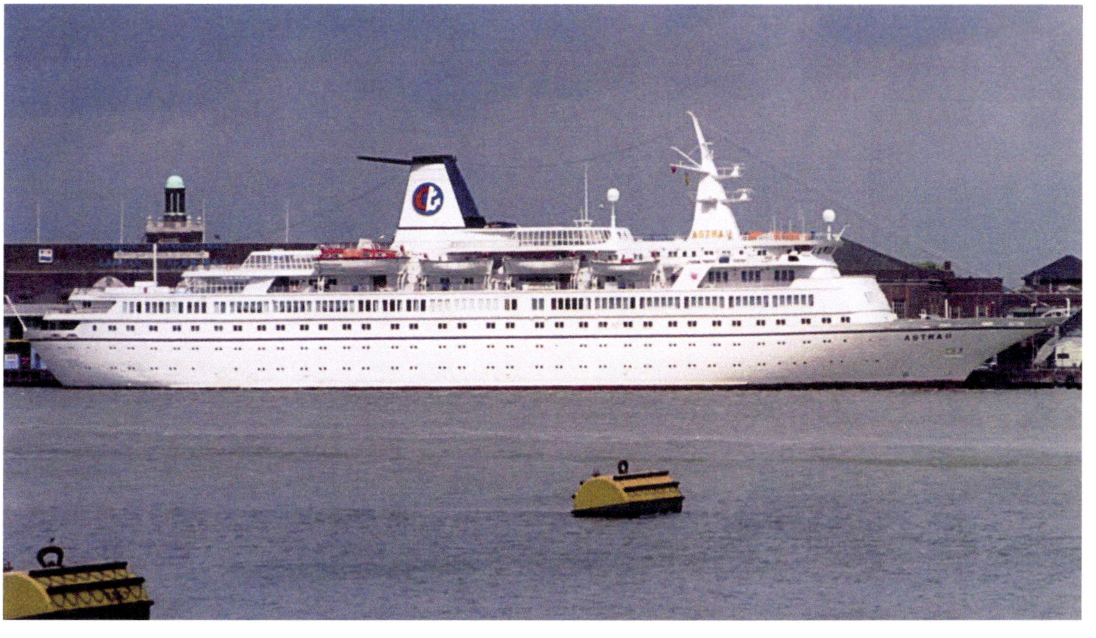

Seen at the London Cruise Terminal (Tilbury Landing Stage) in 1997, the *Astra II*, 1974/9,848 grt, was acquired from Royal Cruise Line, for whom she sailed as *Golden Odyssey*, in 1994. Having cruised for various German companies, she changed hands again in November 2000, eventually becoming a casino ship based at Hong Kong in 2014.

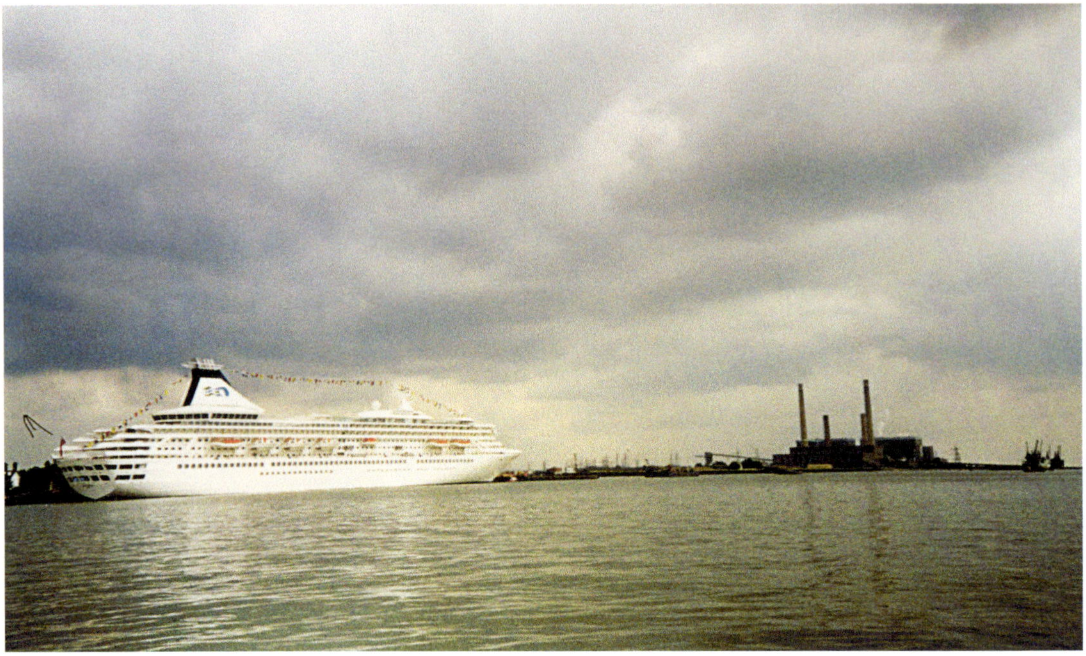

The well-loved British cruise ship *Royal Princess*, 44,348 grt, made several cruises from Tilbury during the 1990s. Delivered to Princess Cruises in 1984, she was the first purpose-built cruise ship to feature balconies. To her right, further downstream, is Tilbury power station in full operation with its two chimneys intact.

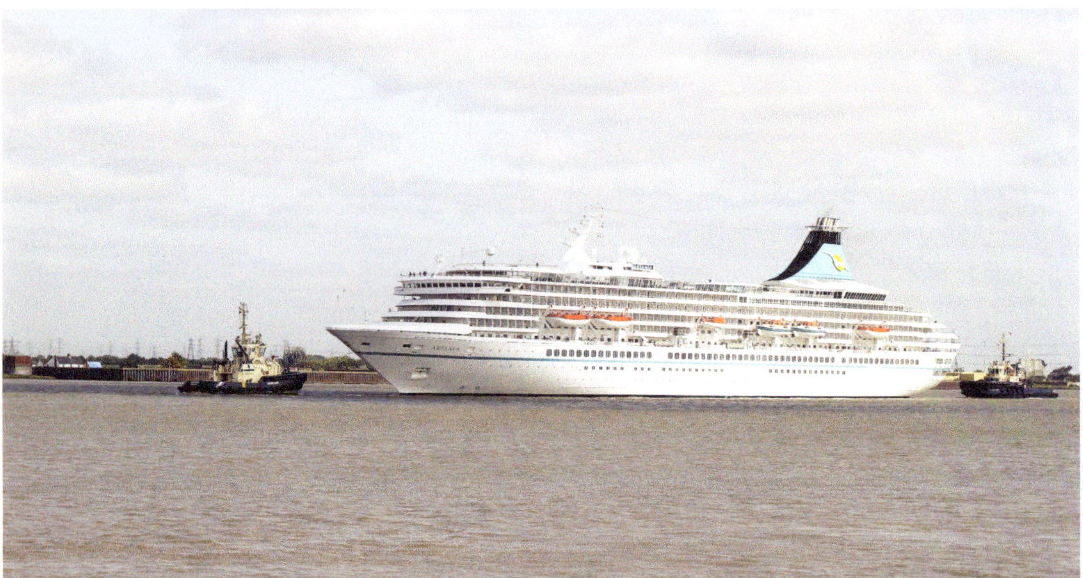

Looking as resplendent as when she was new, *Artania*, formerly *Royal Princess*, makes a welcome return to Tilbury. In 2005 she was transferred to P&O Cruises as *Artemis* before moving on to Artania Shipping in 2011, since when she has cruised for the German cruise operator Phoenix Reisen.

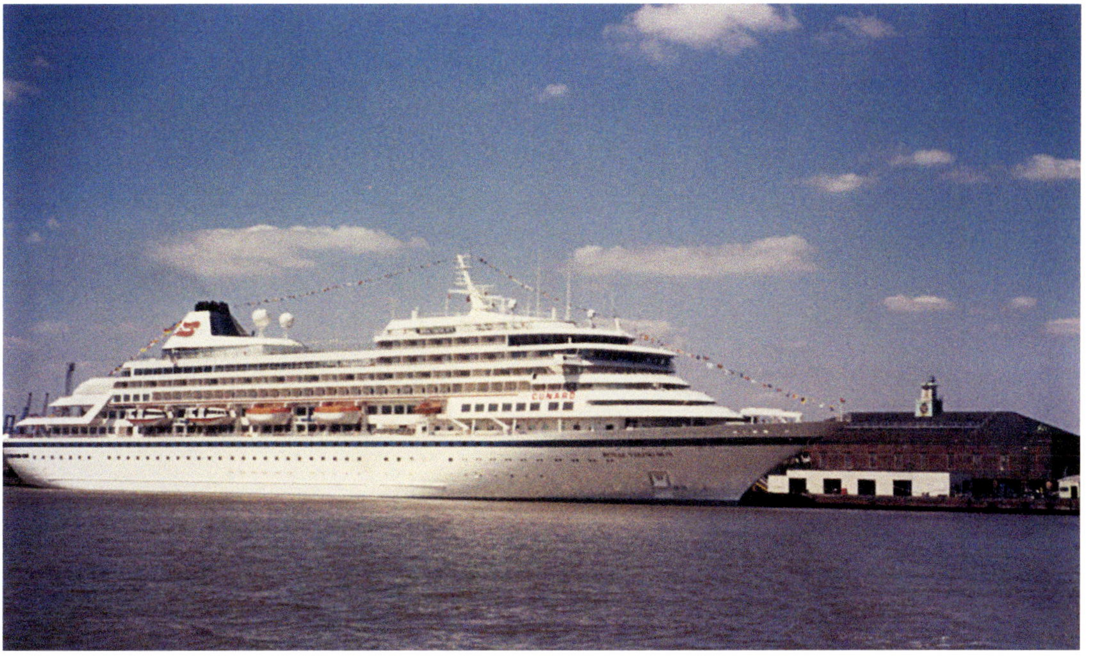

The graceful-looking 37,845 grt cruise ship *Royal Viking Sun* at the London Cruise Terminal during 1997. Completed for the former Royal Viking Line in 1988, she moved in 1994 to Cunard, who retained her name. In 1999 she became *Seabourn Sun* for the Seabourn Cruise Line and transferred again in 2002 to Holland-America Line, who renamed her *Prinsendam*. After a further seventeen years of service, she is due to join Germany's Phoenix Reisen's fleet in August 2019 as *Amera*.

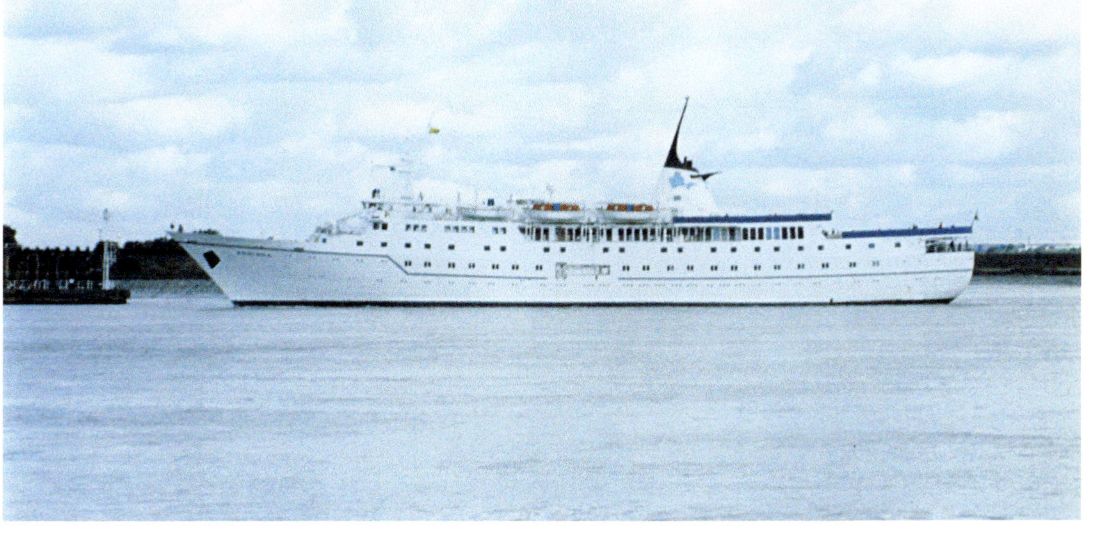

One of the smallest cruise ships to visit Tilbury Landing Stage, the 4,591 grt *Adriana* dates back to 1972, when she was built as the *Aquarius* for Hellenic Mediterranean Lines. Purchased by Yugoslav owners in 1987, she flies the flag of Croatia and since 2015 has been operated by Adriana Cruises.

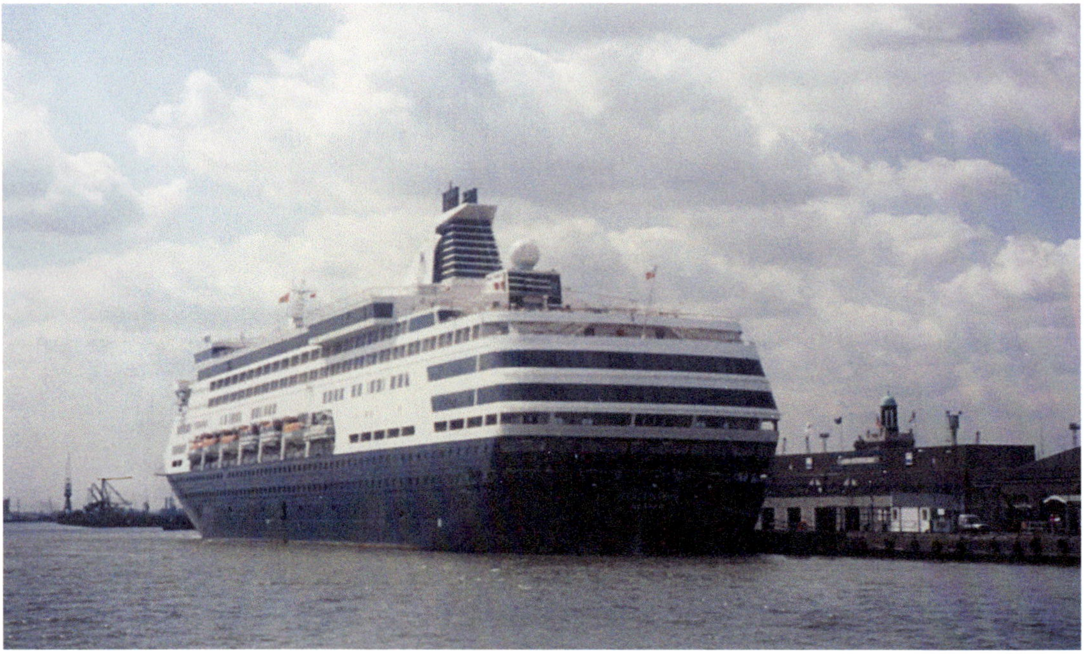

A later view of *Statendam* at Tilbury during the 1990s. She remained in the Holland-America fleet until 2015, when she transferred to P&O Cruises Australia as *Pacific Eden*. But in March 2019 she was acquired by Cruise & Maritime Voyages (CMV) for cruising out of Australia during the winter months and operating annual line voyages between the London Cruise Terminal and the Antipodes under the name *Vasco da Gama*. In the summer season she is scheduled to cruise in Europe for CMV's German brand Transocean.

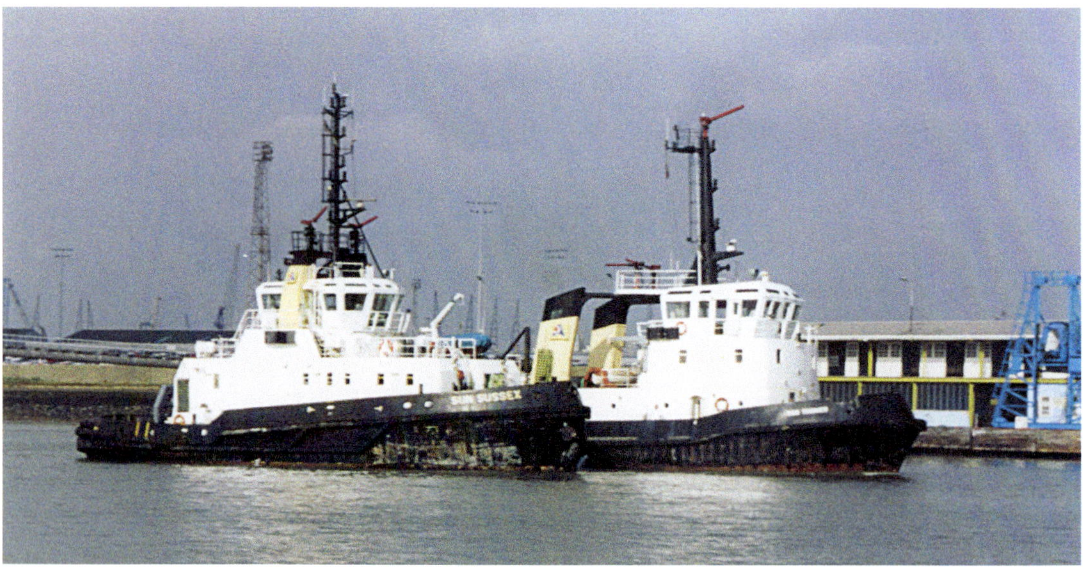

The tugs *Sun Sussex*, 1992/378 grt (left), and *Sun Thames*, 1982/330 grt, both at the time owned by Adsteam, pictured at Tilbury Landing Stage, no doubt awaiting the arrival of a cruise ship. *Sun Sussex* now works elsewhere as *Svitzer Sussex*.

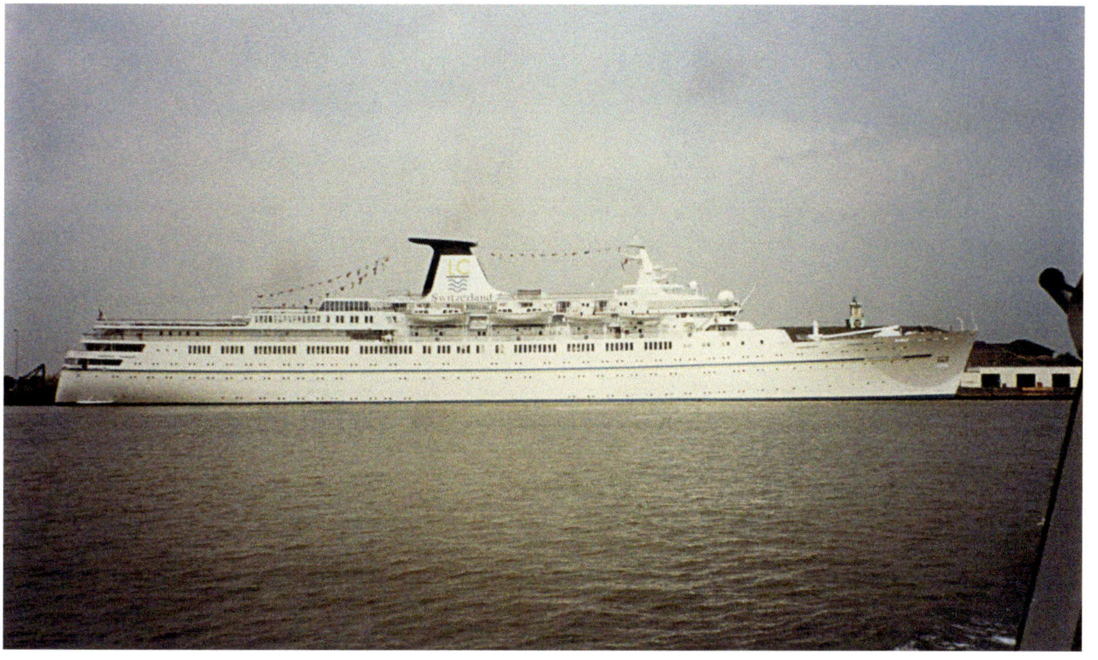

In her original guise as the Port Line cargo vessel *Port Sydney*, the 15,739 grt *Switzerland* would regularly pass Tilbury Landing Stage on her way to Australia. Converted into a cruise ship in the 1970s, she sailed under several names, including *Ocean Monarch*, *Princess Daphne* and the *Switzerland*, as she was seen at Tilbury in 1998. She was broken up in 2014.

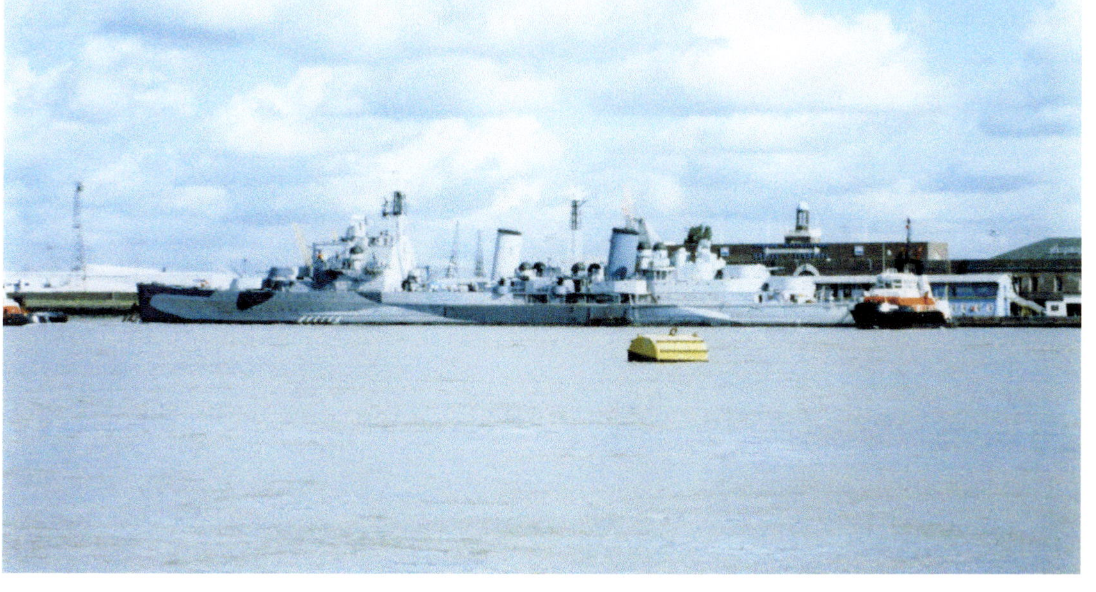

The locals rubbed their eyes in disbelief one June day in 1999 when HMS *Belfast* was nosed gently alongside Tilbury Landing Stage, for this was only the second occasion that the preserved Second World War cruiser had left her moorings in the Pool of London since 1971. She was on her way to Portsmouth for an inspection and the recoating of her hull.

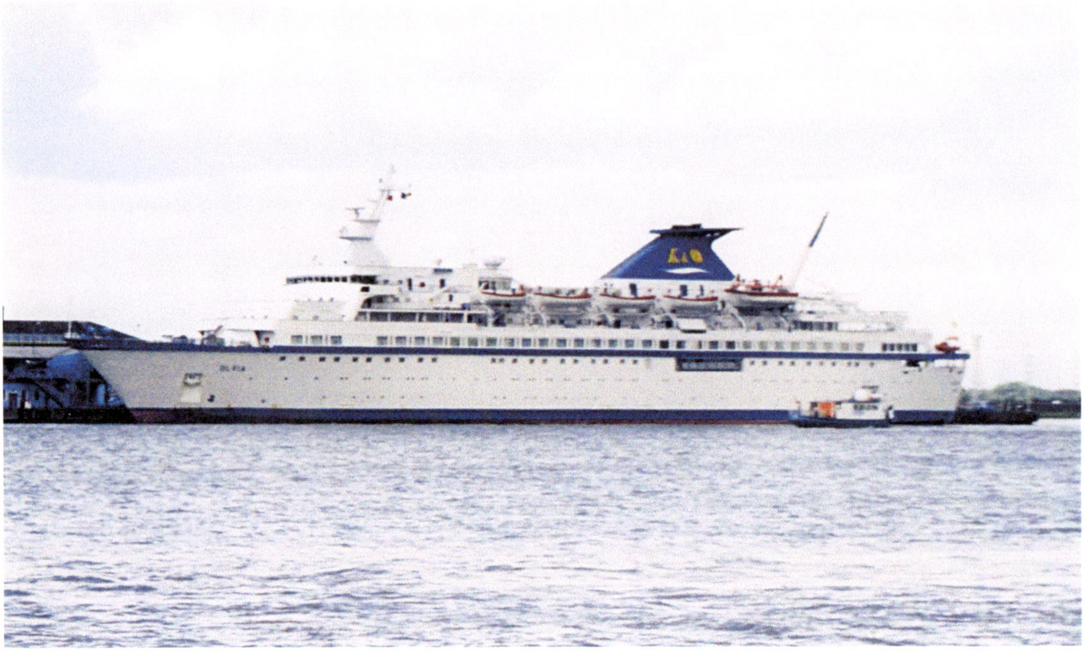

Welcome return: *Kareliya* was sold to Kaalbye Shipping International in 1998 and returned to Tilbury under the name *Olvia*. In 2001 she was laid up before finding employment as a Hong Kong gambling ship. Initially renamed *Neptune*, she currently sails as *Starry Metropolis*.

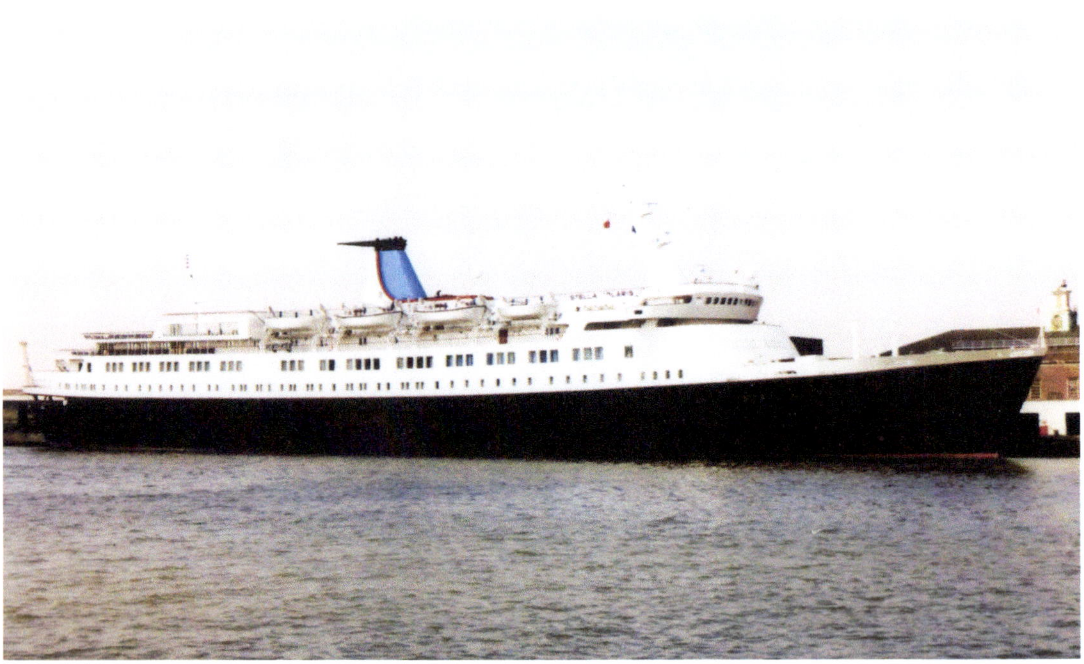

Louis Cruise Line's 10,595 grt *Stella Solaris* at the London Cruise Terminal in the late 1990s. Built as the French liner *Cambodge* in 1953, she was extensively rebuilt in 1970, including a new funnel. She was broken up in 2003.

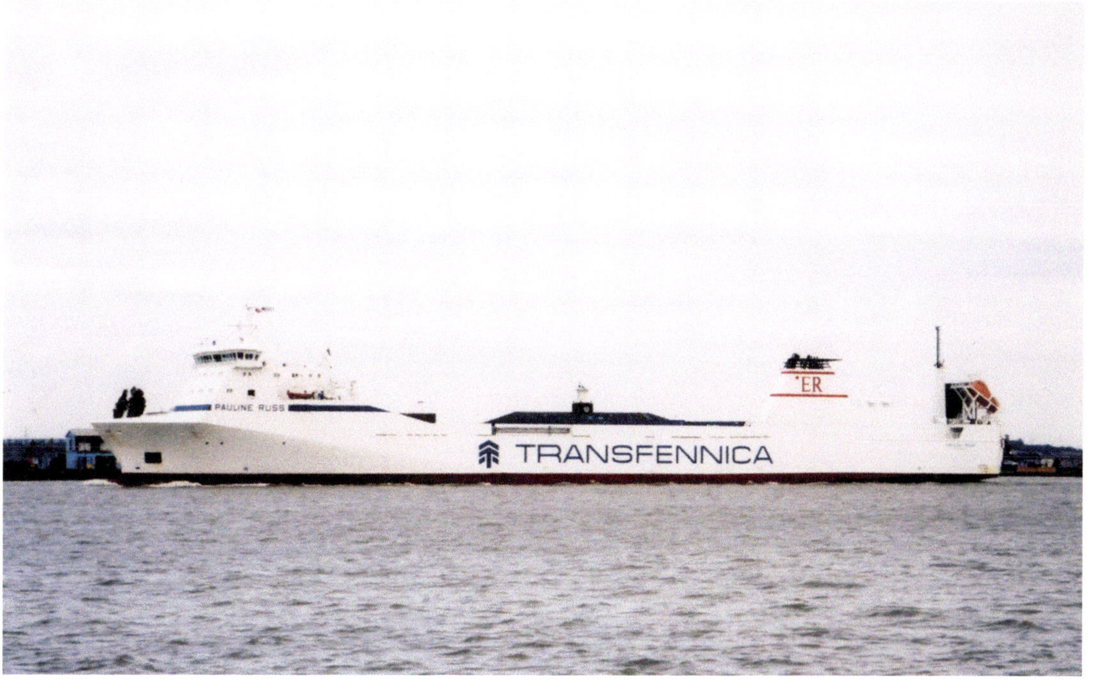

Pictured passing Tilbury soon after her completion in 1999, the 10,488 grt *Pauline Russ* is an extremely adaptable ship that can carry trailers, loaded cassettes, paper products and general cargo as well as containers. Operated by Transfennica, a Finnish company, she is heading for her berth within the docks at Tilbury.

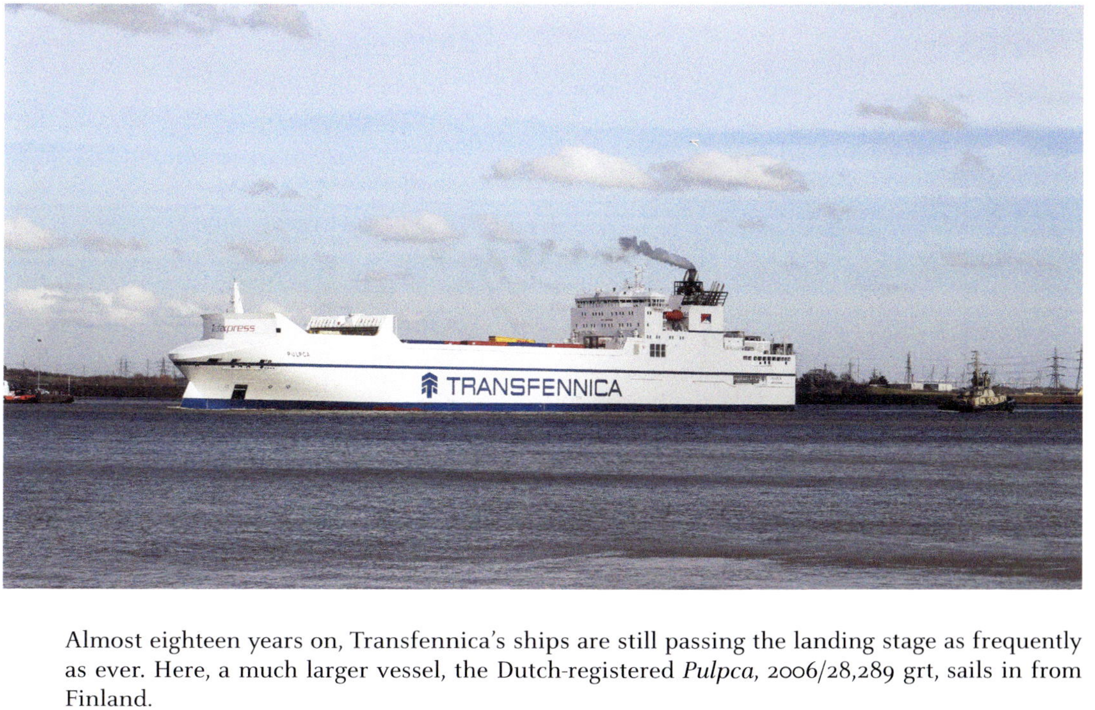

Almost eighteen years on, Transfennica's ships are still passing the landing stage as frequently as ever. Here, a much larger vessel, the Dutch-registered *Pulpca*, 2006/28,289 grt, sails in from Finland.

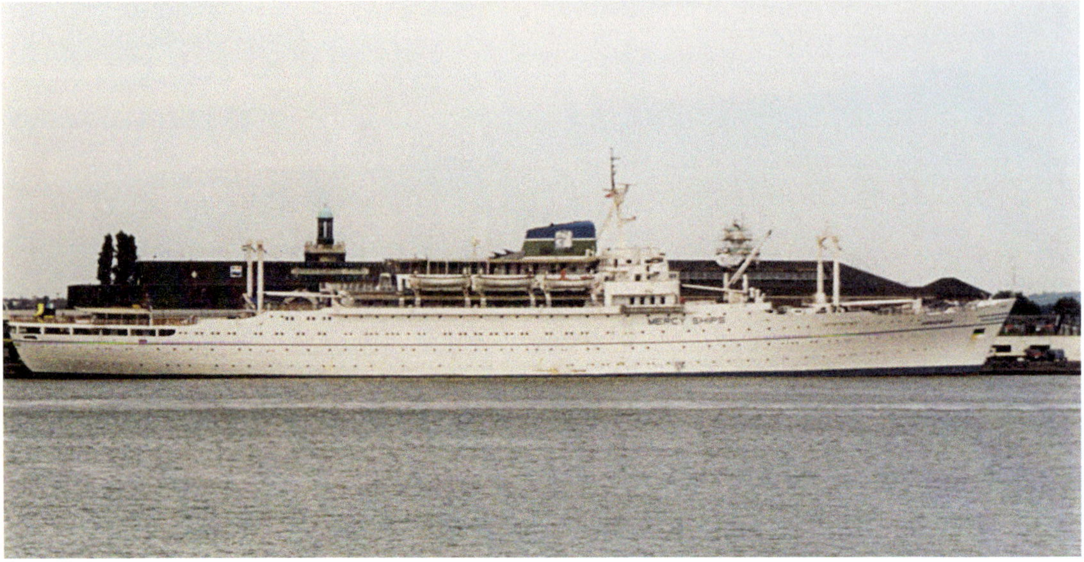

The founder member of the Mercy Ship fleet, *Anastasis*, 11,695 grt, began life as the 1953-built Italian liner *Victoria*. A veritable floating hospital with three operating theatres on board, she made several appearances in the Thames until Mercy Ships, an international charity providing humanitarian aid, withdrew her from service in 2007.

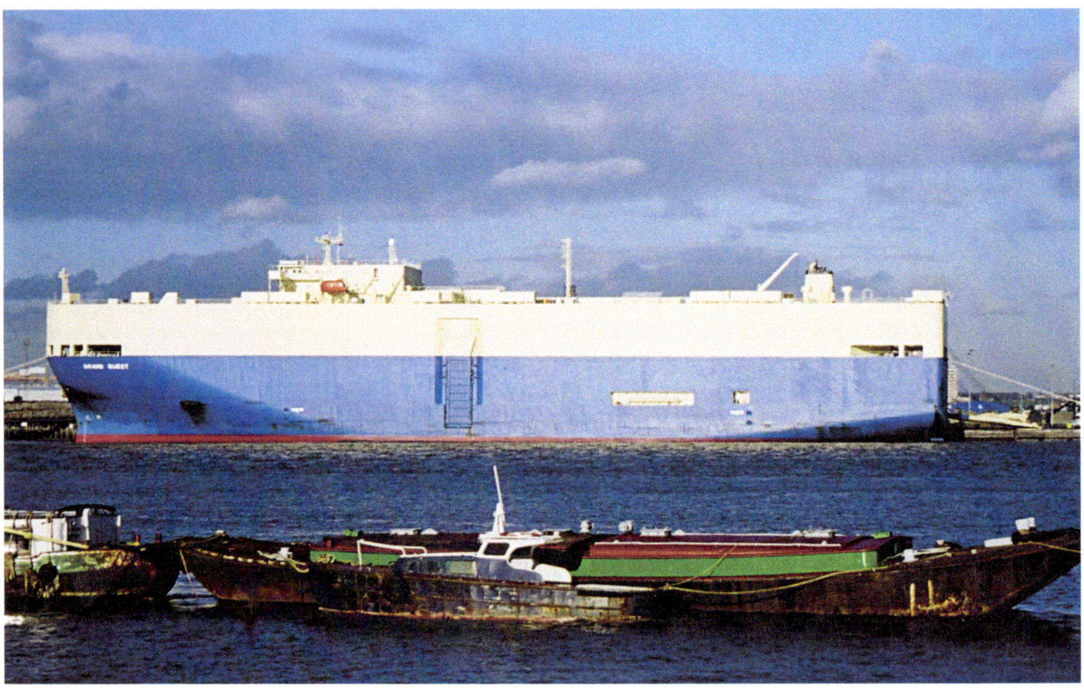

At the western end of Tilbury Landing Stage, a dedicated ro-ro terminal was opened early in the year 2000 for the handling of imported Hyundai cars. Since then some of the largest vessels to enter the Thames have berthed there, including the 50,309 grt *Grand Quest*. Built in 1999, she can transport up to 4,375 cars.

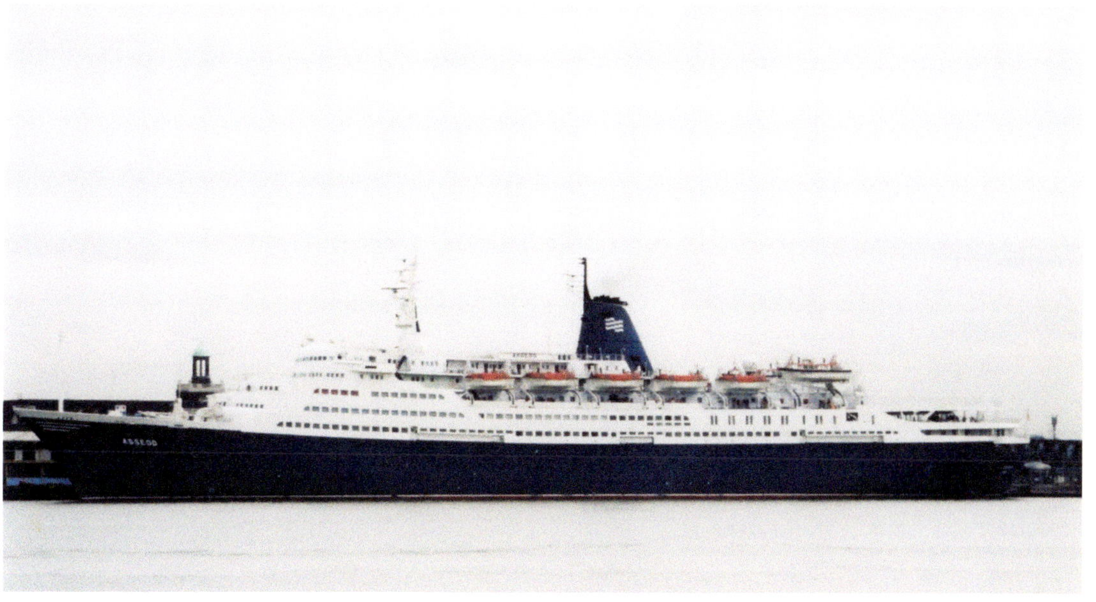

Originally *Shota Rustaveli*, the fourth vessel of the Soviet Ivan Franko class, *Assedo* ('Odessa' in reverse) came out of lay-up in 2001 to make a number of cruises that featured calls at the London Cruise Terminal. She was broken up soon afterwards, in 2003.

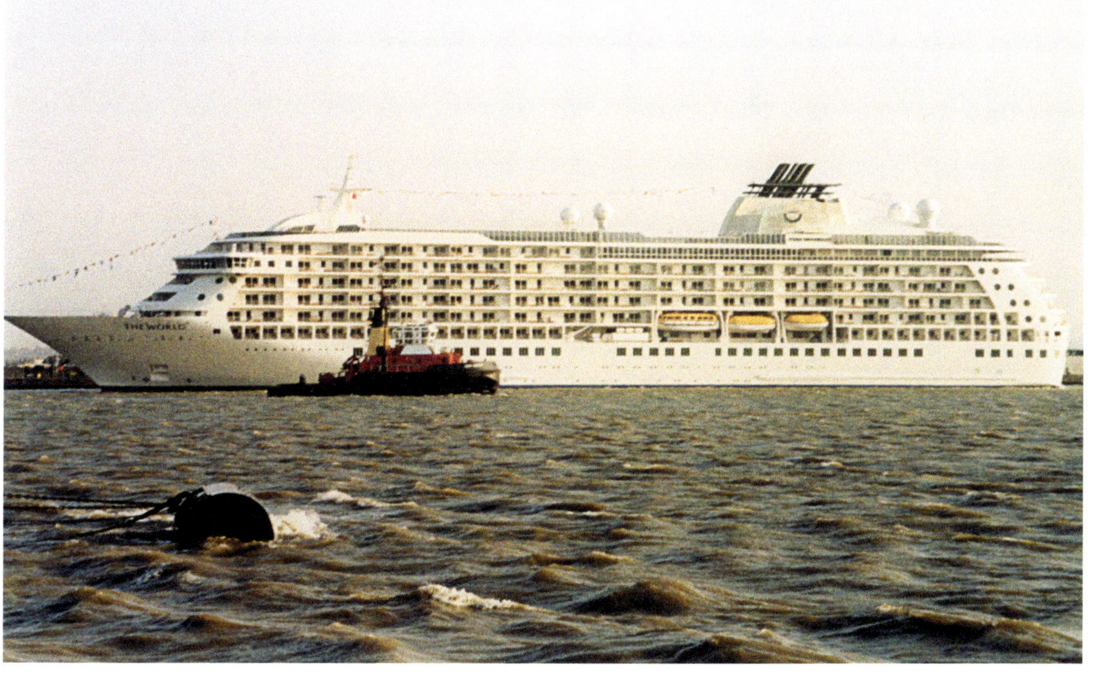

In April 2002 the first ever residential ship, *The World*, 43,525 grt, arrived at the London Cruise Terminal direct from her trials. On board are 110 luxurious apartments, allowing an average occupancy of 390 residents, and eighty-eight guest suites. On subsequent visits to London she has moored upriver at Greenwich.

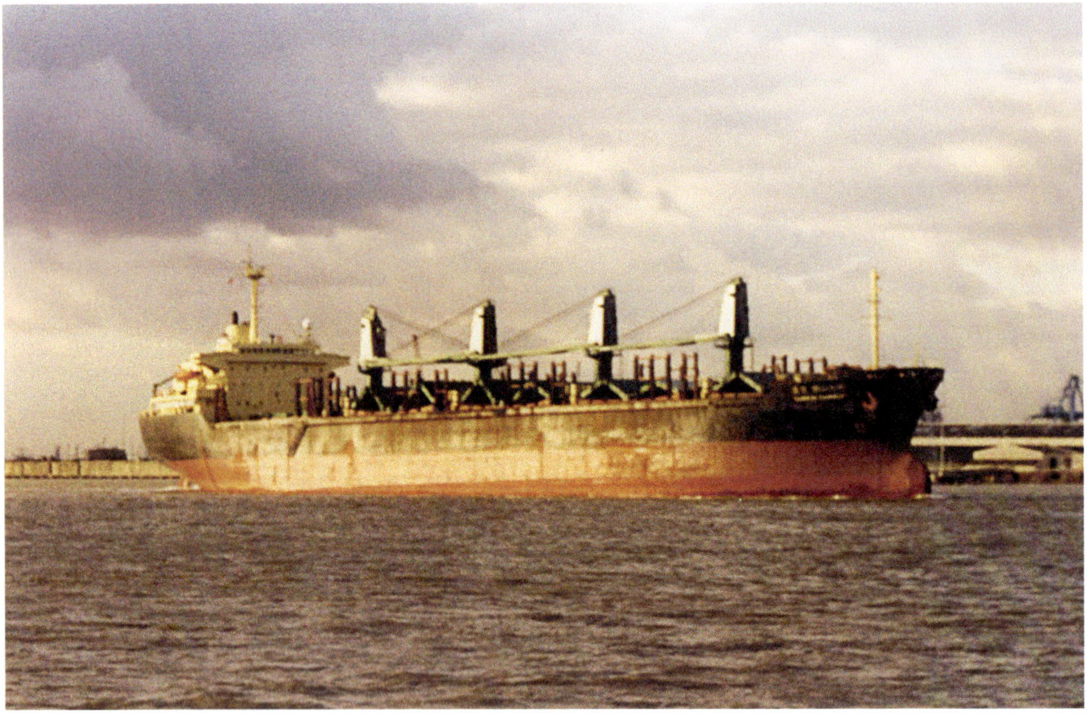

Caught on camera in the early evening sunshine during 2003, the South Korean bulk carrier *Samsun Earnest*, 1986/19,035 grt, passes through Gravesend Reach, having discharged her cargo at the nearby Tilbury Grain Terminal.

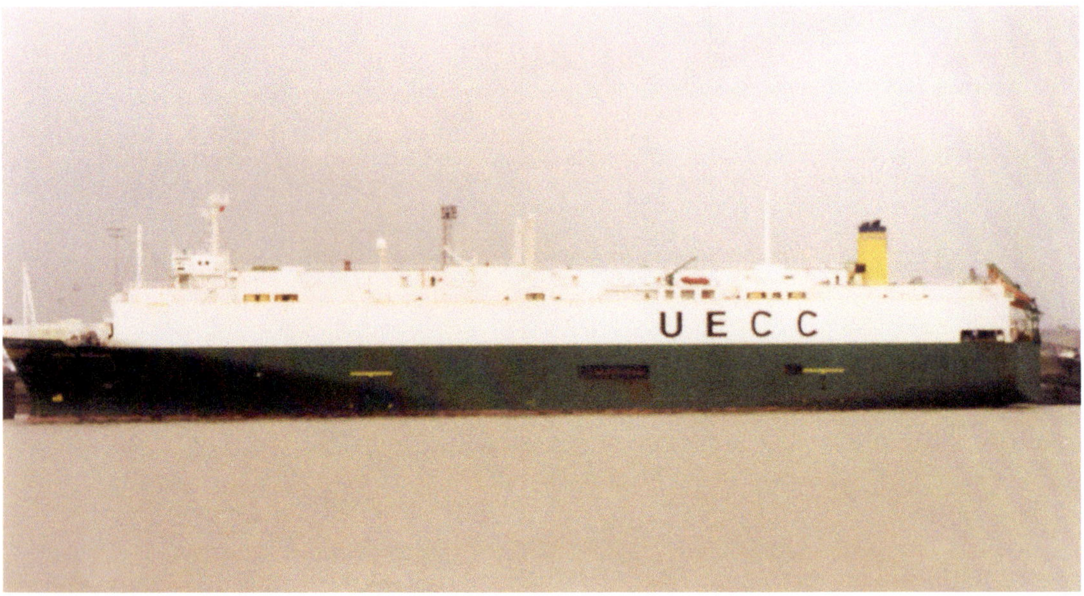

As business at the Tilbury car import facility grew, United European Car Carriers opened a service for importing vehicles from Turkey. Among the ships employed was *Asian Breeze*, 28,117 grt, built in 1983.

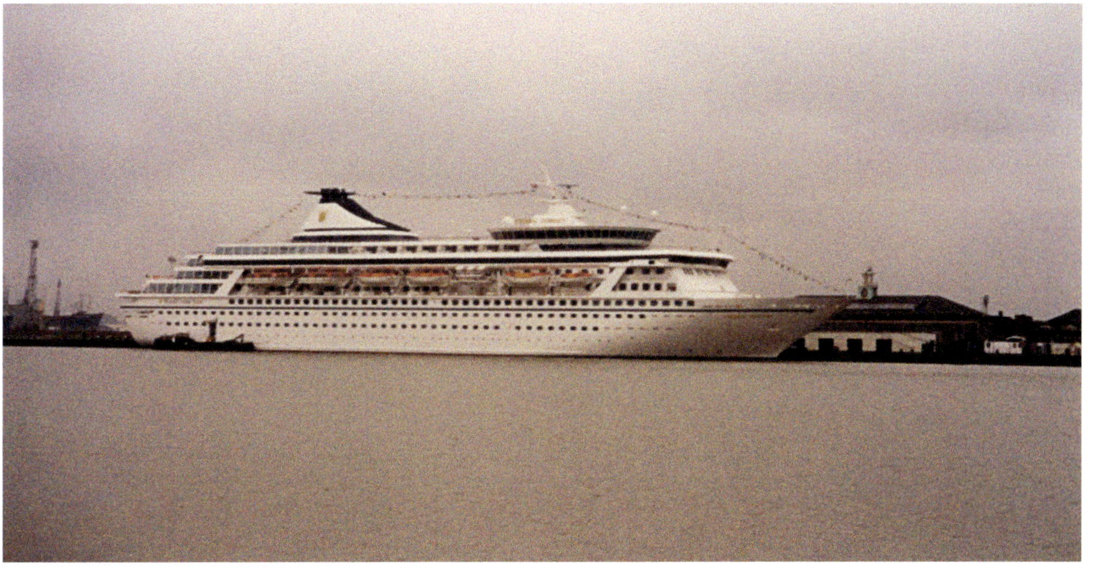

June 2003 saw the arrival of the 34,242 grt *Crown Odyssey* at the London Cruise Terminal. Owned by Royal Cruise Line, she was built in 1988 to accommodate 1,230 passengers. In 1996 she was sold to Norwegian Cruise Line (NCL). She then joined the newly founded Orient Lines before returning to NCL. But in 2007 she was bought by Fred Olsen Lines, who renamed her *Balmoral* and lengthened her by 30 metres. She now measures 43,537 grt and can carry 1,778 passengers.

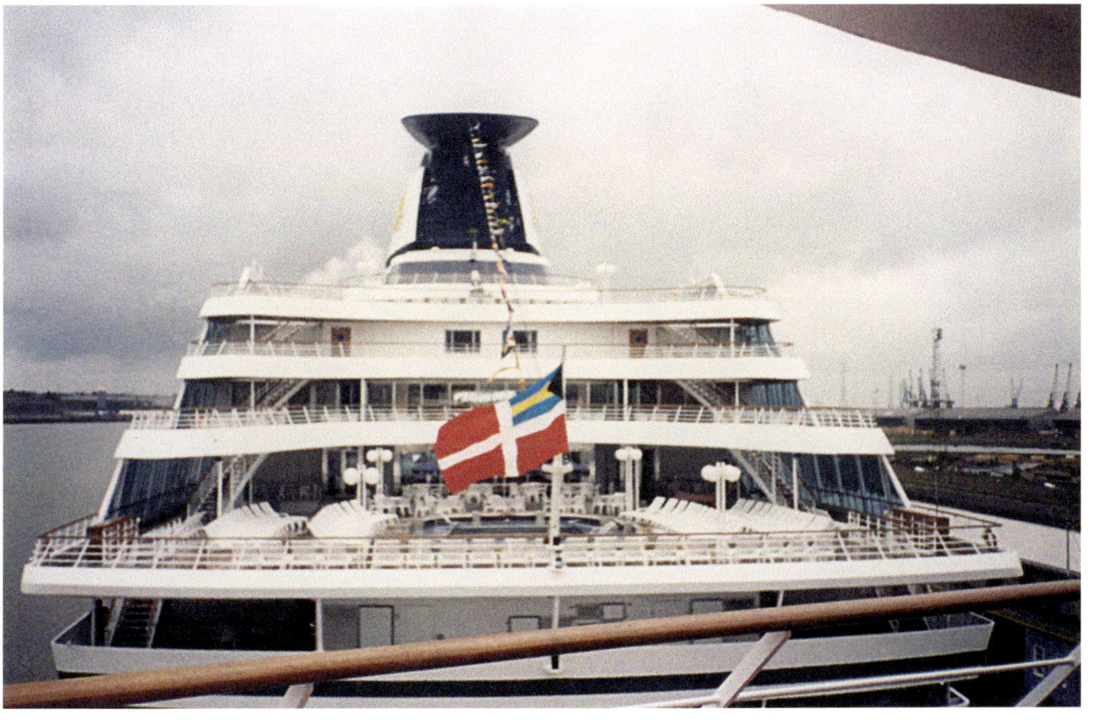

A view of the aft decks of *Crown Odyssey* berthed at the London Cruise Terminal.

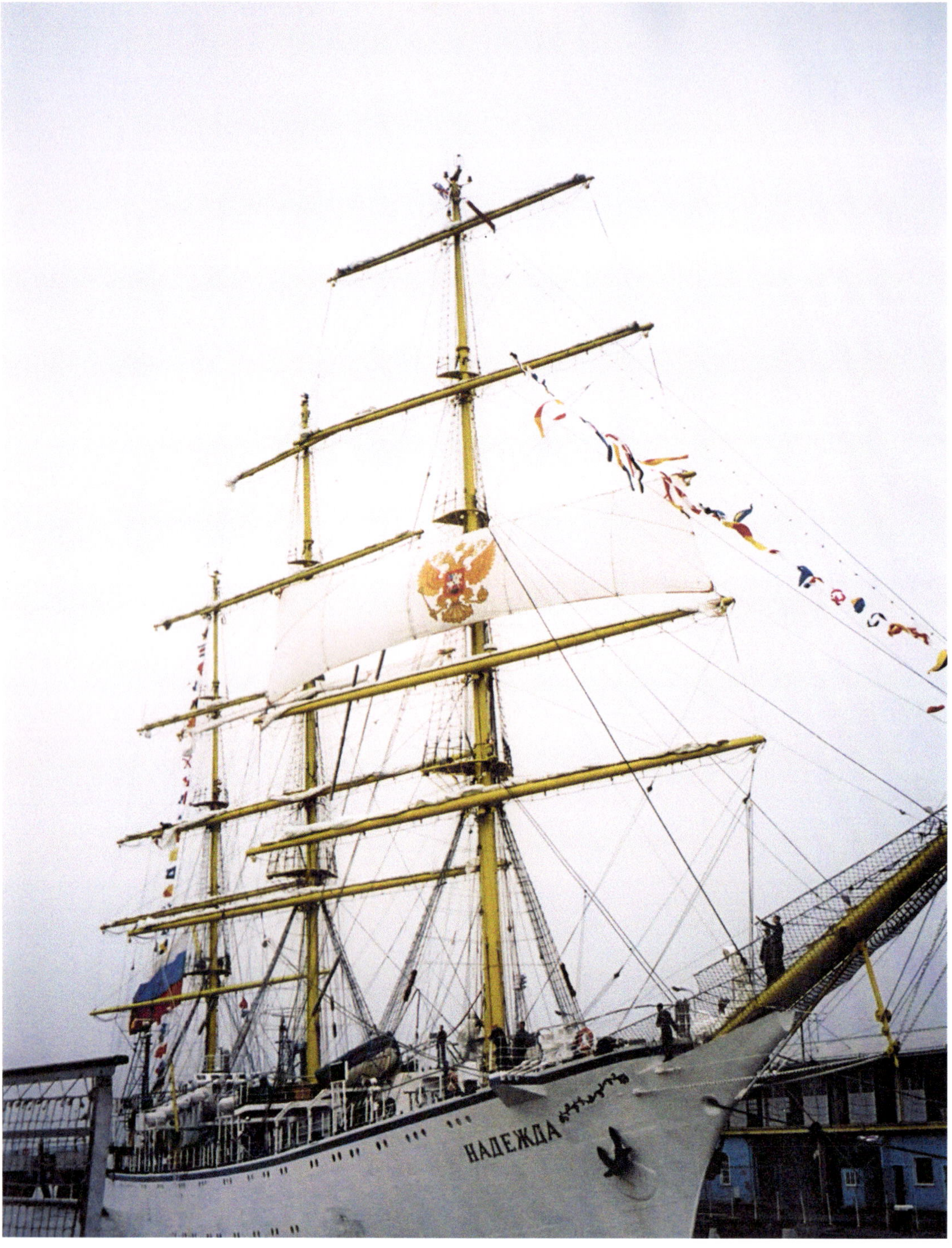

Her masts towering above the London Cruise Terminal, the Russian tall ship *Nadezhda* (Russian for 'good hope') pays a visit to the landing stage in October 2003. Built in 1990, she is operated by FSVE Rosmorport, a Russian organisation that helps train Russian maritime civil cadets. She has accommodation for fifty-one permanent crew and 140 trainees.

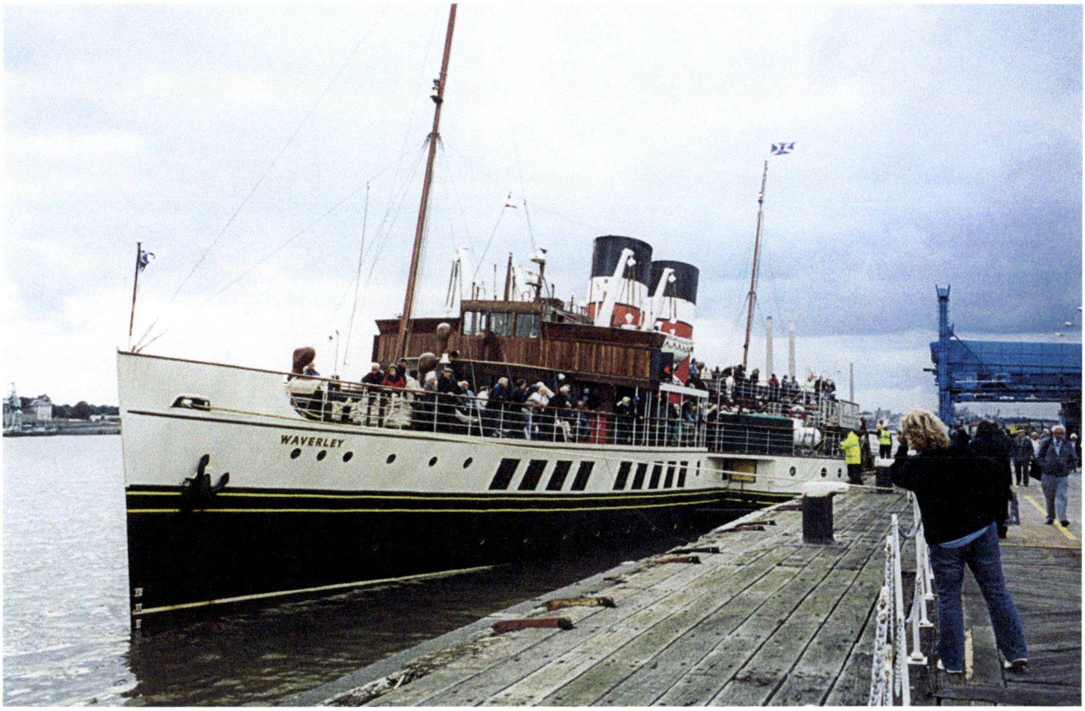

The world's last seagoing paddle steamer, PS *Waverley*, creates great interest as she disembarks passengers at Tilbury Landing Stage following an afternoon jaunt to Tower Bridge. Built in 1947 for service on the Clyde, the 693 grt steamer first called at Tilbury in 1978 and has made visits to the Thames ever since. She was saved from certain extinction in 1974 when she was purchased by the Paddle Steamer Preservation Society.

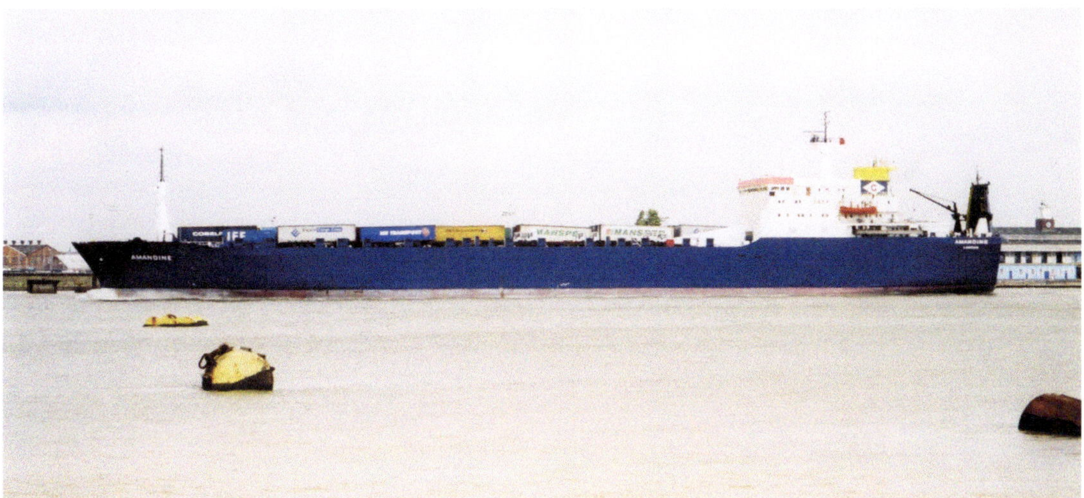

Roll-on roll-off vessels of the Belgian company Cobelfret pass Tilbury Landing Stage daily as they convey cars, trailers and containers between Purfleet and the Ford plant at Dagenham and the Continental ports of Rotterdam and Zeebrugge. The 1978-built *Amandine*, 14,715 grt, joined the Cobelfret service in 1998.

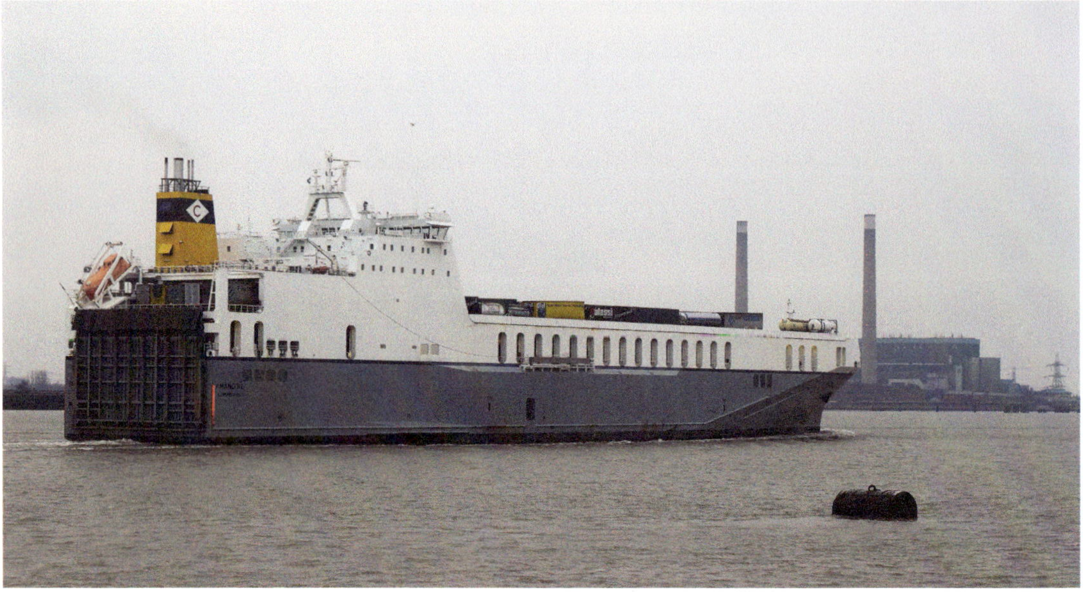

A new, larger *Amandine* was delivered to Cobelfret in May 2011 following her naming ceremony at Greenwich. At 33,690 grt, she can carry up to 336 trailers and containers on her cargo decks.

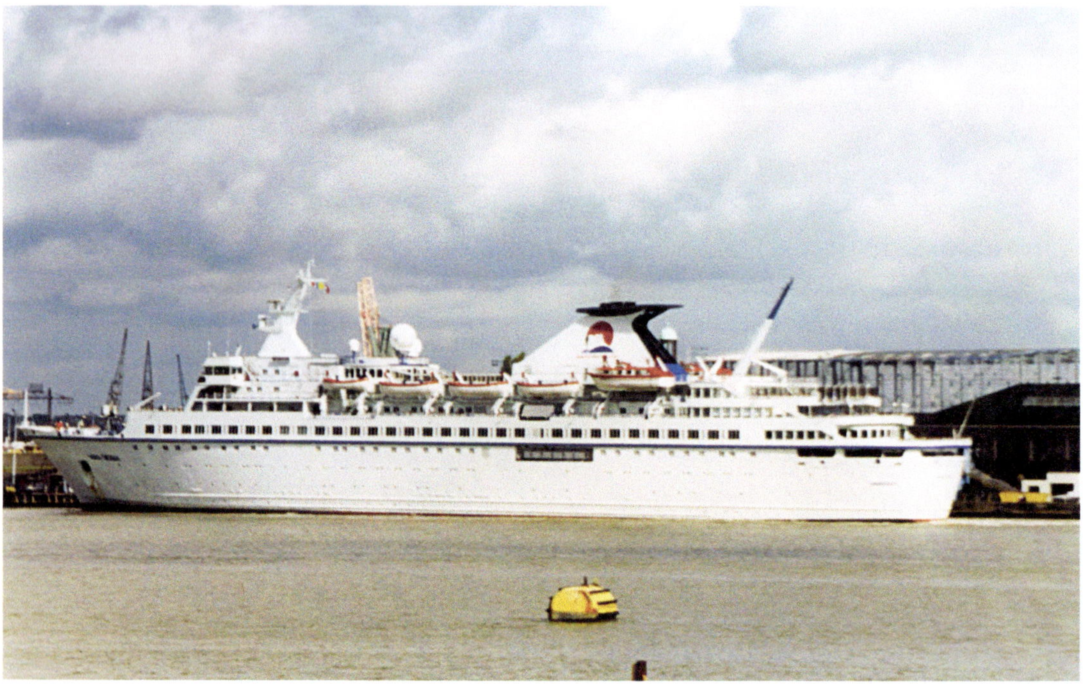

The 15,402 grt cruise ship *Van Gogh* arrives at the London Cruise Terminal in the summer of 2004. Built for the USSR in 1975 as a sister to *Kareliya*, she was cruising for the travel firm Travelscope. In 2009 she was sold to Cyprus-based Salamis Cruises and renamed *Salamis Filoxenia*.

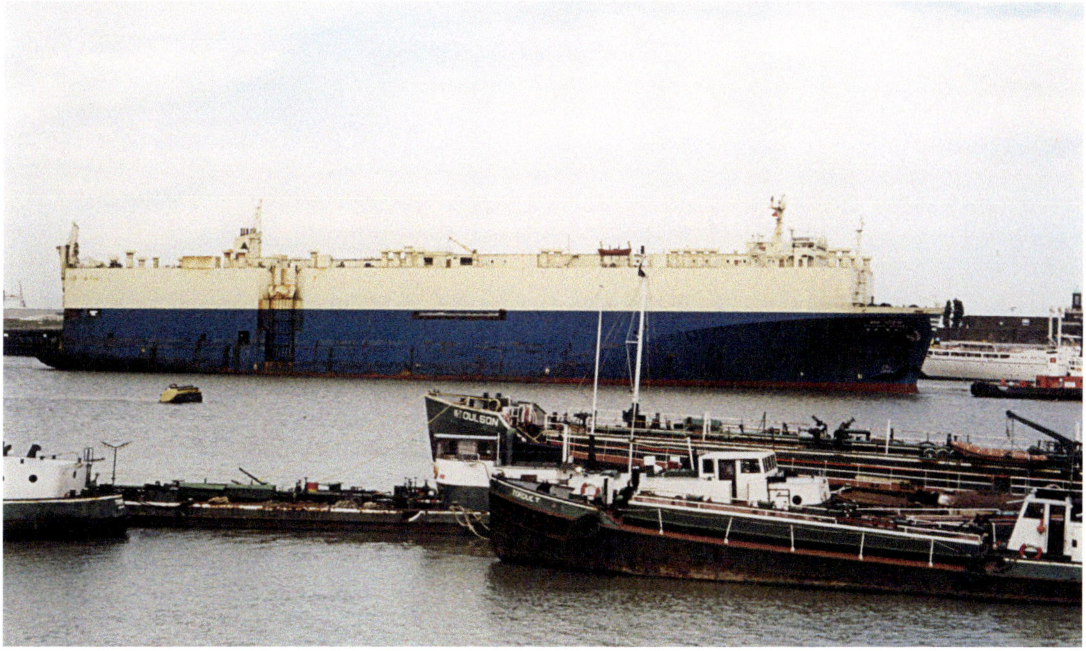

The 55,729 grt vehicle carrier *Asian Captain* sets sail from the Hyundai car import terminal for the Far East. Large vessels moving to and from the terminal pass very close to Tilbury Landing Stage.

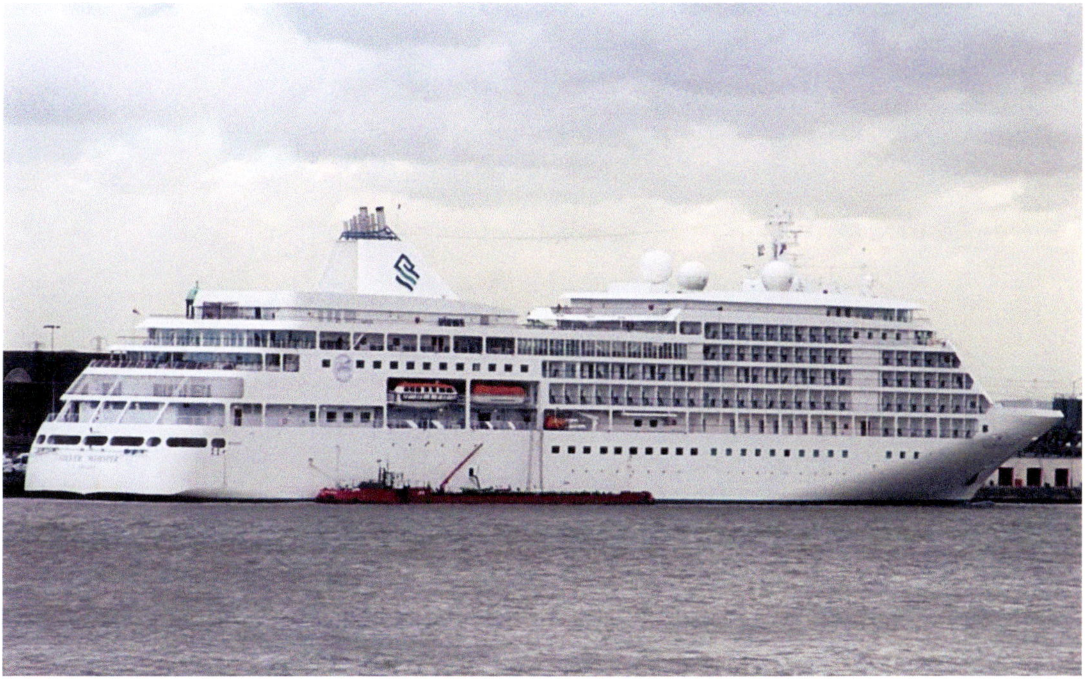

The five-star cruise ship *Silver Whisper*, 28,258 grt, taking on bunkers at the London Cruise Terminal. Delivered to Silversea Cruises in 2001, she accommodates just 382 passengers.

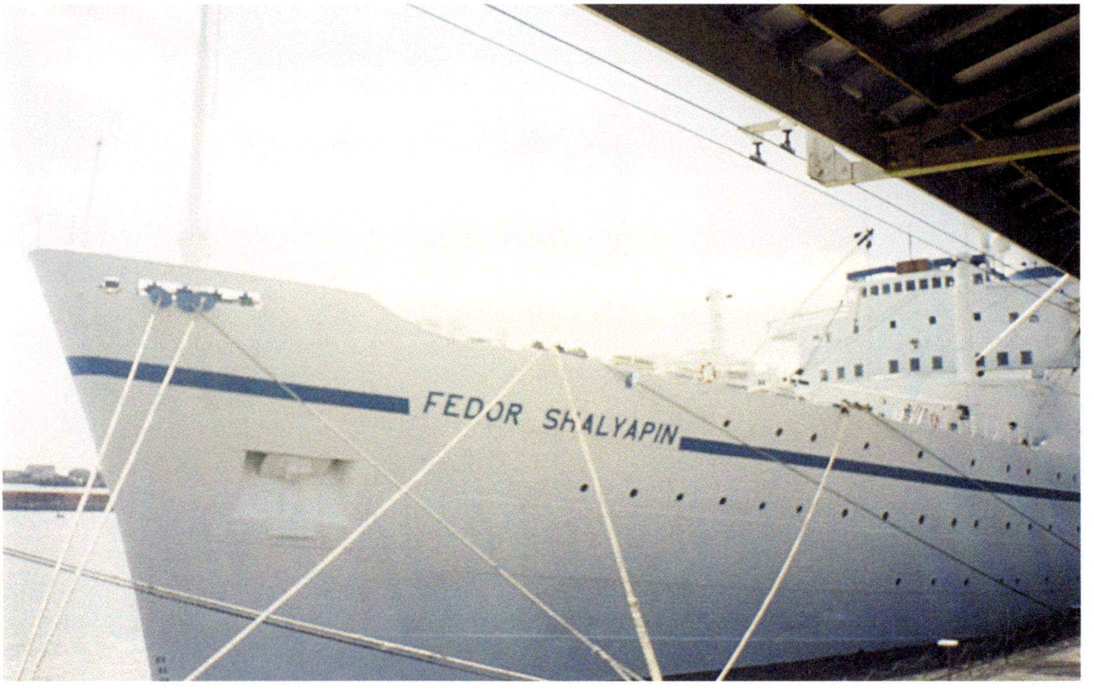

A bow view of the Ukrainian cruise ship *Fedor Shalyapin*. For almost ten years after her final visit to Tilbury she was laid up in the Ukraine before arriving at Alang in February 2004 for breaking up.

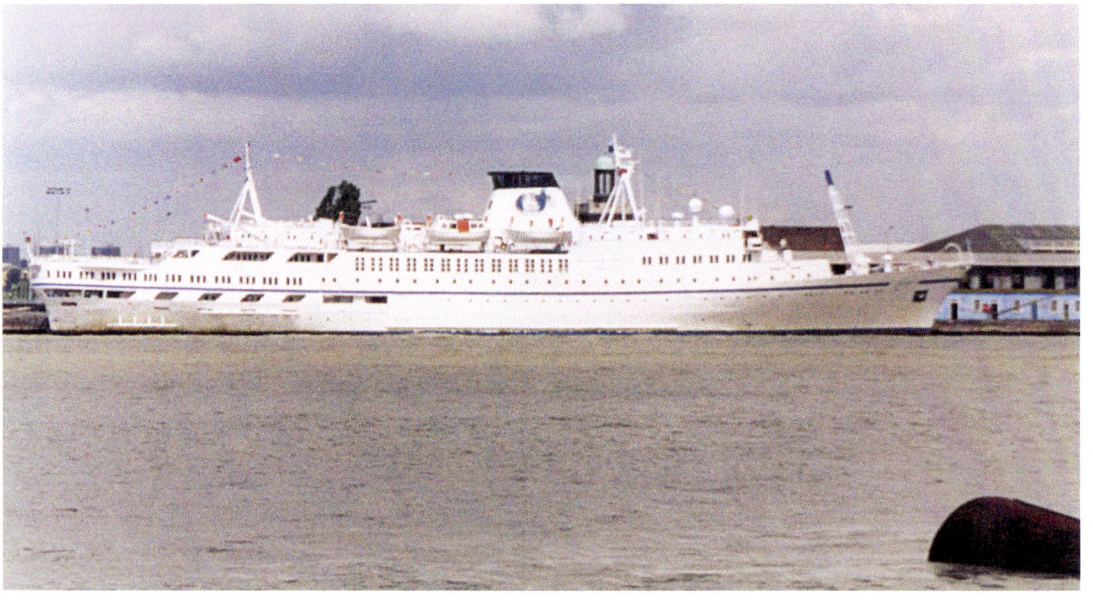

Seen at Tilbury Landing Stage, the little cruise ship *Arion* was built in 1965 as the *Istra*. Following her purchase by Arcadia Shipping Company in 2000 she was rebuilt from the hull upwards and put in service with Classic International Cruises. In 2013, when her operators went into liquidation, she was sold to Portuguese owners and renamed *Porto*. She was scrapped in 2018.

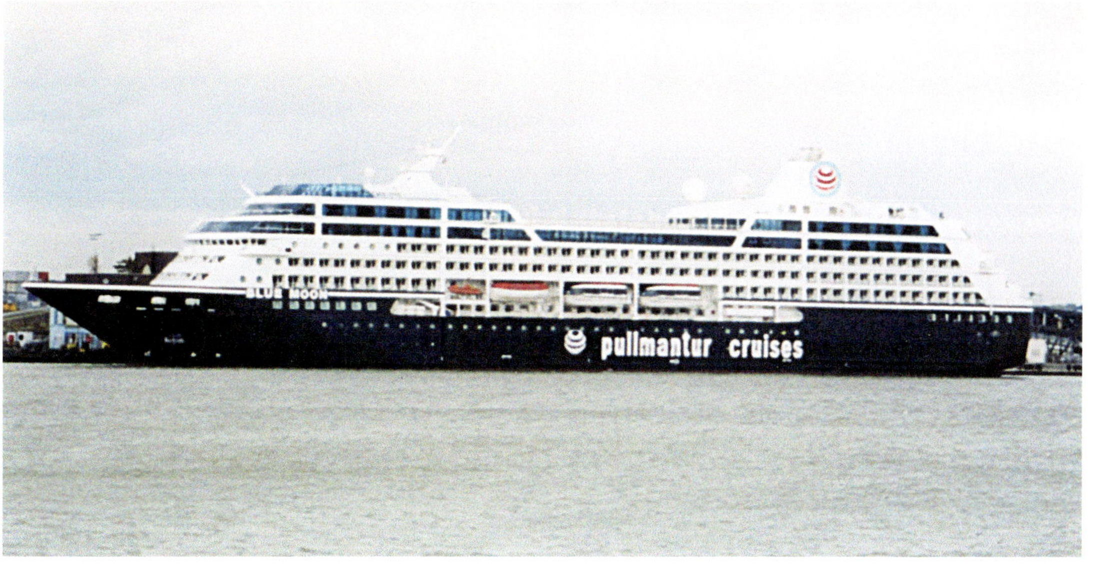

Visiting the London Cruise Terminal in 2006, *Blue Moon*, 30,277 grt, began life in 2000 as the unimaginably named *R7*, the seventh of eight R-class ships built for Renaissance Cruises. Unfortunately, her owners ceased trading in September 2001 and she was laid up in Tilbury Docks until mid-2003, when she was chartered to Germany's Delphin Seereisen as *Delphin Renaissance*. In 2006 she was sold to Pullmantur Cruises as *Blue Moon*. A year later she was transferred to newly founded Azamara Cruises and was renamed *Azamara Quest*, as she still operates today.

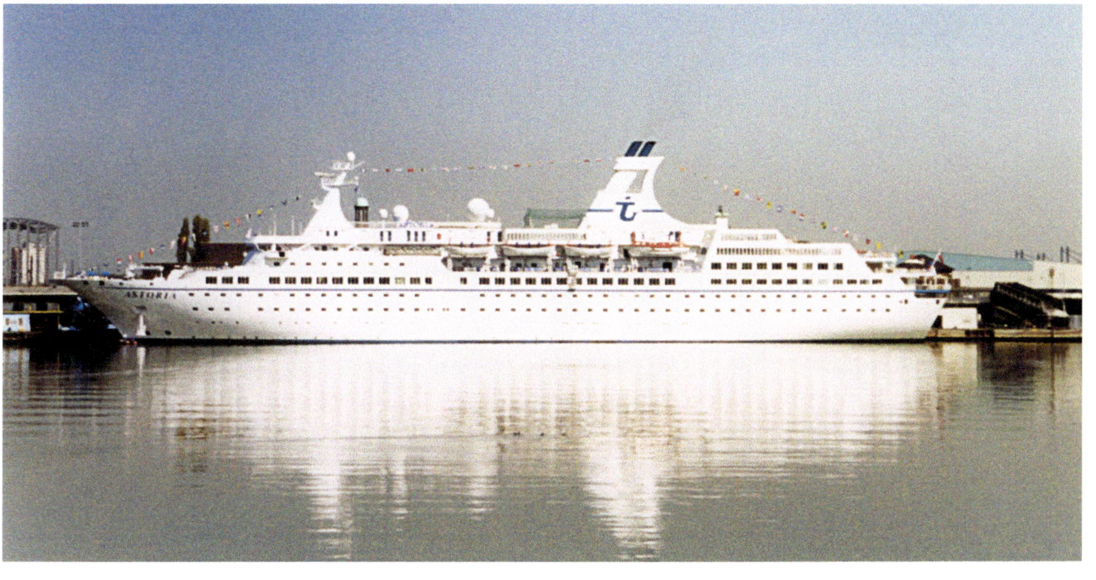

Another ship named *Astoria*. Berthed at the London Cruise Terminal while cruising for Transocean Tours between 2002 and 2010, the 18,591 grt vessel was built in 1981 as *Astor*. Renamed *Arkona* in 1985, she operated between South Africa and Europe until her charter to Transocean. Acquired by Saga Cruises, she became *Saga Pearl II* in 2010 and was also known as *Quest for Adventure* for a while. She made her final cruise for Saga in February 2019.

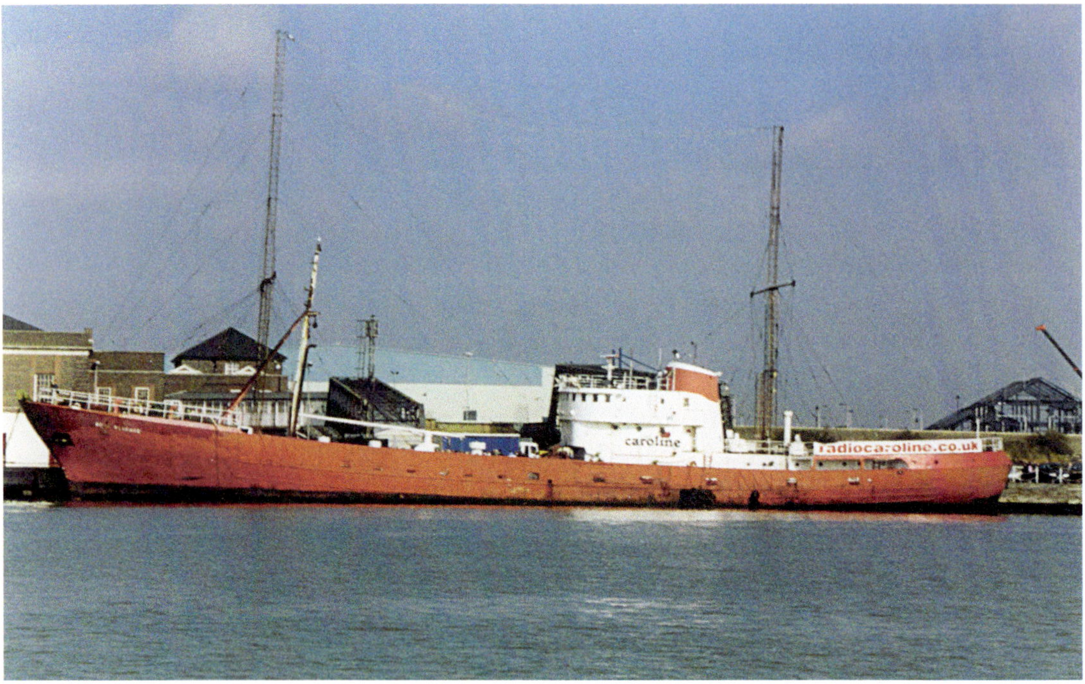

The offshore radio station Radio Caroline began broadcasting in 1964 and up until 1990 employed five different ships. The last of these was a former North Sea fishing trawler, the *Ross Revenge*, which was equipped with a 91-metre-high antenna. In 2007, following a lengthy lay-up, she arrived at Tilbury Landing Stage before moving into the docks, where she was repaired and maintained by volunteers.

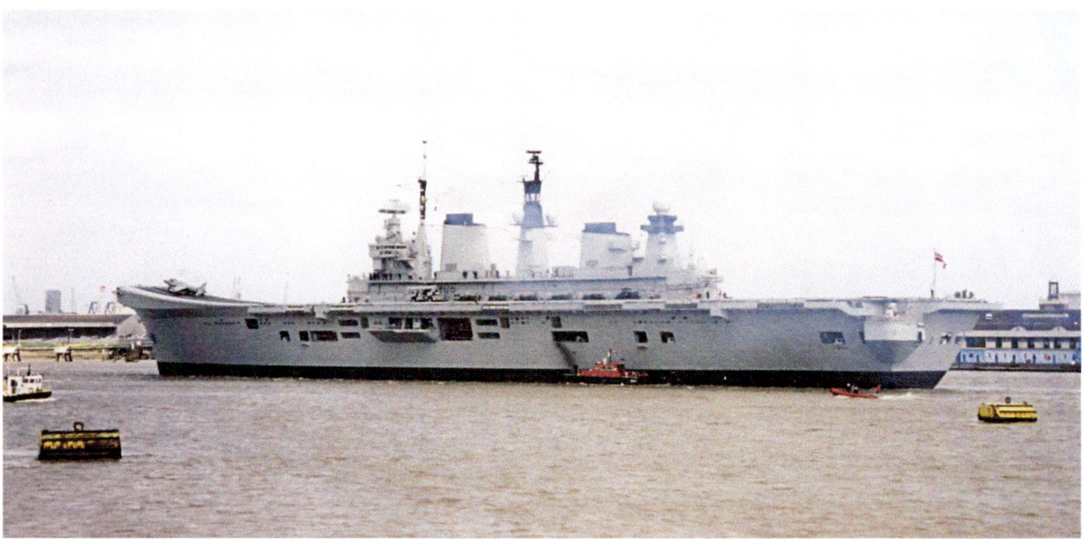

The Royal Navy aircraft carrier HMS *Illustrious*, 22,000 tons displacement, sails past Tilbury Landing Stage for a courtesy visit to Greenwich in 2008. Commissioned in 1982, she visited the Thames for the last time in May 2013 before being taken out of service the following year. She was towed to Turkey for scrapping in December 2016.

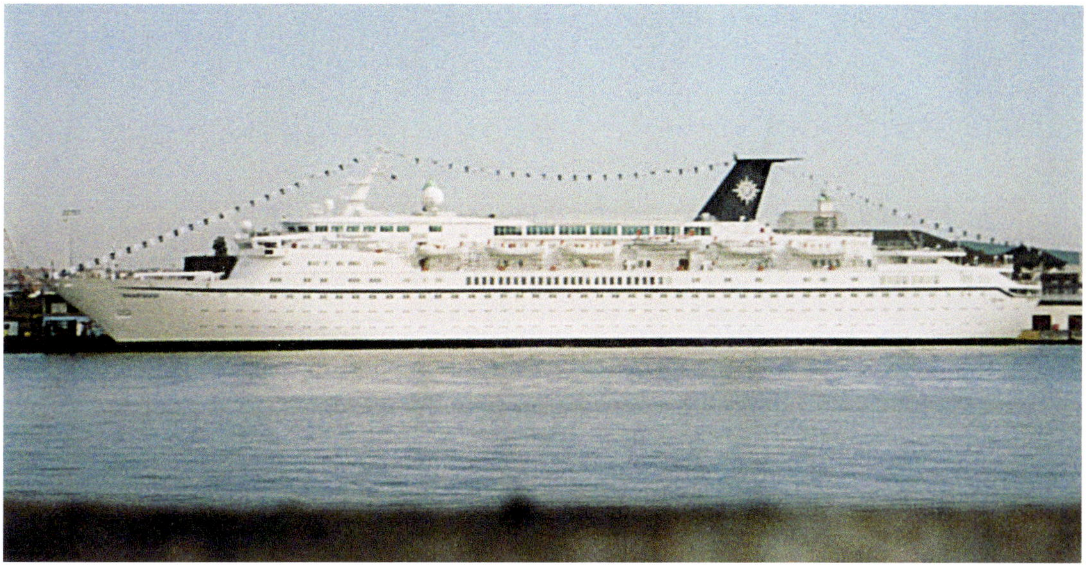

Displaying her smart white hull in the summer sun, the 16,852 grt vessel *Rhapsody* was owned and operated by MSC Cruises. Originally delivered to Cunard in 1977 as *Cunard Princess*, she was one of a pair of cruise ships that became well-known around the Caribbean. Acquired by MSC in 1995, she served the fast-growing cruise concern until 2009, when she was sold to Israel-based Mano Maritime and renamed *Golden Iris*.

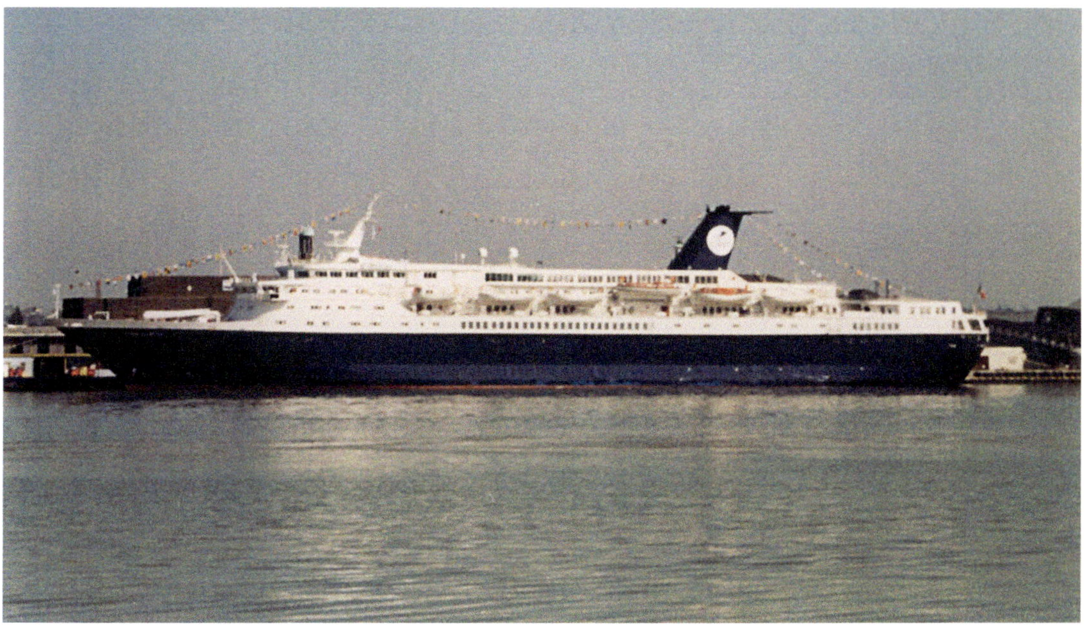

Spot the difference: apart, of course, for the dark blue hull, *Ocean Countess* was almost identical to *Rhapsody*, having been completed in 1976 as her sister *Cunard Countess*. Leaving Cunard in 1996, she undertook several charters and name changes before joining Cruise & Maritime Voyages in 2010 to sail alongside *Marco Polo*. Having made several visits to the London Cruise Terminal, she was laid up but caught fire and was scrapped in 2014.

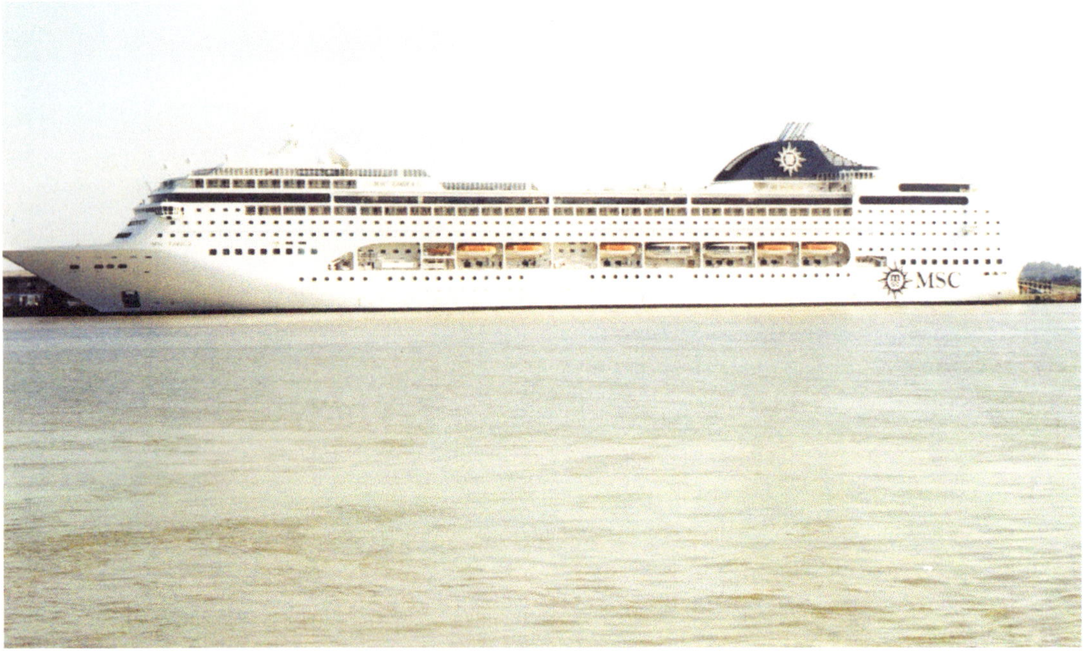

MSC Lirica called at the London Cruise Terminal in May 2009 during a north European cruise. Built in 2003, she measures 59,058 grt and is owned by MSC Cruises, which now operates her in the Far East.

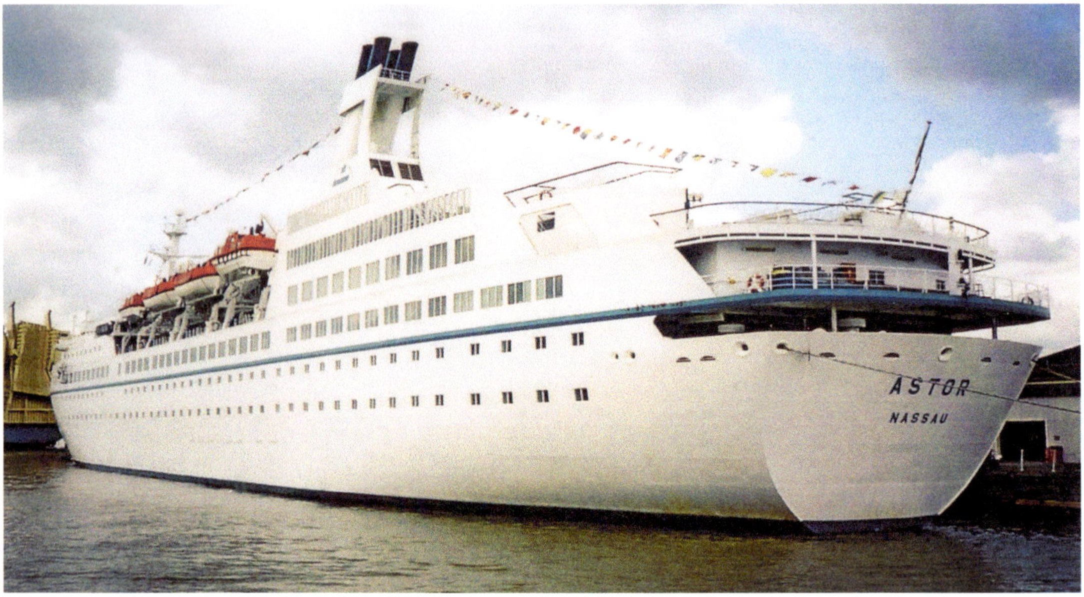

Astor, 1987/20,704 grt, seen at the London Cruise Terminal while under charter to Germany's Transocean Tours. Ordered for a Southampton–Cape Town liner service, she was sold on the stocks to a Mauritius-based concern. In 1998 she passed into Soviet hands as the *Fedor Dostoyevskiy* but cruised for Transocean much of the time. In 2013 her charter passed to Cruise & Maritime Voyages (CMV).

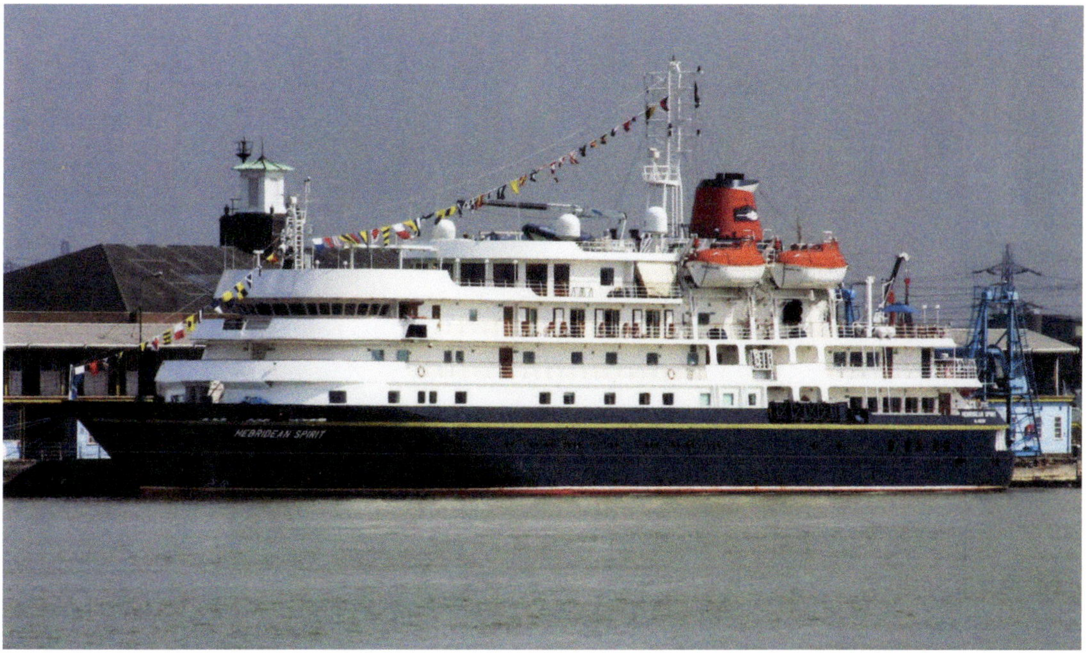

The luxurious little cruise ship *Hebridean Spirit* berthed at the London Cruise Terminal. Built in 1991 as *Renaissance VI*, the 4,200 grt vessel saw a number of name changes before being purchased by Hebridean Island Cruises in November 2000. However, the recession of 2009 forced her sale.

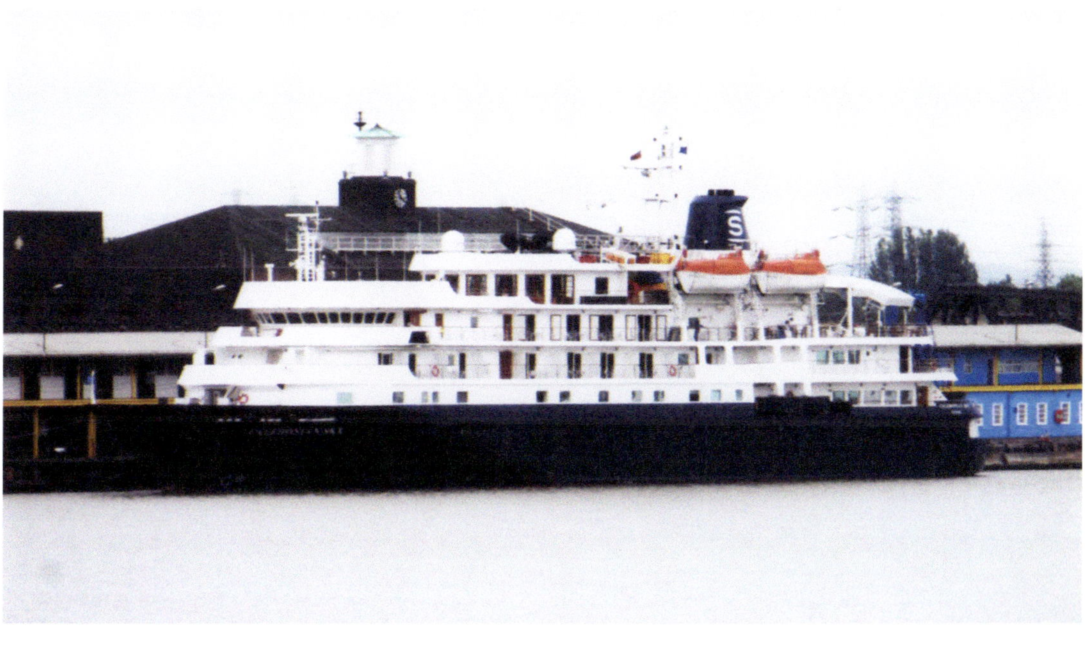

In 2012 the former *Hebridean Spirit* was bought by Noble Caledonia and was renamed *Caledonia Sky*, after which she made a return visit to Tilbury. Accommodating just 114 passengers, she now cruises worldwide.

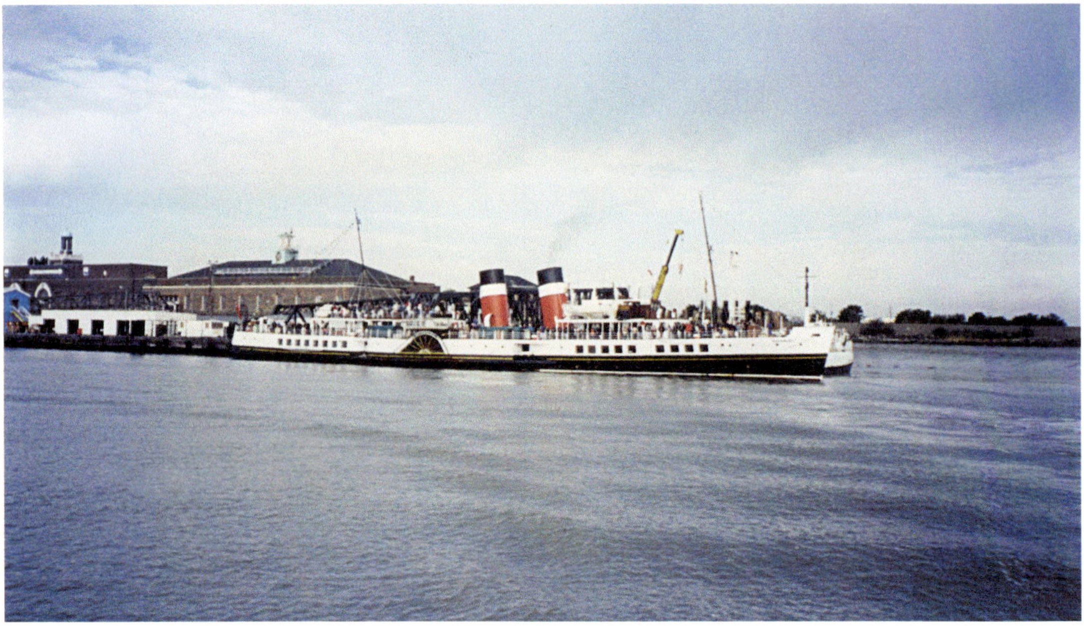

PS *Waverley* sets off from Tilbury Landing Stage on a trip to Southend. Thanks in particular to money awarded by the Heritage Lottery Fund, she has been maintained in excellent condition over the years.

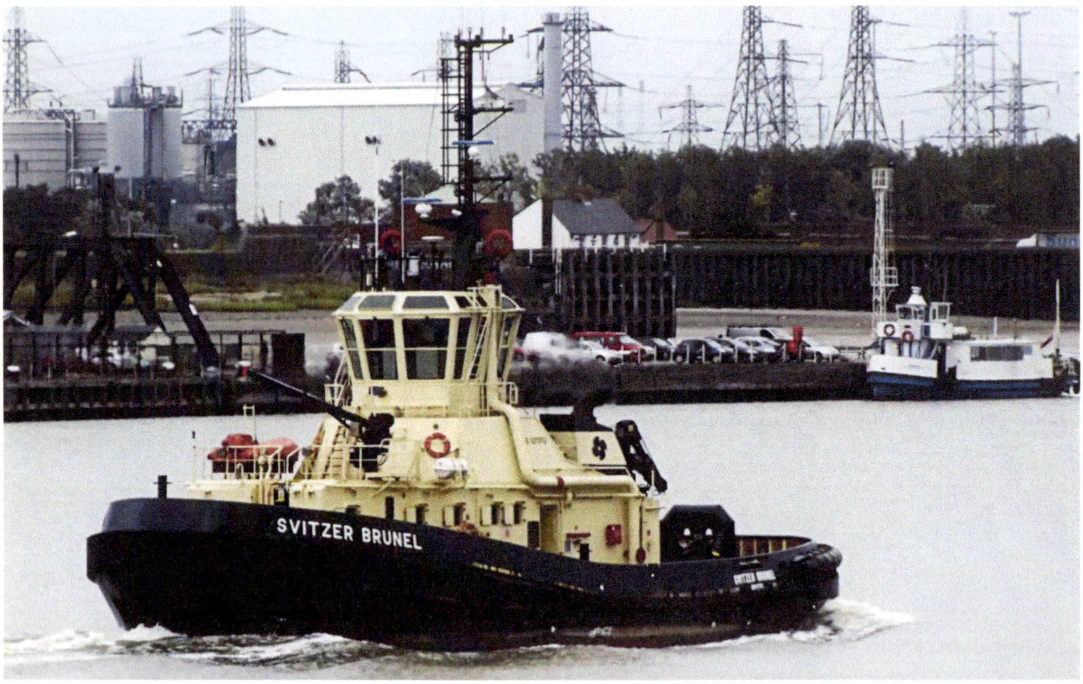

Svitzer Marine's 366 grt tug *Svitzer Brunel* under way off Tilbury. On the landing stage behind her is the little *Duchess M*, which operated the Tilbury–Gravesend ferry service from 2002 to 2017. Jetstream Tours has since taken over the service.

In September 2014 the River Thames was honoured to be part of the 2014 Falmouth to Royal Greenwich Regatta. A total of fifty-one tall ships of various shapes and sizes participated, passing Tilbury Landing Stage and Gravesend's river front as they sailed to their upriver destination. After a four-day stay the vessels made the return journey down the Thames in a Parade of Sail. Hundreds of onlookers lined both sides of the river to witness the event.

Here is a small sample of the long line of ships as they sailed past Tilbury.

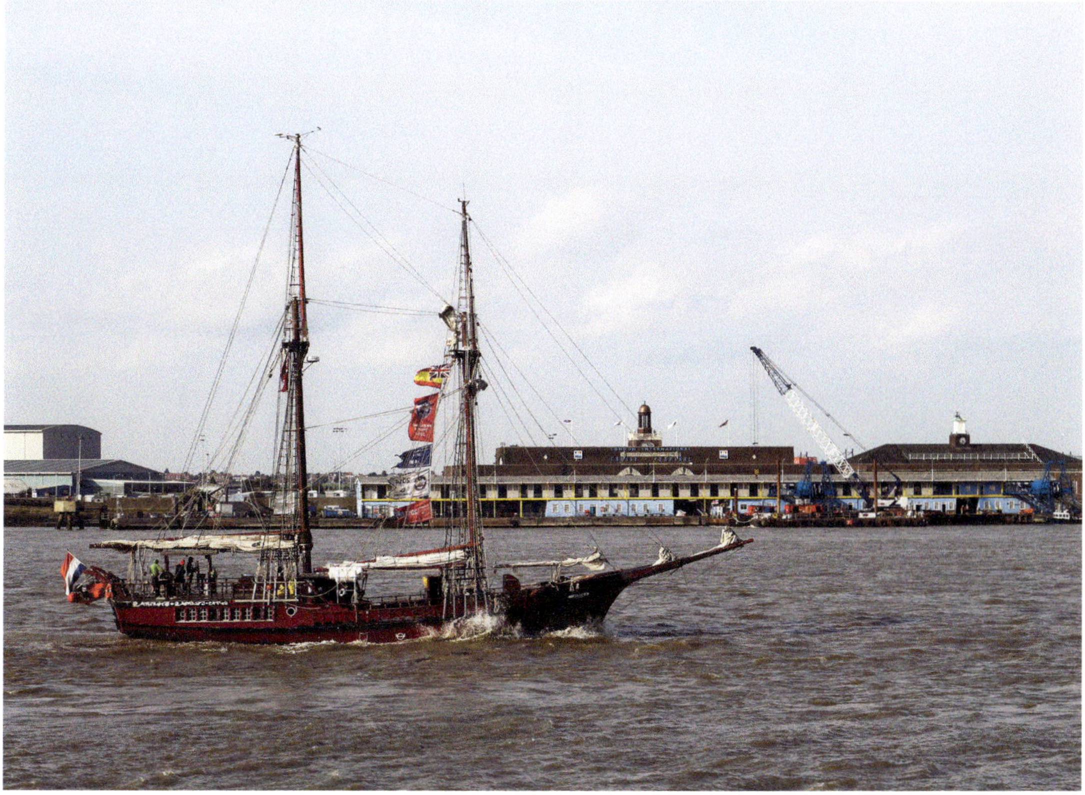

TS *Atyla*, a Dutch-registered two-masted schooner, hand-built in Spain to resemble Spanish vessels of the 1800s. She is 31.28 metres long.

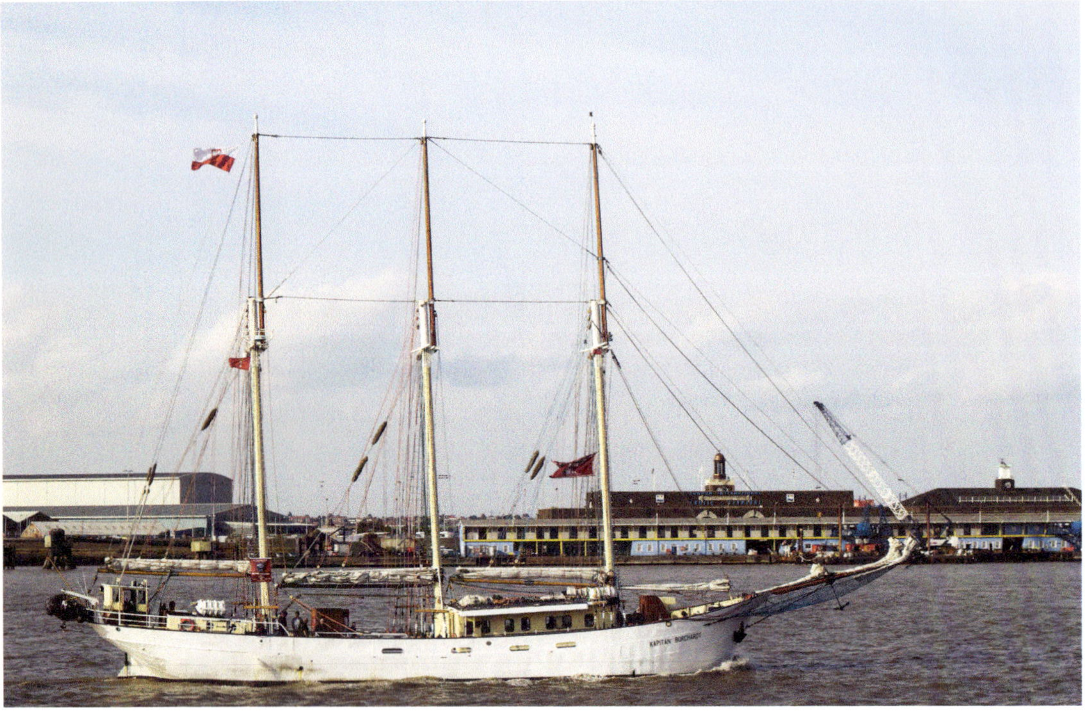

The Polish sail training ship STS *Kapitan Borchardt* has an overall length of 45 metres. Built in 1918 in the Netherlands as an oceanic cargo ship, she is owned by Sklodowsky Yachting Sp.

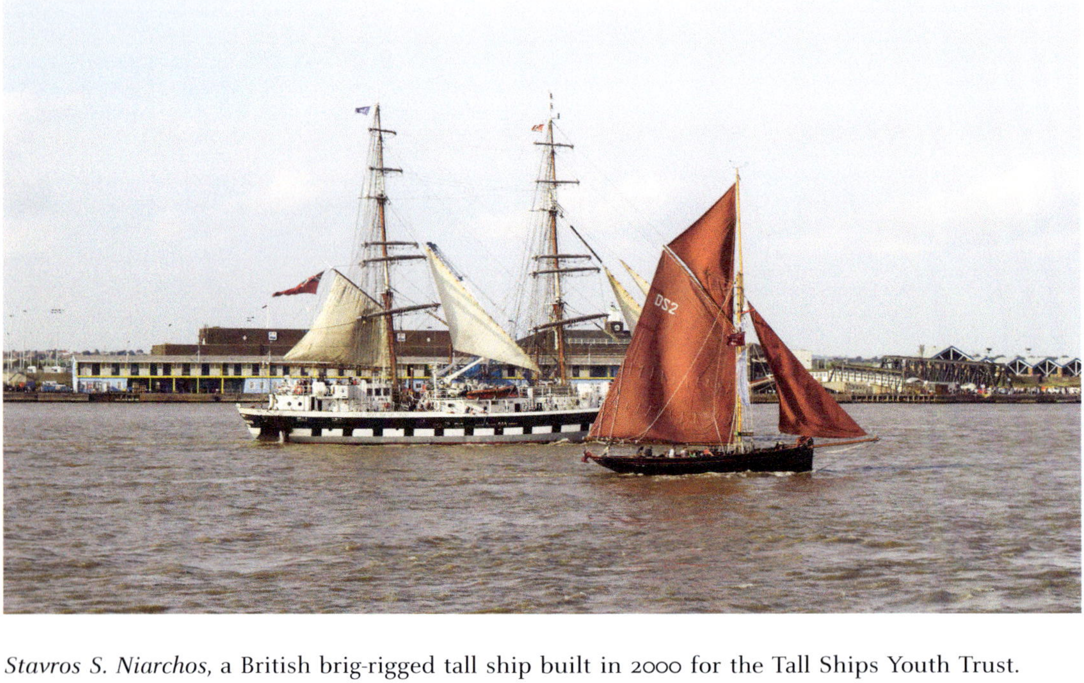

Stavros S. Niarchos, a British brig-rigged tall ship built in 2000 for the Tall Ships Youth Trust. Measuring 50.1 m by 9.9 m, she normally sails with a crew of up to sixty-seven. With her is the smaller British gaff ketch *Queen Galadriel*, built in 1937 and entered by the Cirdan Sailing Trust.

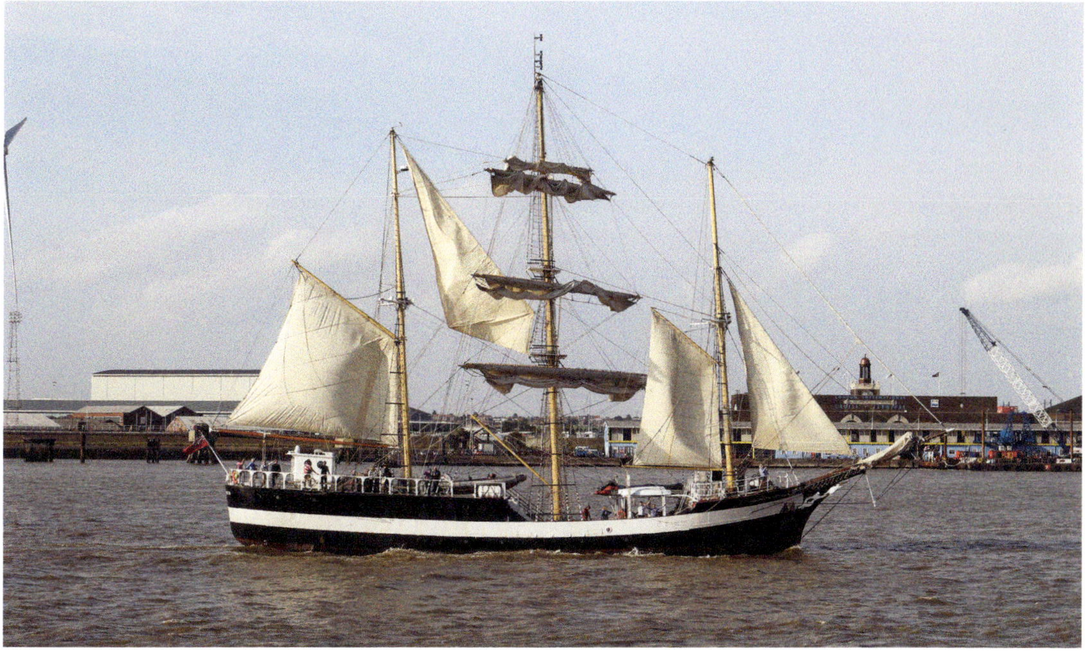

A three-masted training ship, *Pelican of London* was built at Le Havre in 1948. 45 m long, she was originally an Arctic trawler and then a Norwegian coaster until 1995. After twelve years of rebuilding she was completed as a sail training ship in 2007.

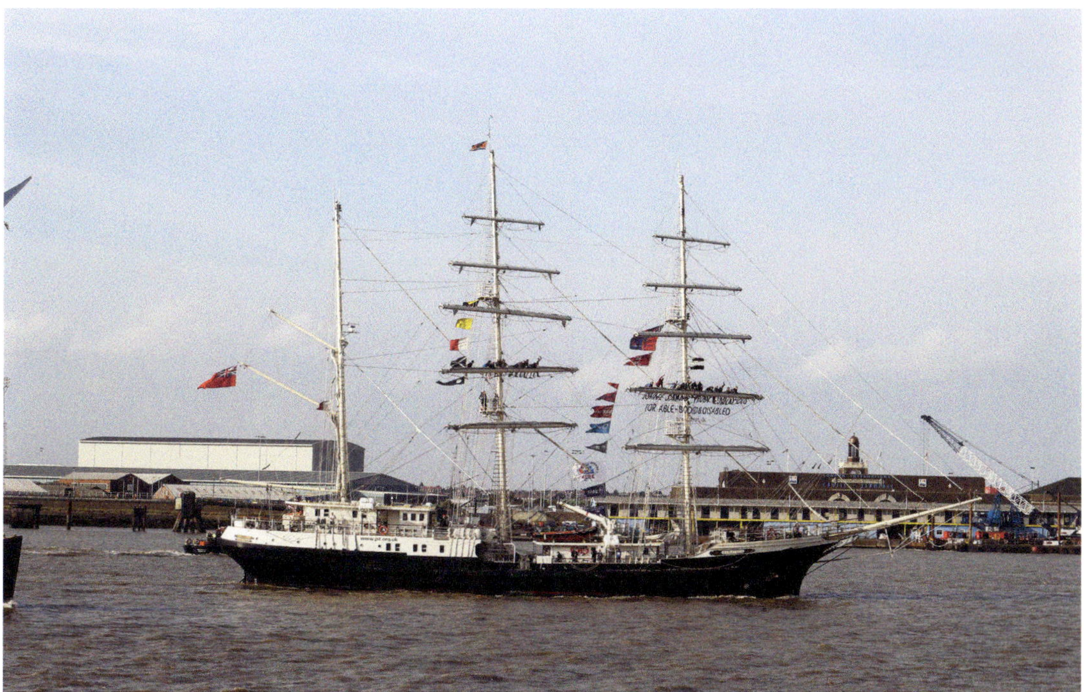

With cadets standing aloft, Jubilee Sailing Trust's *Tenacious* was one of the largest participants.

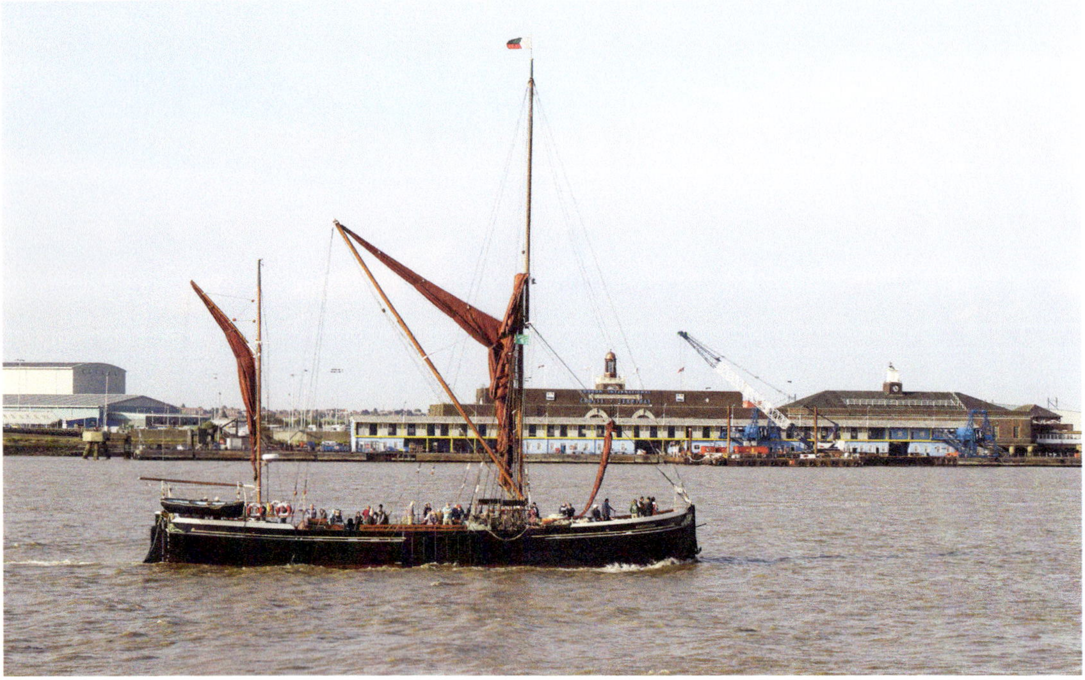

Hydrogen is a Thames barge built at Rochester in 1906. Now the largest surviving wooden barge, she gives cruises for up to fifty guests.

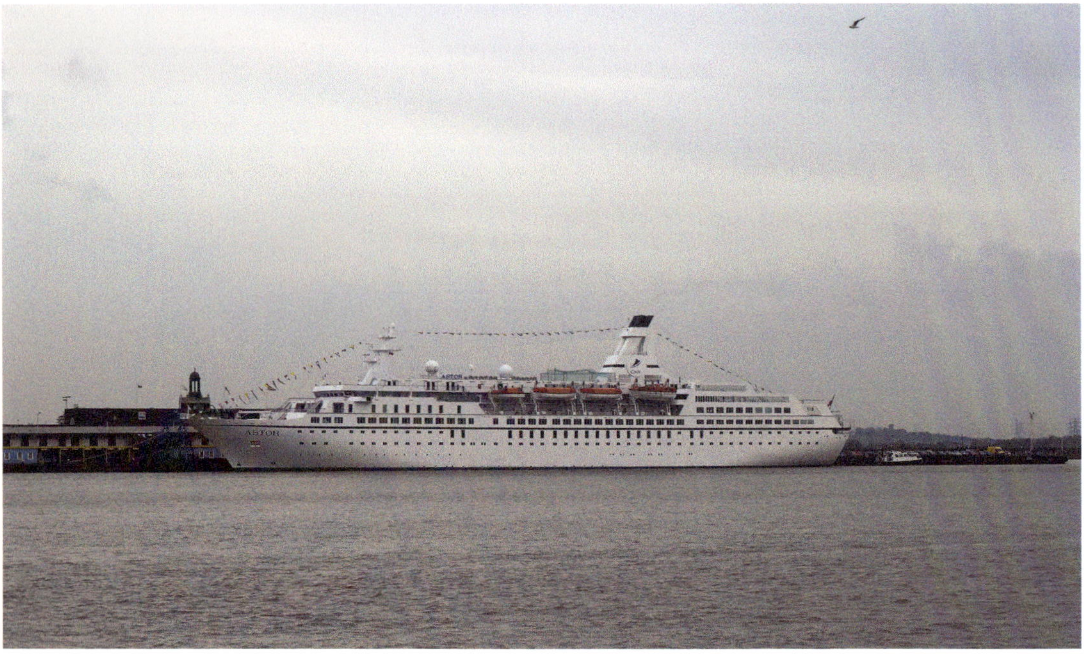

In October 2014 *Astor*, displaying the CMV logo, prepares to leave for Australia. She has since spent each winter cruising in the Southern Hemisphere but is being replaced by Cruise & Maritime's *Vasco da Gama* (ex-*Statendam*) in 2019.

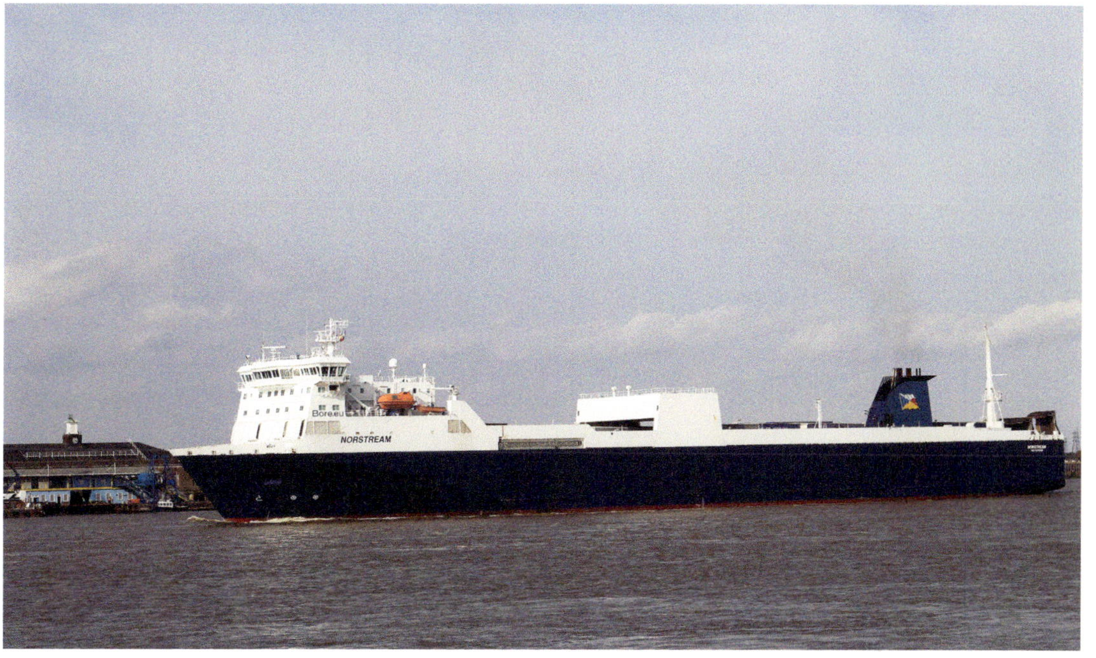

Operated by P&O Ferries, the 20,296 grt ro-ro vessel *Norstream* passes the landing stage every day, sailing between the Port of Tilbury and Zeebrugge. Built in 1999, she is owned by Bore Ltd and carries 2,530 lane metres of freight per crossing.

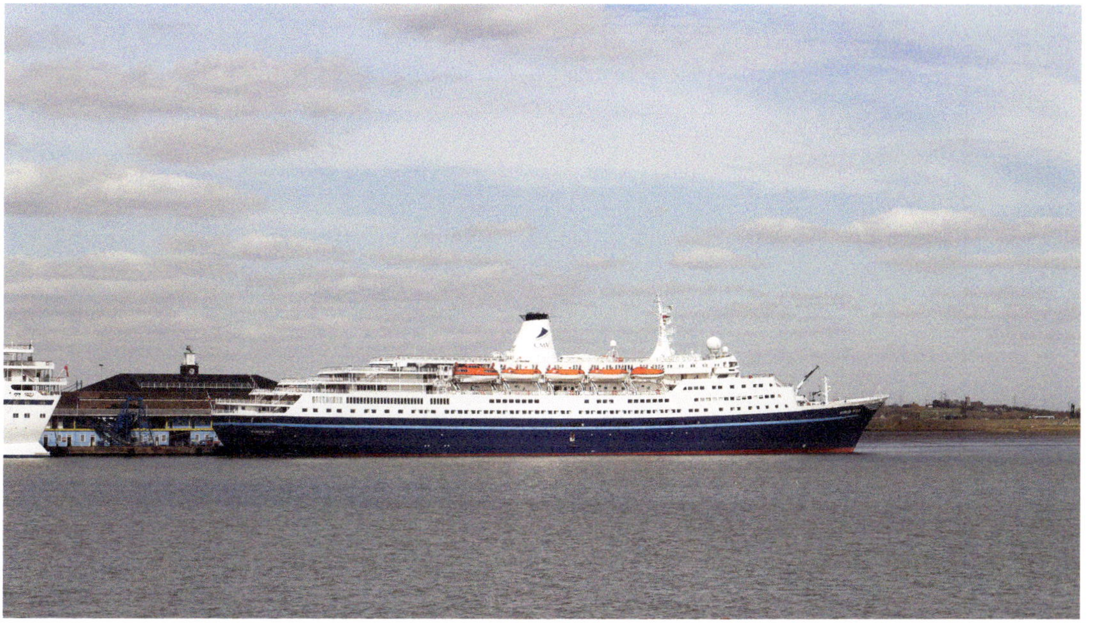

In 2010 the newly established Cruise & Maritime Voyages took over *Marco Polo* as its first ship. Since then she has become a firm favourite with a British clientele, sailing regularly from Tilbury and other UK ports. She is pictured at the London Cruise Terminal in 2015 before embarking on a Baltic cruise.

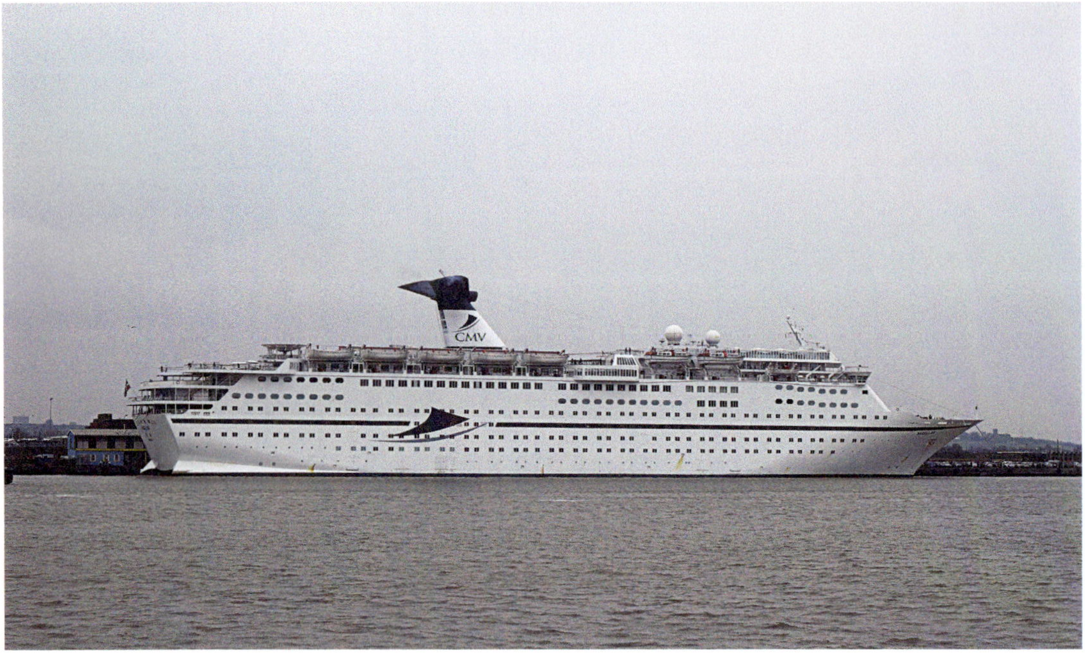

Following its first ship, the *Marco Polo*, Cruise & Maritime Voyages operated comparatively small cruise vessels until 2015 when, encouraged by a healthy demand for bookings, it decided to 'go bigger' by acquiring a former Carnival Cruise Line ship. Rechristened *Magellan* at the London Cruise Terminal in March 2015, the 46,052 grt ship had sailed in the western Caribbean as the *Holiday* before being transferred to Carnival's subsidiary Iberocruises as *Grand Holiday* in 2010.

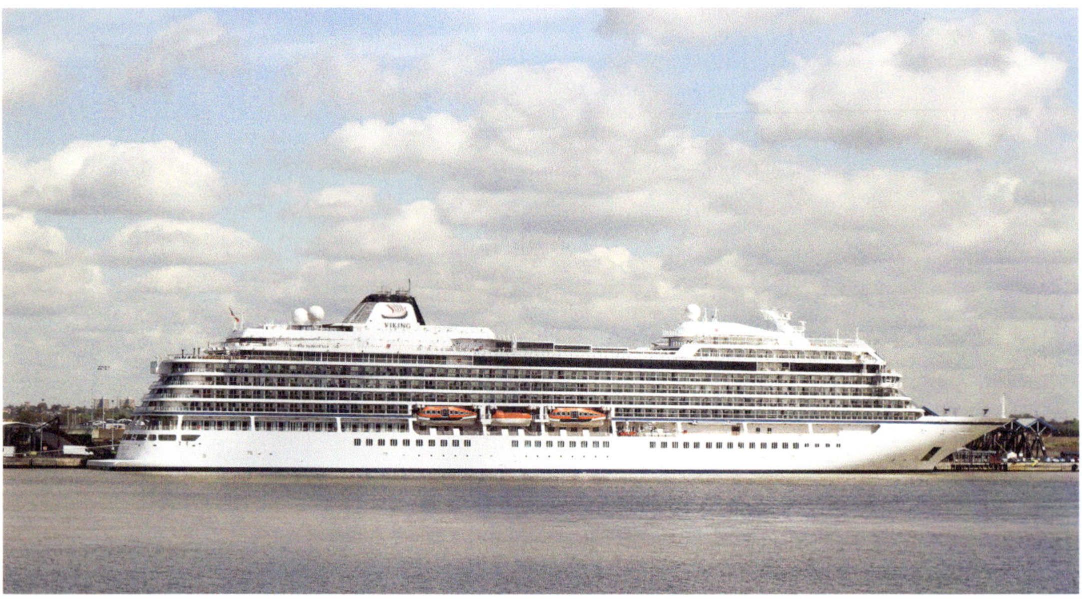

The first ship of the rapidly expanding Viking Ocean Cruises fleet, *Viking Star*, 2015/47,843 grt, pays a visit to the London Cruise Terminal in June 2016. Further ships, all of similar size and design, are to be added to the fleet over the coming years.

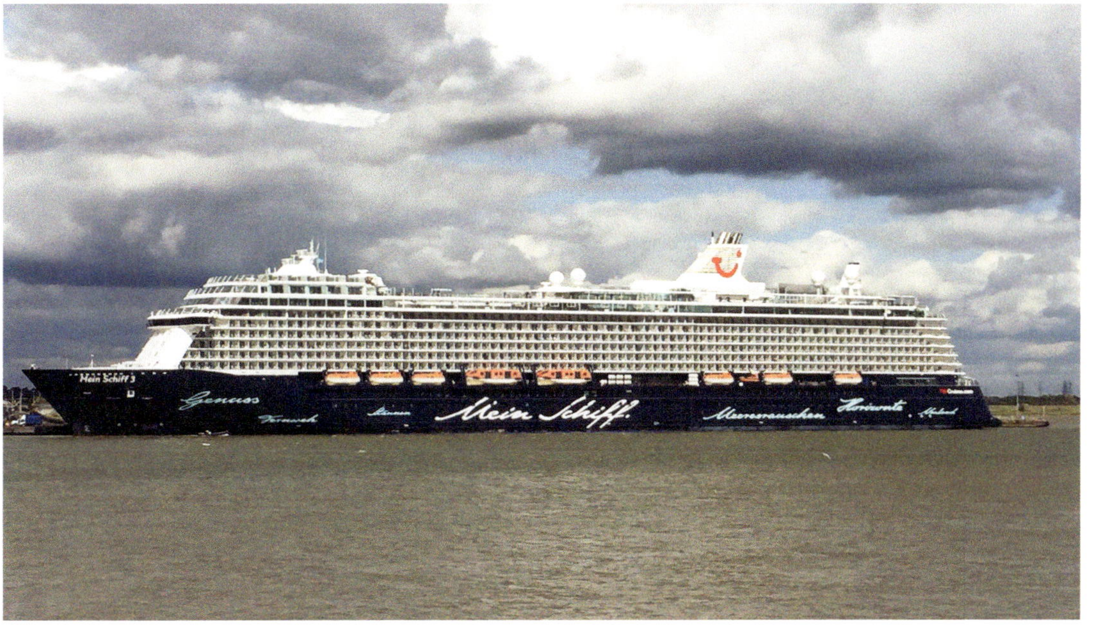

The biggest ever: arriving at the London Cruise Terminal on the morning of 12 September 2017, the 99,526 grt *Mein Schiff 3* became the biggest cruise ship ever to berth there. The 293-metre-long German vessel disembarked her 2,500 passengers for a day out in London, part of a seven-day north European cruise. Completed in 2014, *Mein Schiff 3* is one of six *Mein Schiff* ('My Ship') cruise ships.

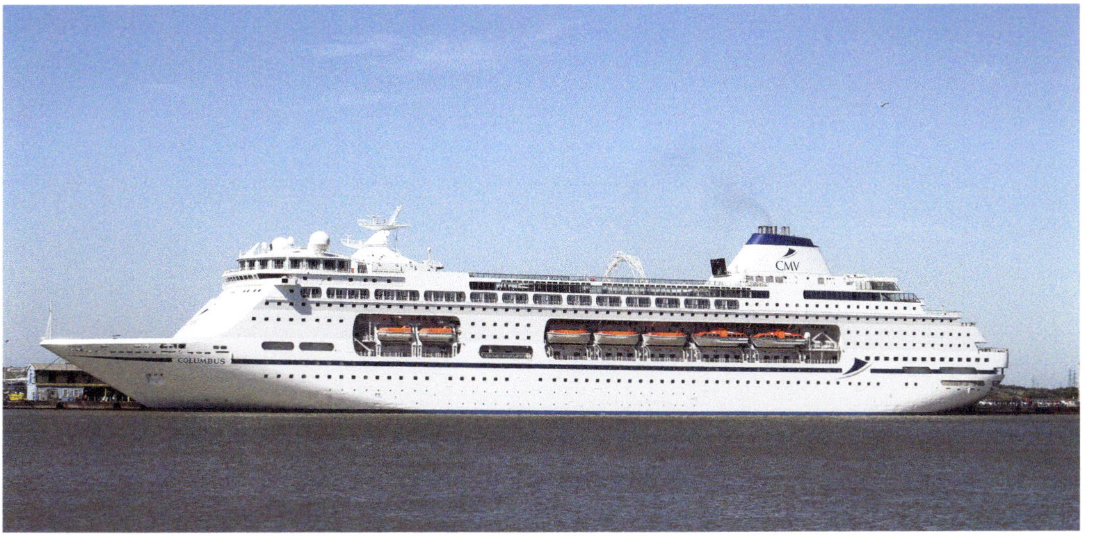

Tilbury's latest resident: the largest cruise ship to join the Cruise & Maritime Voyages (CMV) fleet, *Columbus*, 63,786 grt, was named at a gala ceremony alongside the London Cruise Terminal on 8 June 2017. Boasting an excellent pedigree, she entered service in 1988 as Princess Cruises' *Star Princess* and was transferred to P&O Cruises in 1997, sailing as *Arcadia* until 2003. After five years as *Ocean Village*, she moved to P&O's Australian division as *Pacific Pearl*. Today *Columbus* is regarded as Tilbury's own resident cruise ship.

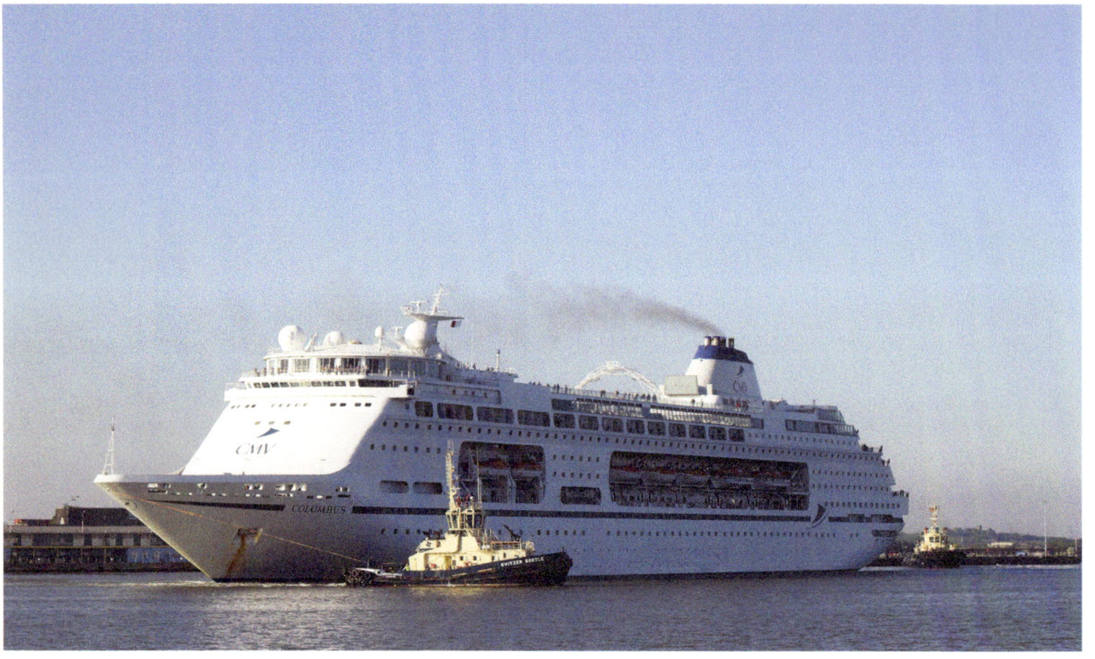

Turning circle: *Columbus* swings around in front of the London Cruise Terminal with the help of two Svitzer tugs, her owner's initials clearly emblazoned on her forward superstructure.

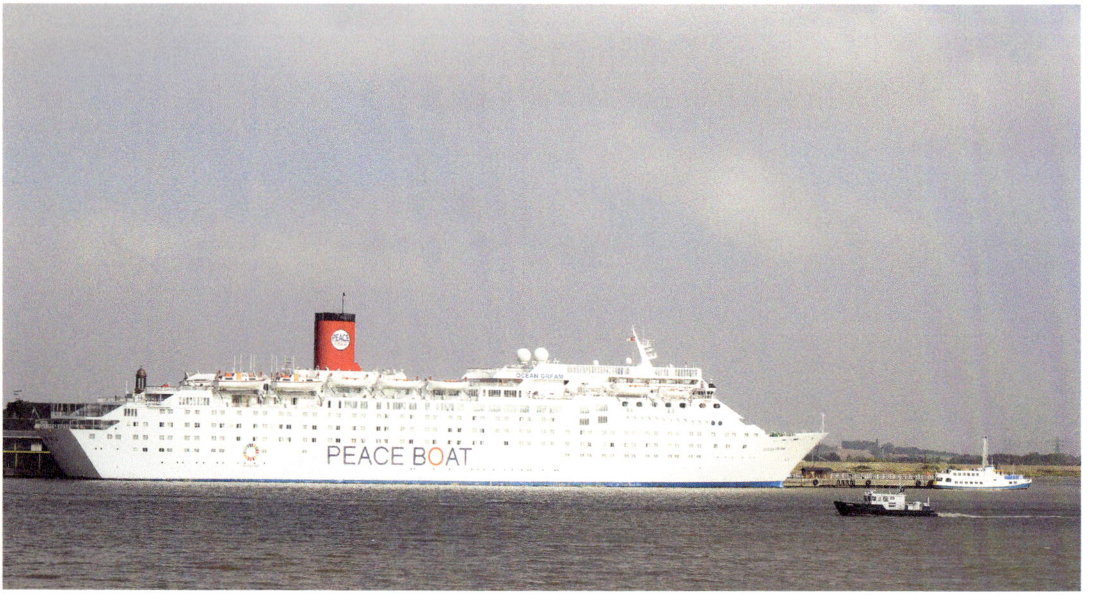

Peaceboat has chartered a number of passenger ships since its inception in 1983 and the latest is the 35,190 grt *Ocean Dream*, which visited the London Cruise Terminal in October 2017 during a global voyage. Built in 1981 as *Tropicale* for Carnival Cruise Lines, she transferred to the Costa Line in 2001, becoming *Costa Tropicale*. In 2005 she moved to P&O Cruises Australia as *Pacific Star* before acquiring her present name in 2008 with Pullmantur Cruises. She has sailed for Peaceboat since 2012.

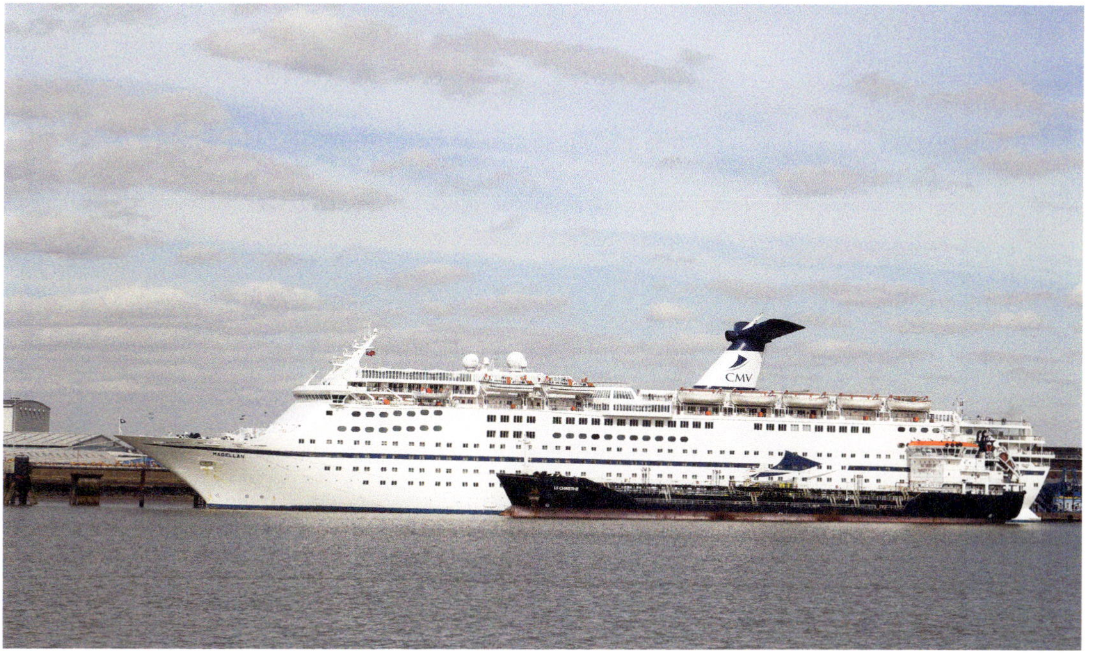

A small tanker passes in front of the cruise ship *Magellan*. On her introduction in 2015 the former Carnival ship became CMV's principal Tilbury-based vessel but has since added various UK regional ports to her cruise schedules.

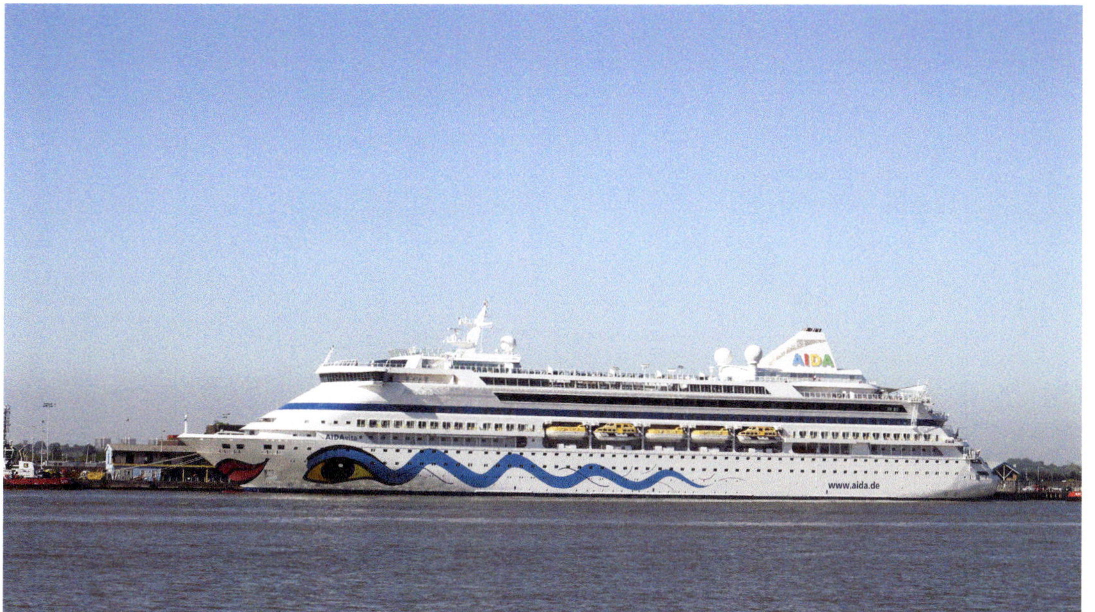

The German cruise ship *AIDAvita*, 42,289 grt, displaying the latest trend in ornately painted hulls at the London Cruise Terminal in May 2018. Operated by AIDA Cruises, she was built in 2002.

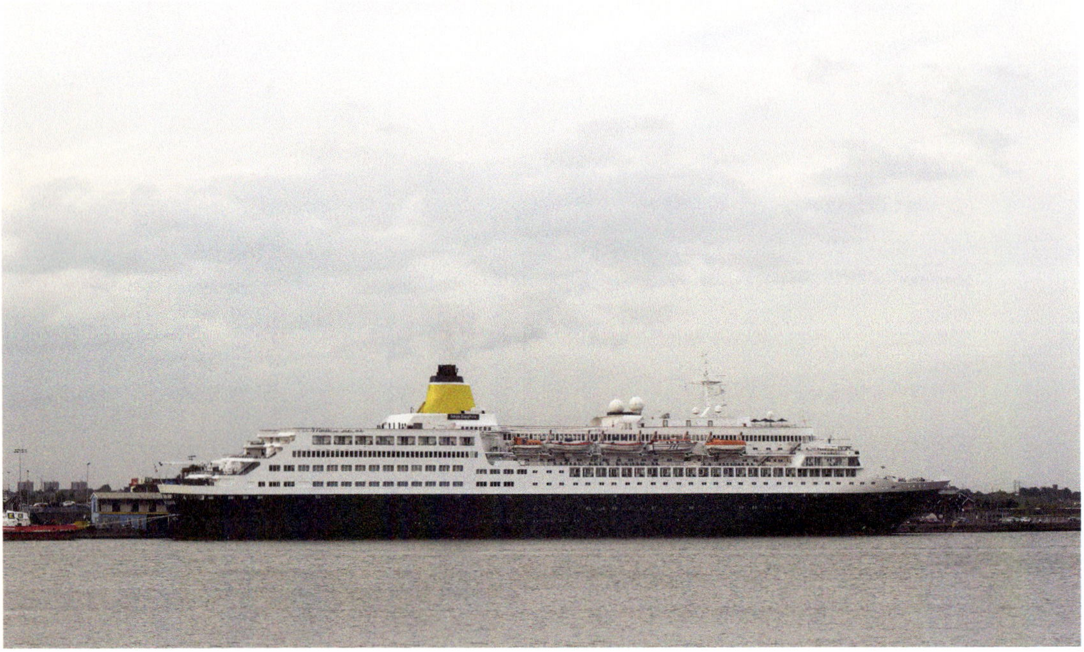

Another visitor to Tilbury in May 2018, Saga's 37,301 grt *Saga Sapphire* has normally cruised out of Dover. She started life as the top-rated German cruise ship *Europa* but is due to be withdrawn from the Saga fleet in 2020.

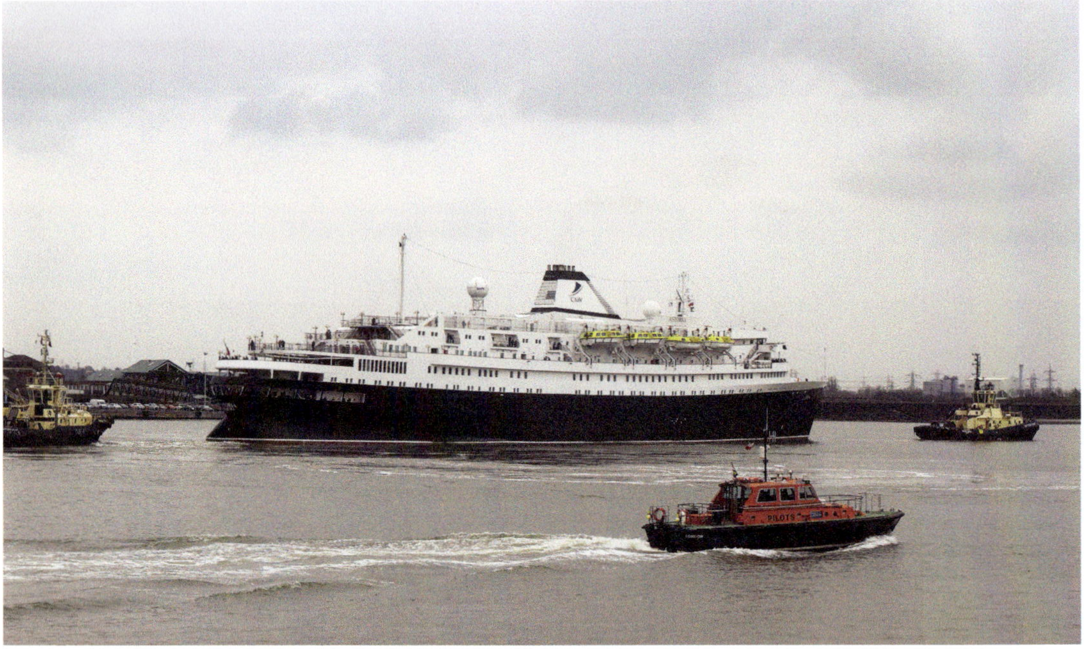

CMV's small cruise ship *Astoria* leaving the London Cruise Terminal in 2018. The world's oldest operational cruise ship, she has experienced eleven name changes in seven decades, yet she continues to be featured in CMV's cruise brochures.

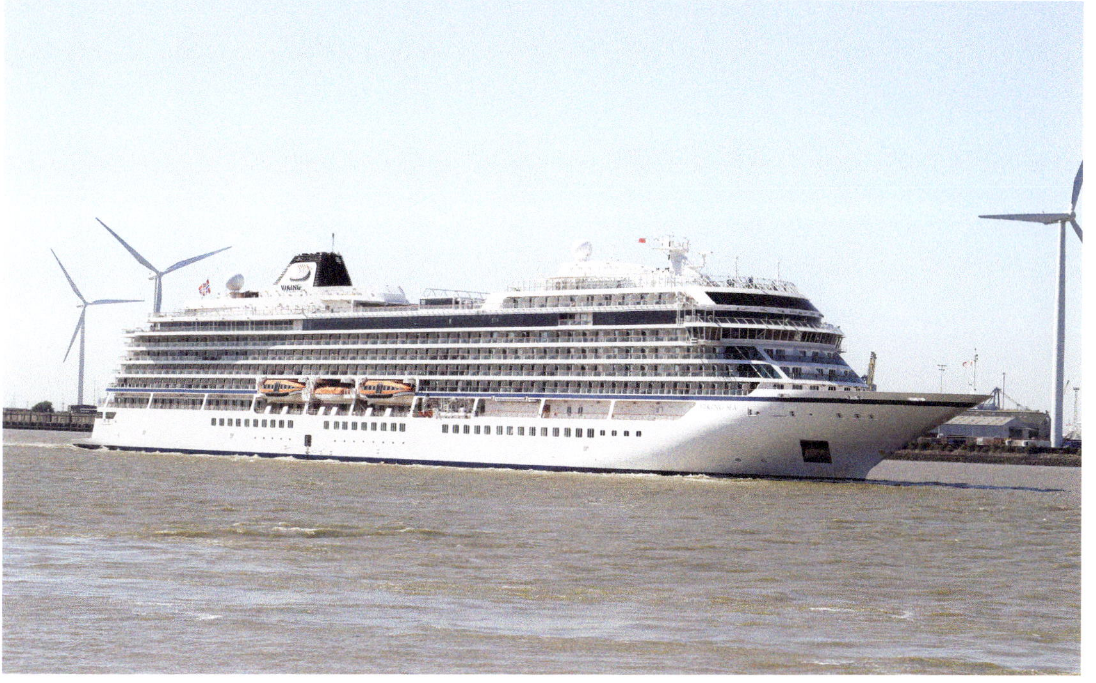

Viking Sea, delivered to Viking Ocean Cruises in 2016, makes a fine sight as she passes through Gravesend Reach following a visit to Greenwich in the summer of 2018.

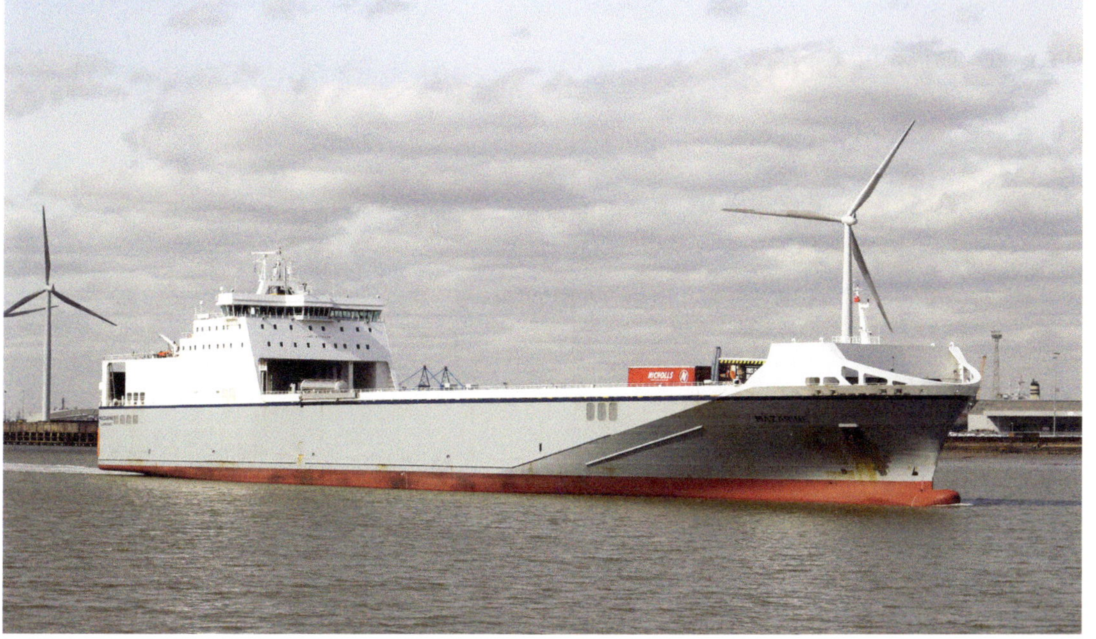

As if to emphasise the continuing regularity of the Cobelfet ro-ro ships, the 25,593 grt *Mazarine* is pictured passing Tilbury Landing Stage during 2018. Built in 2009 and registered in Malta, she was at the time sailing between Purfleet and Rotterdam with additional calls at Dublin.

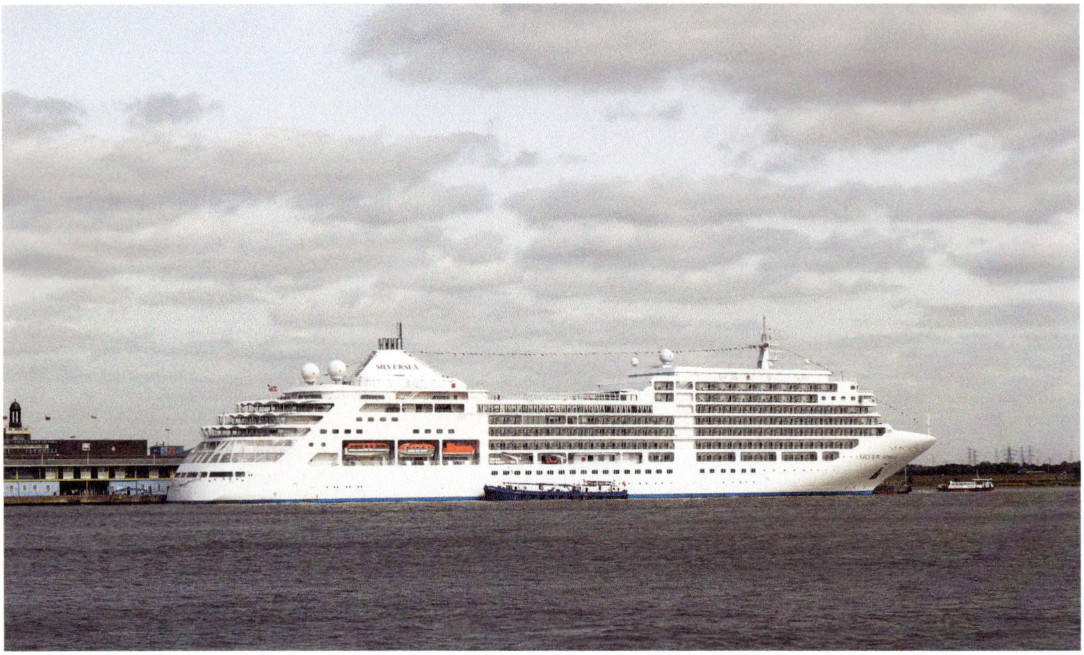

The sixth ship of the Silversea fleet of luxury cruise vessels, *Silver Spirit* visited the London Cruise Terminal in September 2018. Just a few months earlier she had been lengthened by 14.9 metres, increasing her gross tonnage to 39,519 and her passenger capacity to 608.

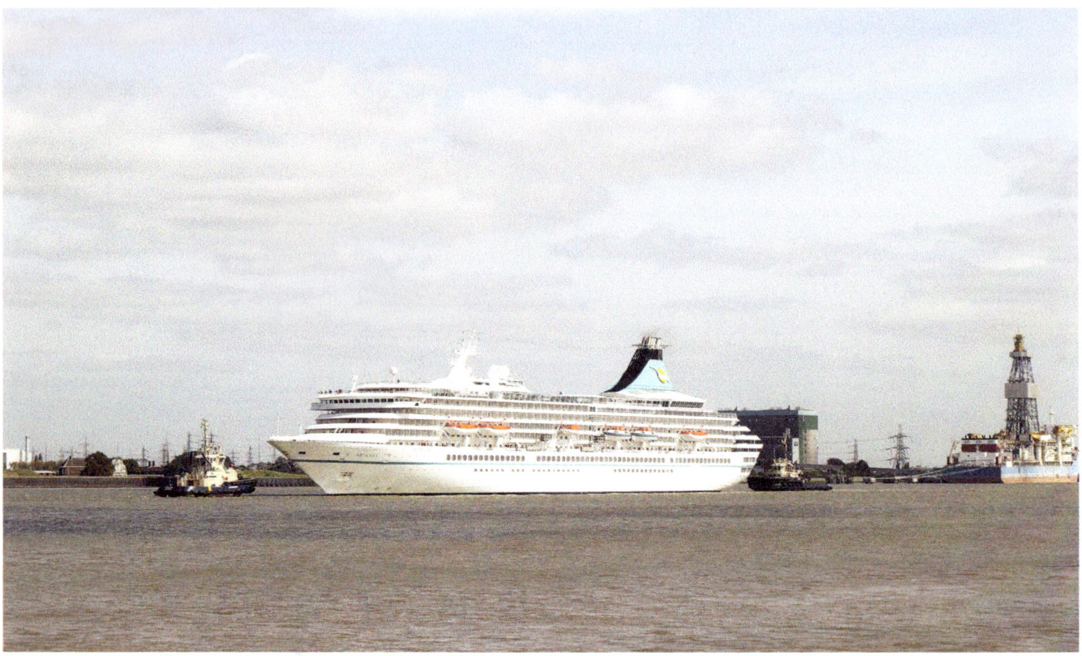

The cruise ship *Artania* heading for the London Cruise Terminal in the autumn of 2018. Behind her the giant 60,316 grt drill ship *Sertao*, the tallest vessel ever to have visited the Thames, lies awaiting sale at the now-derelict Tilbury power station.

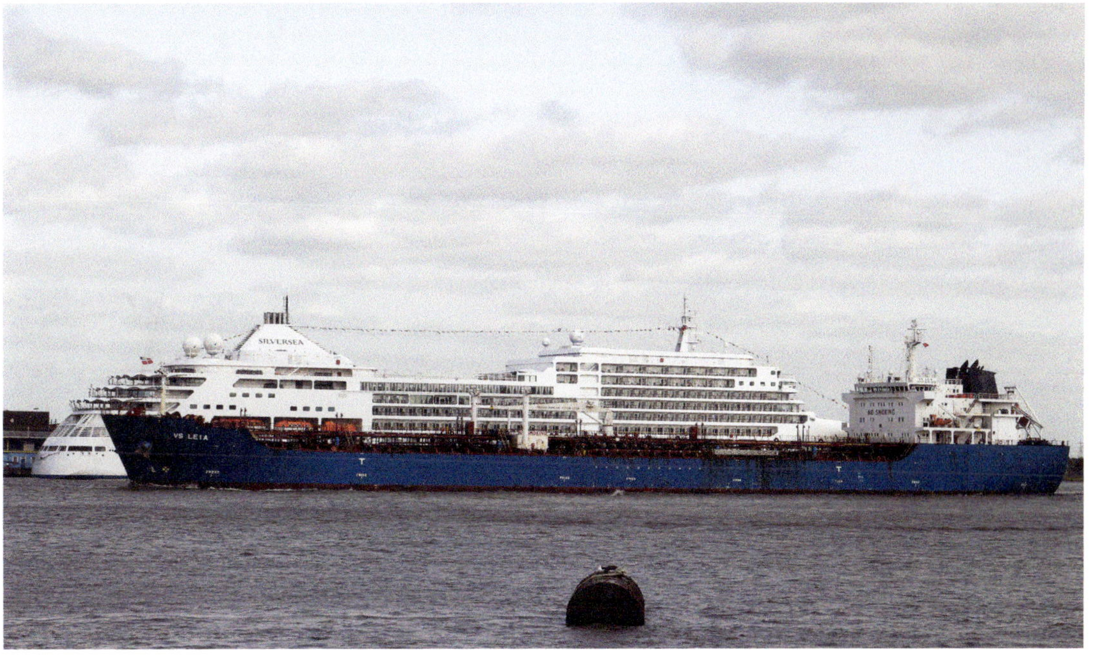

VS Leia, 24,048 grt, a products tanker registered in Malta, passes the cruise ship *Silver Spirit* berthed at the London Cruise Terminal as she makes her way to her upriver berth adjacent to the Dartford Bridge.

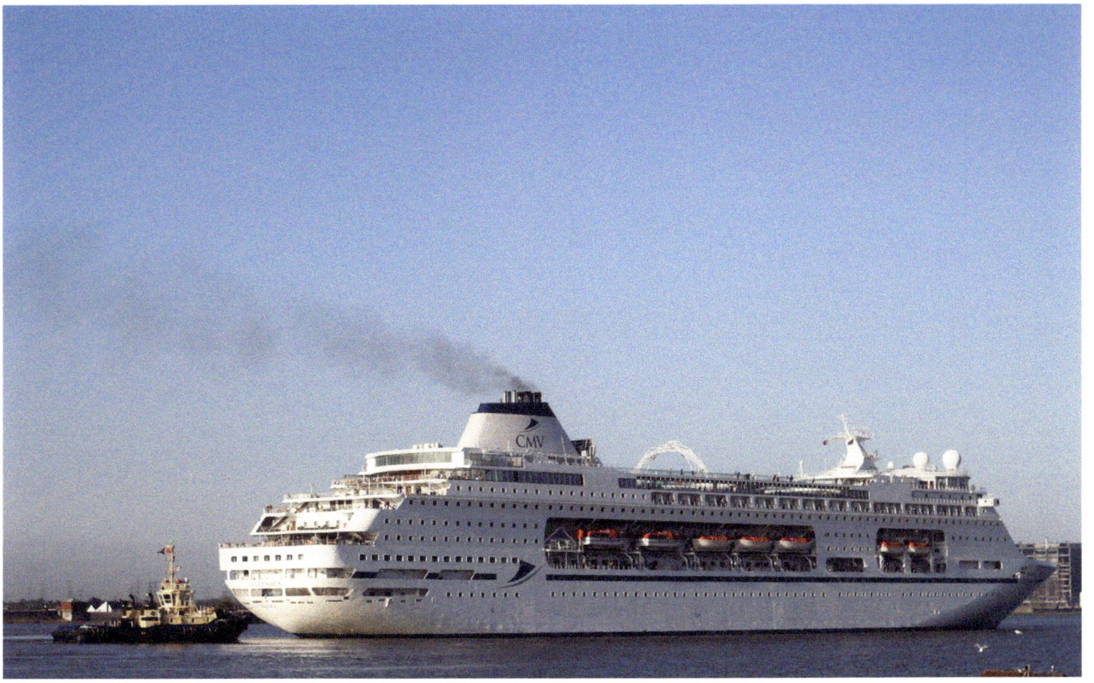

Columbus sets sail on another cruise from Tilbury. She operates year-round from the Cruise Terminal, including two 120-day world cruises in 2019 and 2020.

Acknowledgments

The majority of the photographs used in compiling this book came from my personal collection, but I wish to thank my daughter Rebecca for shooting the recent digital images and Ron Baker of Porthole Productions for allowing the reproduction of the following ship photographs: *Vistafjord* at the landing stage, *Bergensfjord, Britanis, Europa, Jupiter, Stella Solaris, Hebridean Spirit, Caledonian Sky, Svitzer Brunel* and *Contest,* and the Sun tug.